Zoopoetics

Zoopoetics

Animals and the Making of Poetry

Aaron M. Moe

LEXINGTON BOOKS
Lanham • Boulder • New York • Toronto • Plymouth, UK

Published by Lexington Books
A wholly owned subsidiary of Rowman & Littlefield
4501 Forbes Boulevard, Suite 200, Lanham, Maryland 20706
www.rowman.com

10 Thornbury Road, Plymouth PL6 7PP, United Kingdom

British Library Cataloguing in Publication Information Available

Library of Congress Cataloging-in-Publication Data
Moe, Aaron M., 1976-
 Zoopoetics : Animals and the Making of Poetry / Aaron M. Moe.
   pages cm
 Includes bibliographical references and index.
 ISBN 978-0-7391-8662-6 (cloth) -- ISBN 978-0-7391-8663-3 (electronic) 1. Poetics.
2. Animals in literature. 3. Poetry--History and criticism. 4. Ecocriticism. I. Title.
 PN1083.A5M64 2013
 809.1'9362--dc23
                              2013037233
 ISBN 978-1-4985-5043-7 (pbk : alk. paper)

Printed in the United States of America

For my pops, who showed me what resolve looks like;
and for Rebecca, who showed me the wonder that's keeping the stars apart.

Contents

Abbreviations

LG   *Leaves of Grass*, Walt Whitman
CPW   *Complete Prose Works*, Walt Whitman
CP   *Complete Poems, 1904–1962*, E. E. Cummings
P   *The Collected Poems of W. S. Merwin*, W. S. Merwin
PW   *Practical Water*, Brenda Hillman

Preface

Phrases such as "nonhuman animals" attempt to address the HUMAN/animal bias as they foreground that humans, too, are animals. However, the phrase still marks animals by something they are not. They are not human. . . . Moreover, when used multiple times on every page of an argument, "nonhuman animals" becomes tiresome.

In what follows, I use the terms "animal" and "human" full knowing the categories are inadequate—but I use them in the context of continuity and fluidity shared across and amongst ANIMAL↔HUMAN spheres. Animals are makers, too.

When discussing animals, I use the pronouns *he* and *she* over "it." Calling an animal an "it" reflects a long history of Western thinking that perceives the animal as an instinct-driven machine, but as will be demonstrated, many animals have agency in the ways they undergo a bodily *poiesis*. Whereas an "it" possesses no more agency than a stone, a "she" or a "he" acts within an environment with conscious intention. I, along with many others, argue that animals have earned the robust title of gendered pronouns. In a small but significant way, the shift to the pronouns *he* and *she* points to the continuity shared across species in ways I find lacking in the term "nonhuman animal."

It is hoped that zoopoetics opens space within the poetic tradition to see animals in new and productive ways despite how the argument is written in a language fraught with a history of undermining the articulate *poiesis* of other animal makers. And though I am invested in drawing out the ethical implications of zoopoetics and in further augmenting the animal rights movement, the main focus of this book explores how zoopoetics illuminates the process of *poiesis* by humans and other animal makers.

Lewis Hyde's *The Gift: Imagination and the Erotic Life of Property* shapes how I see the exchange of intellectual ideas: a cycle of gift-giving through which hunches and false starts augment into something that has much more weight. Many, many thanks to the following people who have contributed to the momentum of zoopoetics: Christopher Arigo, for initial thoughts at the genesis of zoopoetics, and for the many discussions that helped bring zoopoetics to fruition; Patricia Ericsson, for insight into the field of animal rhetoric; Debbie Lee, for knowing when to ask the exquisite question; George Kennedy and Jana Argersinger, for their mentorship, insights, and friendship; Ken Price, for email exchanges on Whitman's library; Tim McGee, for email exchanges on Aristotle's *semeion*; Brenda Hillman, for email exchanges on "Rhopalic Aubade," ecopoetics, and the radical animism in her work; Michael Webster, for his abundant generosity in circulating page proofs on Cummings, for instigating collective email exchanges amongst Cummings scholars, and for welcoming me into the sphere of the E. E. Cummings Society; Gillian Huang-Tiller, Etienne Terblanche, April Fallon, and all members of the E. E. Cummings Society, for fruitful explorations and exchanges of ideas at conferences; Peter Moe, for sending my way mimic octopi; Ben Merritt, for discussions on Cummings, prime numbers, and gestures; former students, for the invigorating explorations of zoopoetics and ecopoetics in the long-twentieth century.

Portions of my argument on zoopoetics, Cummings, and Merwin first appeared in *Humanimalia: A Journal of Human/Animal Interface Studies*. Parts of my chapter on Whitman first appeared in the *Walt Whitman Quarterly Review*. Initial thoughts on Cummings "(im)c-a-t(mo)" first appeared in *Rupkatha: Journal: On Interdisciplinary Studies in Humanities*. Many thanks to the editors and reviewers of these journals for their contributions.

I also thank the love of my life, Rebecca, for pursuing this dream with me, for your insight into the craft of *poiesis*, and for your support in turning fragments of time into something substantial. Daphne, you kept this dad grounded during the writing of this argument (along with Bridget whom I had not yet met)—thank you both. And Twilight, whose bodily *poiesis* is no more, you wove yourself into our lives and into this argument. You are missed.

In my dream,
the angel shrugged
& said, If we
fail this time, it
will be a failure of
imagination

& then she placed the [earth]
gently in the palm of my hand

Brian Andreas

Part 1   Foundations

Language connected to evolved autonomy

Semiotics

Prelude
The Coat of a Horse

Speech is, after all, breath moving amongst myriad gestures of the mouth. One can still respond to the gestures of the jaw, lips, tongue, and teeth even when no breath accompanies their movement. Forgive me for stating that which is self-evident, but zoopoetics demands a recognition that the jaw, lips, tongue, and teeth are not detached from the body; rather, they are a specific, concentrated, and intensified constellation of highly evolved parts embedded within the communicative zone of a countenance. Though icons such as Auguste Rodin's *The Thinker* encourage us to see language as disembodied, some materiality always already buoys up a word, such as the plosive pop necessary for the lips to say *spit*.

language

Zoopoetics also demands a recognition that animals possess communicative zones as well—zones that may differ from the human mouth. A jockey knows how to read a horse's body, namely, the vast and powerful text of an epidermis enlivened by muscles straining to win. Shelly Scott explores the coperformance of horses and jockeys, arguing that horses have agency, an "intentional exertion of power involving more than merely action or reaction." The two-way communication creates a "symbiosis" between horse and rider, and the horse often "subvert[s] commands" and suggests others through the nuanced and near inscrutable gestures of the flanks, back, neck, and ears—inscrutable, that is, to nonriders.[1] A good rider does not merely observe gestures but feels some of them through his or her feet, ankles, and shins. The symbiosis emerges as horse and jockey read the bodily text that emerges between them.

Faulkner said it best in *As I Lay Dying* when Darl describes Jewel's horse: "Moving that quick his coat, bunching, tongues swirling like so many flames."[2] Like the human tongue, the coat of a horse gestures—but there isn't a focused breath to turn those gestures into speech.

Notes

1. Shelly R. Scott, "The Racehorse as Protagonist: Agency, Independence, and Improvision," in *Animals and Agency: An Interdisciplinary Exploration*, ed. Sarah E. McFarland and Ryan Hediger (Boston: Brill, 2009), 47, 57, 48.
2. William Faulkner, *As I Lay Dying* (New York: Random House, 1964), 12.

Mary Oliver's Zoopoetics.

Chapter 1
Zoopoetics: An Introduction

I know noble accents
And lucid, inescapable rhythms;
But I know, too,
That the blackbird is involved
In what I know.

Wallace Stevens

How does form produce language?

When I first envisioned zoopoetics, I gravitated to poems inextricably bound up
with the intensity of animal *poiesis*—poems with gestures playing with an animal's gestures and vocalizations. Most of the poems within this argument explore intense, but nonviolent, human-animal interactions. They are poems borne
out of respect, wonderment, and care for animals. Recently, though, I discovered
Ray Gonzalez's "Rattlesnakes Hammered on the Wall" published in 2005. The
poem exemplifies zoopoetics, for its form has been shaped by an attentiveness to
the snake's *poiesis*. When the second stanza shifts from shorter iambic beats
("alive and writhing against the wood") to longer dactylic beats ("their heaviness whipping the wall"), the weight and agony of the snakes' bodies emerge in
the heavier line. Through the heavier line, I feel the tempo of each thud.

But the main event is not the poem's form; it is the content. The snakes, in
all of their tormented agony, magnetize the speaker of the poem as does the bewildering question, *who would do such a thing?* Unlike so many poems
throughout the following pages, this one confronts the reader with what Simon
Estok calls ecophobia. The speaker of the poem—and the reader—grapples with
the irrational fear and hatred of snakes that drives a barbaric display of human
dominance.[1] Above all, the poem makes readers attentively witness the snakes'
agency amidst the abject cruelty inflicted upon them:

Seven of them pinned in blood by
long, shiny tails, three of them still

alive and writhing against the wood,
their heaviness whipping the wall

as they try to break free,
rattles beating in unison,

hisses slowly dying in silence,
the other four hanging stiff

like ropes to another life,
patterns of torn skin dripping

with power and loss, the wonder
of who might have done this

turning to shock as all seven
suddenly come alive when

I get closer, pink mouths
trembling with white fangs,

lunging at me then falling back,
entangled in one another to form

Whitman

twisted letters that spell a bloody
word I can't understand.[2]

That "bloody / word" cannot be looked up. It is part of, to echo Walt Whitman, the "dictionaries of words that print cannot touch."[3] The "bloody / word" seems to be beyond language . . . or preceding it. The printed poem comes close to touching the word, especially when "all seven / suddenly come alive . . ."—but reading the poem pales in comparison to a face-to-face encounter with such articulate rage. I sense, though, a subversion in the final moments of the poem. The speaker of the poem may think he "can't understand" the snakes' "twisted letters," but then again, he does. Many readers do, too. As Gonzalez exposes the snakes' collective protest, he finds a way to give the writing bodies *voice*. The seed for zoopoetics emerges in the poem's turn from the snakes to the letters, for the "twisted letters" of the snakes' bodies generate the energy of the origin of poetry—amplified here by violence. As mentioned above, part of the poem's materiality—the rhythm of its lines—emerges from an attentiveness to the snakes' *heaviness whipping the wall*. These snakes, like Stevens' blackbirds, are involved in what the poet knows: the "accents" and "lucid, inescapable rhythms" of poetry.[4] I see "Rattlesnakes Hammered on the Wall" as a stark example of how an attentiveness to animals shapes the making of human poetry.

David Abram [handwritten marginalia]

The zoopoetic process, though, has roots. In *The Spell of the Sensuous*, David Abram reminds us that human-animal interactions contributed to the invention of some letters. The Hebrew word for what became *Q* is the same Hebrew word for *monkey*. Likewise, the Hebrew word for what became *A* is the same Hebrew word for *ox*.[5] The tail still swings in the *Q*, and flipping the *A* upside down reveals the ox's head and two horns. The making of these letters, like the making of some poems, is bound up with an attentiveness toward animals, so much so that monkeys and oxen join the list of blackbirds and snakes concerning what the poet knows.

I argue, though, that the roots of what I call zoopoetics reach further back than the invention of the *A* and the *Q*. In *Poetics*, Aristotle suggests that the "general origin of poetry" involves, in part, the impulse or instinct to "imitate." The ability to imitate, for Aristotle, gives humans "advantages over the lower animals," for humans are "the most imitative creature[s] in the world."[6] Despite the anthropocentric emphasis, Aristotle does not discount the imitative capabilities of other animals; he merely emphasizes who he thinks imitates the most. The difference is one in degree and not in kind. Many animals not only participate in that crucial aspect of *poiesis*, that is, *makings* through their innumerable nuances of bodily movement, symbolic gesture, and in many cases, symbolic vocalization, but many also imitate. Aristotle emphasizes the human sphere; he does not have a Darwinian vantage point. I extend Aristotle's thinking to include other animals, for many species participate in the process of discovering innovative imitations through an attentiveness to another's gestures and vocalizations. Innovative imitations of gestures contributed to the evolution and emergence of animal rhetoric, and they helped shape the evolution of poetry and poetics in the Euro-American tradition.

In what follows, I trace the implications that emerge from an animal's ability to imitate. I assume (but also defend) that animals partake in what Aristotle calls the "general origin of poetry." I expose how some human poets continue to imitate animals throughout the process of making their poems, and I suggest that for all animal makers, including humans, an *attentive* disposition precedes imitation.

Zoopoetics calls for looking at alphabetic language differently. Max Nänny makes an excellent case for the iconicity at work in a range of poems written within the alphabetic system.[7] Iconicity (where form mimes meaning) encourages an attentiveness to the spatial, temporal, visual, and auditory dynamics of a poem. Gonzalez's "their heaviness whipping the wall" exemplifies a temporal iconicity, for instance, as the timing of the stresses conjures up the tempo of the thudding bodies. Iconic poems move away from emphasizing the "meanings" of words and toward a word's shape, gestures, and therefore implied movement. As the iconicity increases, a poem gestures much more like ideogrammatic systems of the East. I contend that some iconicity in poetry and poetics of the long-twentieth century emerges from a poet's attentiveness toward animals.

For Western readers, though, iconicity is difficult. Richard Lanham highlights the tendency in Western culture to look through words rather than at them,

[handwritten marginalia, right margin: *Animals can imitate — so can plants.*]

and Brian Rotman exposes how alphabetic systems function as if language is something "invisible"—something that exists less in the body and more in the interiority of the mind. Rotman observes that alphabetism has reigned as the "West's dominant cognitive technology . . . and the medium in which its legal, bureaucratic, historical, religious, artistic, and social business has been conducted."[8] Rotman's project, though, moves toward materiality, bodily gestures, textual gestures, and images prevalent in digital writing spaces. Zoopoetics likewise moves toward material gestures of text, but it focuses on a micro-universe within alphabetism: the poetic tradition.

This introduction establishes some of the interrelationships between human gestures, animal gestures, and human language. In the chapters that follow, I integrate other foundational concepts with explorations of specific poets and their work. Here, I expose the crucial role of gestures across human and animal spheres including rhetoric, the origin of language, evolution, animal communication, and the Euro-American poetic tradition. The gesture is not a minor event in animal ways-of-being, nor is it on the periphery of poetry and poetics. And when, in many cases, a poet discovers new gestures through his or her engagement with animals, the process of *poiesis* becomes a multi-species event.

The Breakthrough in Rhetoric

Several theorists, philosophers, and poets have already begun a revaluation of gestures, but I begin with the rhetorician George A. Kennedy. In 1992, *Philosophy and Rhetoric* published Kennedy's controversial "A Hoot in the Dark: The Evolution of General Rhetoric." In 2010, Diane Davis argues that Kennedy's "Hoot" is a "seminal essay that should also have been pathbreaking"—and it is, now, in retrospect.[9] At the time, the field generally disregarded Kennedy's ideas. Debra Hawhee attended Kennedy's talk a year after the publication of "A Hoot," and she recounts the "whispers, sidelong glances, and muttering" amongst the crowd "all of which bespoke a slight panic about his—and the field's—direction."[10] However, for Davis, Hawhee, and others working in the field of animal rhetoric, Kennedy's "A Hoot" has become a pivotal cornerstone.

Kennedy argues that "we"—that is, humans and animals—"share a 'deep' universal rhetoric," and he establishes an evolutionary and taxonomic framework to support this claim. In order to map some of the "universal rules of the rhetorical code," Kennedy suggests that "the various historical meanings of rhetoric" could be seen as individual "species," and that these species must be part of a common "genus"—a genus he defines as "rhetorical energy."[11] The materiality of bodies generates this energy through "physical actions, facial expressions, gestures." Kennedy reminds readers that "body language"—that is delivery, the fifth canon of classical rhetoric—is "prior to speech."[12] The various species of speech emerged out of a common genus shared by many animals characterized by the energy of gestures, inflections, bodily movement, and gesticulations. As the essay progresses, Kennedy describes the communication of crows and other birds, rattlesnakes, octopi, primates, insects and so forth with the "categories of traditional rhetoric"—such as ethos, pathos, logos, delivery, invention, arrangement, style, memory—thereby demonstrating the rhetoric at work across species lines. If rhetorical nomenclature aptly describes animal interactions, some profound commonality diffuses the supposed HUMAN/animal divide. "Speech," Kennedy deduces, "would not have evolved among human beings unless rhetoric already existed."[13]

Though Kennedy locates all rhetorical systems within an evolutionary and taxonomic framework—thereby casting human language as but one species amongst innumerable that all share a common origin—he nevertheless leaves the question of animal languages open. Reading closely, however, reveals that the issue has little to do with language. It has to do with agency: "Whether animals can be said to have languages is controversial . . . but there is no room for doubt that animals communicate among their own species and with other species; *what is in doubt* is the *extent of their intentionality and consciousness* of sending and receiving messages and the resulting question of whether some animals have a sense of self and of mental individuality." Kennedy's groundbreaking work helps us consider how many animals may partake in rhetorical energy, but he backs away from attributing agency to animals as they gesture and vocalize with a purpose, for an audience, in a specific time and place. Even if he sees conscious intention within the "ritualized socializing that involves reassuring 'contact calls'" amongst crows—or within the "groups of birds living apart from others of their species [who] develop local 'dialects' and individuals [who] introduce new vocalizations by combining segments of song, rather like phonemes, into new utterances, rather like sentences"—the field was not ready for such an argument.[14] He had to doubt animal agency. Arguing for animal agency along with a universal rhetoric would have been too much for the field of rhetoric in the early nineties.

Zoopoetics assumes animal agency. I recognize, though, that many humans still regard animal agency with circumspection, and so in what follows, I take time to defend it. For now, I offer a list of several other phrases that contribute to an understanding of the agency at work in what Kennedy calls the "rhetorical energy" of an animal's gestures and vocalizations: Paul Patton's "the somatic framework of interspecies communication" from his 2003 "Language, Power, and the Training of Horses"; Debra Hawhee's 2006 discussion of how the "bodily poetics" at work in Kenneth Burke's rhetoric stems from animal ways-of-being; Donna Haraway's 2008 "material-semiotic exchange" between companion species and humans; Hawhee's "bestial rhetoric" that further extends Kennedy's ideas in "A Hoot"; and Diane Davis' 2011 "creaturely rhetorics" that exposes the rhetoric within the social fabric of animal communities.[15] This list cannot do justice to the nuances of each writer's position—nor is this the time to articulate each writer's project. The list, though, highlights the recent emergence of phrases that contribute new ways of seeing an animal's agency as rhetorical/poetic beings. Moreover, the list gives weight to the initially circumspect ideas of Kennedy. It is much easier to work with "rhetorical energy" in light of Haraway's "material-semiotic exchange."

Zoopoetics

Zoopoetics has a relatively brief history of use. Jacques Derrida first used the word in *The Animal That Therefore I Am* in reference to the sheer abundance of animals in Kafka's work—"Kafka's vast zoopoetics"—and Chris White conflates zoopoetics with zoosemiotics, or the sign systems of nonhuman animals, in his 2008 dissertation *Animals, Technology, and the Zoopoetics of American Modernism*.[16] In previous articles on zoopoetics, I provide an initial architecture for the term, but that architecture needs further clarity and expansion.

Though zoopoetics has a brief history of use, one scholar has articulated a facet of zoopoetics without using the term. In "Emily Dickinson's Animal Pedagogies," Colleen Glenney Boggs develops the term "animal orthography" through an attentive reading of Dickinson's "Many a phrase has the English language."[17] Though Boggs draws on theories from Akira Lippit's "Magnetic Animal," her theory of animal orthography emerges from Dickinson's meta-poem about the ways animals shape the process of making. In the poem, Dickinson gravitates to the whippoorwill whose vocalizations continue "Breaking in bright Orthography" while the speaker tries to rest. The *Oxford English Dictionary* defines "orthography" as the "branch of knowledge which deals with letters and their combination to represent sounds and words," and Boggs exposes how "Dickinson locates animal presence in orthography, in writing itself."[18] To extend Boggs' exploration, Dickinson's choice of "Whippowil" has implications. The etymology of whippoorwill leads us not to a Greek or Latin root but to the bird's *poiesis*: "echoic, from the bird's note."[19] In 1709, the word emerged from the zoopoetic process of attentiveness, imitation, and innovation. Indeed, the innovative moment Dickinson speaks of emerges as the bird's song quite literally bursts into human language every time someone utters "whippoorwill." Furthermore, the whippoorwill's song ushers the speaker into a "stir"—or the initial stirrings of a creative moment. As a result, the whippoorwill, as co-maker and muse, earns a political status as a "Saxon" by the end of the poem, something I return to in the multispecies polis of Brenda Hillman's *Practical Water*.

Boggs suggests that animal orthography is not a minor event in Dickinson's "poetic enterprise," and she proceeds to explore how the fly, too, bursts into the sounds of human language in "I heard a Fly buzz - when I died."[20] Animal orthography is undoubtedly consanguineous with what I call zoopoetics; however, as I demonstrate, zoopoetics expands the poetic tradition to include other makers than humans.

The starting point for zoopoetics is as follows: Zoopoetics is the process of discovering innovative breakthroughs in form through an attentiveness to another species' bodily *poiesis*.

The definition intentionally leaves the subject undefined. As the prelude, interludes, and postlude of this argument demonstrate, more species than one discovers new forms through an attentiveness to another species. The definition also emphasizes an attentiveness to *another species* rather than conspecifics (animals of the same species). I agree with the ethologist Hal Whitehead that when the pod of humpback whales joined another pod from the Indian Ocean basin—and when they adopted the rhythms, cadences, and pitches of the new pod's songs—they underwent a "cultural revolution."[21] I add that the whales discovered a new way of being, a new bodily *poiesis*, through an attentiveness to other humpback whales. Clearly, an attentiveness to conspecifics *can be* the catalyst for breakthroughs in form; however, when one attends to the bodily *poiesis* of a different species, the breakthroughs are often that much more bewildering.

Etymologically, *poetics* comes from the Greek *poiesis* meaning *to make*, while *zoo* comes from the Greek *zoion* which means *living being*. In "The Secret of the Zoo Exposed," Cummings complicates and yet clarifies this well:

> Nobody seems to know what the word "zoo" implies. The word, generally speaking, suggests little more than a highly odoriferous collection of interesting and unhappy animals. Whoever takes the trouble to look it up in a dictionary will find that "zoo" comes from the Greek *zoon*, meaning "animal." The mis-apprehension that zoos have to do with animals would appear to be universal. Actually, however, the syllable "zoo" originates in that most beautiful of all verbs, *zoo*, "I am alive"—hence a zoo, by its derivation, is not a collection of animals but *a number of ways of being alive*. As Hamlet might have put it: "to zoo or not to zoo, that is the question."[22]

In step with his poetic vision, Cummings turns *zoo* from a noun into *the* verb underwriting his life's work as a maker, something he states in another short work as the "indescribable Is" of being alive.[23]

The etymological context along with the definition provided above suggests two complimentary foci of zoopoetics. First, zoopoetics focuses on the process by which animals are makers. They make texts. They gesture. They vocalize. The sounds and vocalizations emerge from a rhetorical body, a poetic body, or rather a body that is able *to make*. This assumes agency, that "intentional exertion of power involving more than merely action or reaction."[24] It casts animals in the verb of making, and as the interludes explore, some animals have discovered innovative breakthroughs in their makings through an attentiveness to another species' bodily *poiesis*. The second focus of zoopoetics emerges out of the first. It exposes how the gestures of animals—and the vocalizations embedded in those gestures—have shaped the making of human poetry. Though Derrida used zoopoetics to generally refer to the presence of animals within any genre, I focus primarily upon poetry. More than any other written genre within the alphabetic system, poetry gestures. And when the textual gestures re-enact, re-create, mimic, or respond to the gestures of animals, the making of the form includes the presence of animals.

Gestures

Understanding gestures, then, becomes crucial to the project of zoopoetics, and I draw on the work of Brian Rotman, Sir Richard Paget, William Blake, E. E. Cummings, George Kennedy, Charles Darwin, and Aristotle in order to delve into the primacy of gestures in human language and across ANIMAL↔HUMAN spheres. Rotman provides a threefold hierarchy of gestures. At the highest cognitive level, some gestures are "encoded entirely by a linguistic system," such as American Sign Language. Since they are coded, they can be transmitted horizontally amongst one species and even across species as is the case with many primates. But there are also what Rotman calls "emblem gestures" that are "not captured by a code." Rotman provides a long list of emblem gestures, and even though he focuses on the human sphere, his list suggests many emblem gestures cross species lines:

> [Emblem gestures include] holding up the palm, jerking the thumb, kissing one's fingertips, pointing, snorting, smacking one's forehead, squeezing a shoulder, bowing, slapping someone on the back, giving the shoulder, biting a knuckle, flourishing a fist, tapping the nose, shrugging, chuckling, beating one's breast, giving the finger, winking, and innumerable other visible, haptic, auditory, and tactile disciplined mobilities of the semiotic body.[25]

Any human who has spent time with animals can readily generate a list of emblem gestures that create the interspecies fabric of a sense of belonging. Emblem gestures make Donna Haraway's interspecies "material-semiotic exchange" possible.[26] My cat routinely kneads my lap, but not the laps of other family members. I see her action as one of gratitude for feeding her each morning, and I return her kneading by gently massaging behind her ears. The emblem gestures create a social fabric, a bond not any less significant than the hand-clasp grooming amongst chimpanzees,[27] and it is these bonds, created and sustained by emblem gestures, that generate culture.

Gesticulations compose Rotman's third category of gestures, the "fleeting, often barely discernible, seemingly idiosyncratic and indefinite gestures of the fingers, hands, arms, shoulders, and face." Rotman sees gesticulations to be "connected . . . to the substance of what is being narrated" and later, he provides an example. When a human enters a rhetorical situation, she or he listens not so much to the "isolatable sonic entities" of "speech sounds," but rather "to the movements of the body causing them." Rotman suggests that a listener attunes him or herself to the "gestural origins" carrying a word rather than to the words' denotative meaning.[28] Gesticulations generate, to use Kennedy's term, rhetorical energy. And even though gesticulations are often unconsciously performed, they can quickly morph into a more conscious emblem gesture, such as the sudden foregrounding of a hand of a speaker—accompanied by a forward lean and a nod—all of which gestures to another person to participate in the conversation.

But there is a more profound connection between gestures and speech: the philologist Sir Richard Paget's "gesture-speech theory." In 1930, he published *Human Speech*, a work that explores the gestural origin of speech across myriad languages, including those with Indo-European roots and Proto-Polynesian roots. He argues that the "*continual* use of man's hands for craftsmanship . . . drove him to find other methods of expressing his ideas—namely, by a specialized pantomime of the tongue and lips." He continues, "Gestures, which were previously made by hand, were unconsciously copied by movements or positions of the mouth, tongue or lips." Sir Paget draws on Darwin's notion that when cutting with scissors, the mouth unconsciously mimes the action, or when children learn to write, their faces become contorted. When humans "gesticulated with [their] hands," the mouth, lips, tongue, and jaw "unconsciously followed suit." He sees the "tongue, lips, and jaw" as "understudies" of the rhetorical body. When the hands became occupied elsewhere, they "were already proficient in the pantomimic art."[29] The theory hinges on the observation that the pantomimed gestures of the mouth, when air passes through them, creates sounds. These sounds evolved into speech.

Though I cannot argue that Sir Paget offers the definitive origin of language, he nonetheless presents a cogent and contributing factor. He highlights over sixty Indo-European roots—though, as noted, his work explores languages with other roots as well—in which the mouth, tongue, lips, and jaw reenact the emblem gestures—to draw on Rotman's term—created by other parts of the body. The many pantomimed gestures the mouth reenacts include "reach up"; "feel, stroke"; "draw back suddenly"; "stab or spear"; "shoot (with bow and arrow)"; "sew"; and even involved processes such as "strip grains from the stalk collect take a handful and scatter" and "pick berries collect them bury in the ground."[30] Breath, passing through the gestures of the mouth, creates sounds, and even though distance separates today's English language from the emergence of the Indo-European roots, the gestures remain. Concrete examples include the word *gush* from the root *ghu* meaning *pour* "in which the mouth is made has hollow as possible with protruded lips"; *lick* from the root *ligh* where the tongue actually licks the palate; *suck* from the root *suk* meaning *to flow*, and Sir Paget notes how the word can be spoken either by blowing out (which is what speech became) or by sucking in (which is, according to the theory, the origin of the speech-sound); and *smile* from the root *smi*, the "smiling gesture." It is difficult to say "smile" without *smiling*.[31]

Many of the pantomimed gestures listed above began with the mouth already, but Sir Paget also uncovers gestures that migrated across the body. The tongue, when saying *hither*, reenacts the gesture of a hand/arm waving someone to come near by "protruding, withdrawing, and bending up its tip as it re-enters the mouth."[32] Likewise, to say *creep* the tongue "creep[s] toward the lips"; to say *grip* the lips and jaw reach out to *grip* something; saying *rip* "shows the bending back action, R, together with the gripping action in front –IP; the tongue moves forward (to indicate the ripping motion), while the lips follow on, and hold the ripped portion"; and to say *bloom* the mouth becomes an "expanded mass" resembling the way in which one's hands would gesture a *bloom*.[33]

Poets know this. What often can be mistaken as onomatopoeia is really Sir Paget's theory of the pantomimic reenactment of a word's gestural origin. Two brief citations illustrate this. When one reads aloud the famous lines "And what shoulder, & what art, / Could twist the sinews of thy heart?" the motion of the jaw and cheeks *twist*.[34] They make the same motion that occurs, unconsciously, when I wring out a large towel as if my lips, cheeks, and jaw help my hands, and the fact that Blake ensures that the jaw and cheeks twist twice, back-to-back— once with the word *twist* and once with the first syllable of *sinews*—suggests a poetics that draws on the body's presence within the performance. To my knowledge, lexicons of poetry do not have a name for this phenomenon. It is *not* onomatopoeia, for the words do not re-sound the extratextual event. It is close to iconicity (where form mimes meaning)—but it is not the form of the poem on the page but rather the form of a performing mouth that mimes the meaning. This could be called *pantomim-opoeia*, for the poem encourages a pantomime of the mouth.

E. E. Cummings' "!" provides another example:[35]

!

o(rounD)moon,how
do
you(rouNd
er
than roUnd)float;
who
lly &(rOunder than)
go
:ldenly(Round
est)

?

Though the materiality of the printed page gestures through the iconicity of the rising letters *R-O-U-N-D* that mimes a rising moon, the poem also plays with the materiality of the reader's mouth. Readers unfamiliar with Cummings' *oeuvre* may be tempted to read more linearly than nonlinearly, but there are many ways to descend into the last line's question mark before rising back up to the exclamation mark through the capital letters *R-O-U-N-D*. Along the way, readers can float through the text thereby creating many readings, such as *o moon, how do you float, round , rounder than round, who, who [is] wholly, holy, go, goldenly, rounder than roundest R-O-U-N-D.* When the moon rises, it makes not a sound, but to say *round*, the mouth undergoes a most colossal gesture of enacting rOUNdness. The poem plays on this gesture, for the assonance encourages a crescendo in volume and an increasingly robust gesturing of a round mouth. The long *u* sounds—such as *moon, do, you, who* that all require the lips to stretch far in front of one's nose—acrobatically and suddenly explode into roundness due to the long *o* sounds and the diphthong created by the *ou* of *round* and *ow* of *how*—such as *o, rounder, round, how, wholly, rounder, goldenly, rounder, roundest, R-O-U-N-D*. The mouth becomes the roundness of the full moon rising, and as the poem emphasizes the pantomimic performance of speech, it plays with the gestural origins of language. The mouth, as an understudy, unconsciously mimicked the emblem gesture of hands shaping something that is round. When breath passed through the gesturing mouth, another root emerged.

Sir Paget's theory suggests that the emblem gestures of the body migrated to the concentrated locus of the jaw more and more as humans used their hands for other tasks, and his theory helps extend Kennedy's ideas. Indeed, delivery—the rhetoric of the body—did not merely precede language, it is the source out of which language emerged. Hawhee, when discussing Sir Paget's work, highlights how Sir Paget's theory suggests that the etymology of a word lies not in a "root 'meaning'" but a "root motion." "Paget's physio-philological theory," Hawhee summarizes, "figures speech as a bodily, mimetic, even affective art . . . spreading from body part to body part."[36] Though the West privileges the cerebral intellect over the body, language has its roots in the body and the body's capacity for rhetorical energy.

And if Sir Paget's ideas extend Kennedy's, so Kennedy's ideas illuminates Sir Paget's. To Sir Paget's credit, he does begin the chapter "The Origin and Development of Speech" discussing the gestures and vocalizations of animals—and he did arrive at his theory "partly through study of animal gestures,"[37] but his enormous project focuses on the evolution of *human* speech. I see Kennedy's idea of the common genus shared by many animals—rhetorical energy—necessary in order to further diffuse the arbitrary boundaries between several binaries including MIND/body, LANGUAGE/gesture, HUMAN/animal. The mouth, as it gestures to perform speech, demonstrates the pervasive presence of the body in language. Moreover, if language emerged from gesticulations that became emblem gestures that then migrated to the mouth—and if these gestures are still reenacted through the speaking mouth—then gestures ought to be given much more prestige than they currently carry. This may be one reason why a poet like E. E. Cummings emphasizes how gestures (human/animal/textual) are prime numbers, irreducibly so.[38] One ought not dismiss the intra- and interspecies communication amongst animals as something that is not *language* when gestures are woven throughout the fabric of *human* language to this day—despite the bias within alphabetism to see language as something that resides purely in the "mind."

And it is not just human gestures that shaped the origin of speech. Zoopoetics gravitates toward pantomimes that emerged from an attentiveness to animals. Words such as *growl* and *roar* are much more than merely onomatopoetic. A speaker attuned to the gestures of his or her mouth realizes how, with

little effort, the lips, jaw, teeth, cheeks, and perhaps even the eyes enact a snarl-
ing pantomime of another species' bodily *poiesis* each time the words are performed.

Sir Paget's "gesture-speech theory" and Rotman's "emblem gestures" en-
liven the work of earlier thinkers who also valued human and animal gestures:
Darwin and, despite the human emphasis in *Poetics*, Aristotle. In *The Descent of
Man*, Darwin sees many animals exhibiting signs of wonder, curiosity, imitation,
attention, imagination, and reason. He discusses the "considerable powers of
intercommunication" amongst ants through their antennae, and then observes
how, in a similar fashion, human fingers, "through Braille, . . . could have become the main instrument for language." He continues, "it happened, though,
that gestures migrated to the vocal chords, and thus the voice emerged as the
technology in which language emerged for humans"—which is a seed for Sir
Paget's theory. To support his claim that fingers could have become a highly
exquisite communicative zone of language, Darwin notes how a "dumb, deaf,
and blind girl . . . was observed to use her fingers whilst dreaming." In *The Expression of Emotions in Man and Animals*, Darwin provides an abundant survey
of what could be called emblem gestures of a wide range of animals.[39] For Darwin, then, speech is not something that divides humans from other animals, for
"speech" is not limited to the mouth. It can happen, and does happen, through
many other parts of a body.

Though less robustly than Darwin, Aristotle nonetheless also recognized
how rhetoric is not limited to the mouths of humans. He documented his observations of the ways animals articulate ideas through their bodies in *History of
Animals*. Some animals receive "learning and instruction, some from each other,
some from humans." Implicitly, Aristotle acknowledges an animal's ability to
teach through an intentional making of signs. Aristotle observes that such teach-
ings are only possible because many animals not only "hear sounds" but also
"distinguish the differences between the signs."[40] The word for *signs* is the
Greek *semeion*, meaning *signified, inferred from a sign*—and it is the same word
used sixty-two times by Aristotle throughout *Rhetoric*.[41] Later in *History of Animals*, Aristotle illustrates animal signs at work within the "great complexity" of
hives and thus the "working methods and way of life" of bees. Many phenomena
he discusses require an exchange of signs—or what could be called a rhetorical
energy of emblem gestures—on the part of the bees. Two examples include the
worker bees who notice a robber bee and orchestrate a killing outside of the hive,
and prior to swarming, the collective hive creates a sign where a "monotonous
and peculiar hum is made for some days, and two or three days beforehand a
few bees fly around the hive."[42] Aristotle's language, though, does not give us
any indication, either way, concerning his thoughts about whether bees—or other animals—possess agency in the making of these signs; regardless, he identifies the rhetoric of the body of many species in a work that, until now, often
remained at the periphery of rhetoric.

One way, therefore, to see continuity between ANIMAL↔HUMAN spheres is
through emphasizing the role of gestures. Aristotle suggests animals sustain

their own rhetoric through bodily signs; Darwin recognizes how arbitrary the mouth is, since it is merely one location of a body capable of the work of generating language; Sir Paget exposes the latent vestiges of gestures still present in human speech; Rotman emphasizes how emblem gestures help create and sustain culture; and Kennedy suggests that such gestures comprise a "rhetorical energy" shared across ANIMAL↔HUMAN spheres. As gestures played a role in the origin of human speech, and as human speech still contains vestiges of this origin, human makings differ from animal makings in degree and not in kind.

To return to an earlier claim from the prelude, when I say *spit*, my mouth enacts the emblem gesture of spitting. Or rather, with little additional effort, I look like I spit when I say *spit*. Breath turns the gesture into speech. Just because other animals' emblem gestures have not fully migrated to their mouths ought not diminish the exquisite *poiesis* they craft as makers. Anyone who has spent qualitative time with animals knows this; anyone who has watched *Planet Earth* has witnessed this; and anyone who has read studies from ethology has marveled at this. Humpback whales work together, coordinating the blasts of their air bubbles to corral krill in order to feed, and one can imagine how an individual or a collective group experienced the breakthrough that their air bubbles could be used as a tool, and one can imagine the emblem gestures and vocalizations disseminating the idea through the pod.[43] Sub-groups of orca have developed their own dialect, an example of "vocal culture."[44] YouTube videos readily circulate scenes of adult orca teaching their young how to generate a wave to wash a seal off an ice-floe (through what Aristotle would call clear signs, *semeion*). And to date, over 9 million viewers have watched the YouTube video, taken from *Planet Earth*, of ants and the Cordyceps fungus. What interests me is how an ant can recognize the symptoms emerging through the bodily *poiesis* of an infected member of the colony, gesture for help, carry the infected member far away, and drop the infected ant to the jungle floor. That way, when the fungus sprouts out of the ant's brain, and when the fungus shoots illimitable spores through the air, the colony may be safe. Ants, orca, humpback, and humans have all undergone the evolutionary process of an acquisition of a range of gestures (and, in some cases, vocalizations) to get work done. Emphasizing the role of gestures in both ANIMAL↔HUMAN spheres exposes the continuity of what could be called (after Kennedy's multispecies rhetoric) a *poiesis* shared by many animals.

The Question of Anthropomorphism

Readers circumspect of animal agency, though, may wonder if zoopoetics is founded on anthropomorphism, and therefore, upon a fallacy. Anthropomorphism is only a fallacy when one is a staunch humanist who does not see continuity between ANIMAL↔HUMAN spheres. Cary Wolfe argues that the humanities are "now struggling to catch up with the radical revaluation of the status of nonhuman animals" in today's culture—a revaluation incited by the work in ethology and field ecology. This work has dulled what he calls "the old saws of anthropocentrism" such as "language, tool use, the inheritance of cultural behaviors" that at one time divided ANIMAL↔HUMAN spheres.[45] I suggest, though, that the question of agency lurks behind these "old saws," and some thinkers even within animal studies hesitate to embrace animal agency. John Berger, for instance, in his influential *Why Look at Animals?* sees animals responding to "signals" rather than to signs. "What distinguishes man from animals," he argues, "[is] the human capacity for symbolic thought, the capacity which was inseparable from the development of language in which words were not mere signals, but signifiers of something other than themselves." Berger cites a long passage from Aristotle but then dismisses it for being "too anthropomorphic." Berger then claims that "behaviorists would support [his] objection" of Aristotle's attribution of "gentleness, cross-temper, [and] sagacity" to animals—which behaviorists he does not say.[46] To extend gentleness to another requires conscious intention, something Berger withholds for humans alone despite how even some housecats extend gentleness everyday. Not as a signal, but as a sign. An emblem gesture of nuzzling.

It is no surprise, then, that several theorists in animal studies address the supposed fallacy of anthropomorphism. After exposing the complexity of anthropomorphism in their introduction to *Animal Spaces, Beastly Spaces: New Geographies of Human-Animal Relations*, Chris Philo and Chris Wilbert call for a "guarded anthropomorphism" necessary to explore how animals have responded, with agency, to the "many ways in which animals are 'placed' by human societies in their local material spaces"—a response in which "animals destabilize, transgress, or even resist human orderings."[47] Likewise, in the chapter "Animals" from *Ecocriticism*, Greg Garrard distinguishes a range of anthropomorphisms (and zoomorphisms where humans are given animal attributes) from "crude" to "critical."[48] Cartoon animals exemplify crude anthropomorphism, while recognizing an animal's rhetorical agency exemplifies critical anthropomorphism. As many animals share a common genus—a *poiesis* of the energy of the gesture—attributes crisscross along the supposed human/animal divide, rendering it a blurry borderland full of possibility. Critical anthropo- and zoomorphisms are necessary to understand that borderland.

Bees, ants, humpback, orca, horses, cats, dogs, and many other species possess a degree of agency in the making of signs. In some cases, humans must anthropomorphize to explore the continuity. One way I intentionally anthropomorphize animal gestures and zoomorphize human gestures is through the term "bodily *poiesis*." Poetry, poetics, poet, are terms generally reserved for the human sphere, but the bodily *poiesis* of animals extends that sphere through its implied anthropomorphism. However, bodily *poiesis* of animals also suggests a zoomorphism of humans. That is, the *makings* of animals illuminate the bodily *poiesis* of humans. Through the material body, humans still badger, quail, bear, and leapfrog in all of our animality.

Animal Agency

Much is at stake surrounding the agency of animals. Some may see animal agency as something self-evident, bolstered by a mountain of anecdotal evidence. Others seek scientific, quantitative proof. Still others recognize how the issue of animal agency enmeshes itself within a long history of assumptions about animals. What is agency? Does agency function apart from or in conjunction with instinct? Do all animals possess agency? How might any answer to these questions be proven? What are the implications of animal agency?

The notion of agency—consciousness intention—is complicated further by the observation that humans possess many facets of agency, including kinesthetic or athletic agency, social agency, cultural agency, rhetorical agency, and artistic agency. One might see the drive behind philosophical and scientific inquiry to be distinct facets of agency as well. What facets of agency do animals possess, if any?

To navigate such questions, I first trouble the shallow understanding of "instinct." The long standing assumption about animals is that they merely possesses a "mindless instinct" based more on reaction than conscious intention. A brief reflection on human instinct exposes the shortcomings of such thinking. In the first Olympiad in ancient Greece, the statues of two gods overlooked the contests: Hermes and Kairos.[49] As messenger to the gods, Hermes presence suggested to the spectators and participants that the events had a cosmic audience. The presence of Kairos is more provocative. Kairos was often depicted with wings on his shoulders, wings on his feet, and a long forelock of hair.[50] He swoops in swiftly, and only the most aware are able to seize the forelock—seize the opportune moment—and act. At the first Olympiad, the presence of Kairos suggests the champions must possess something more than skill, strength, and endurance; they must possess the wisdom to know *when* to make their move. As the pack of runners nears the finish line, they will, at some moment, enter the *kairotic* moment. One may lose stamina if the breakaway occurs too early, but breaking away too late has consequences as well. An awareness of the "now or never" moment is an awareness of *kairos*, and for the Greeks, victory depended on such wisdom.

Most human athletic contests—including soccer, volleyball, baseball, football, wrestling, and so forth—likewise hinge on knowing *when* to act. How does one characterize such knowledge? The athlete "knows" in "her gut." The decision is not based on "reason." Any athlete knows how paralyzing over-thinking and over-calculating a split-second burst can be. An athlete may simply say it is *instinctual*. One may be more comfortable with the term *intuition*. To blur the human and animal spheres, one might call this knowledge an *instinctual intuition*.

Regardless, my point here is that the wisdom to act within the *kairotic* moment—even as it lies more closely to "instinct" than to "reason"—involves agency. No one would dare accuse an Olympic runner of lacking agency in the crucial moments when the race is decided—even if she or he made the decision to breakaway based on a gut feeling. The runner has conscious intention.

Many animals, likewise, possess conscious intention as they navigate the "now or never moment" in prey-predator dynamics. For the predator, survival depends on knowing *when* to pounce. For the prey, survival also depends on timing, on knowing when to leap away. Animals (including humans) grapple with *kairos* when they play as well. In *When Species Meet*, Haraway articulates how, as a team, she and Cayenne navigate the *timing* of the race. She speaks of the "tiny but fatal glitch in timing" as a reason behind a breakdown during the contest—often a breakdown of communication. Haraway's father, in a letter to Donna, shares "I marveled at the split-second timing required for you and Cayenne to communicate with each other."[51] In light of Haraway's emphasis on *when* in her title further speaks to how *kairos* permeates interspecies interactions. And yet, the perspective that animals other than humans navigate *kairos* is poorly represented in the field of rhetoric. In the collection *Rhetoric and* Kairos: *Essays in History, Theory, and Praxis*, few contributors point toward the non-human sphere, and when they do, it is more of an aside. Carolyn Hill, for instance, explores first and foremost the physical (and yet almost mystical) resonance that impacts the decisions a writer makes, and she draws on the analogy of a child learning to swing. The most powerful kick, ill-timed, generates no momentum. (Likewise, the most powerful point, ill-timed, generates no argumentative momentum.) In her essay, Hill suggests that such awareness of this kind of resonance may be experienced "at all levels, human or nonhuman," but she does not explore further the ways animals learn how to capitalize on well-timed bursts of physical movement, not unlike the child learning to swing.[52]

Kinesthetic agency—the agency to navigate the *kairotic* moment in the space-time continuum—provides a foundation for other facets of agency. An animal's gestures and vocalizations turn the movements of the body into material signs. Some of the material signs are involuntary, requiring little conscious intention (bristling hair, the rattlesnake's rattle). Other material signs involve voluntary, conscious intention. As the hair bristles, the wolf times his or her snarls, growls, and snaps—with agency—in response to the threat's movements. The coiled snake sways this way and that, with a level of agency as well, prior to the split-second strike. The ritual of social grooming, experienced by many mammals, involves licks, nuzzles, purrs, and many other material signs that move beyond involuntary actions.

Though I hold the perspective that many animals possess multiple facets of agency, I limit the exploration to two of them: 1) animals possess the kinesthetic agency necessary to navigate *kairotic* moments; and 2) animals possess the agency of a bodily *poiesis* necessary to make signs and to navigate rhetorical situations. Such situations include interacting with conspecifics in order to cultivate a social sense of belonging, or intimidating another animal, or, in the case of many birds, alluring a mate. Undoubtedly, many other species have mental events that point toward other facets of agency, but such an exploration is beyond the scope of this book.

Moving to the next question—*do all animals possess agency?*—I recall Derrida's observation of the complete "asininity" of the category of "animal." In *The Animal That Therefore I Am*, Derrida rails against how humans use the term "animal" in a way that effaces the peculiarities of each species and each individual within a given species.[53] One cannot make a claim concerning *all animals* in light of the drastic differences between a roly-poly, a platypus, and a hummingbird. Though one cannot make a universal claim about all animals, I contend that many animals, including invertebrates, possess, to one degree or another, what I have called a kinesthetic agency. Grasshoppers and spiders, for instance, capitalize on opportune moments as do orca, orangutans, and elephants. The later grouping of "higher" animals can be seen crafting *kairotic* moments, or actively bringing about such moments. Likewise, many animals possess the agency to make signs, and though humans readily observe the phenomenon in "higher" animals, one cannot discount the complex social interactions of ants and bees sustained by the making of signs.

But how does one "prove" the agency of bodily *poiesis* of an ant or a bee? Like the ability of animals to empathize, scientists may one day prove the agency of animals. However, a mountain of anecdotal evidence preceded the discovery that some animals possess mirror neurons and therefore the ability to empathize. It is beyond the scope of this argument to "prove" animal agency; rather, I contribute to the thinking that provides a perspective necessary to see it and experience it. In *Zoopolis: A Political Theory of Animal Rights*, Sue Donaldson and Will Kymlicka also recognize the importance of animal agency, and the difficulty to prove it. They observe, however, that many humans do not see animal agency because the human has failed to respond and to reciprocate. When a human responds to and reciprocates an animal's initiation for social interaction, the human witnesses the animals "greater . . . capacity" of agency. Donaldson and Kymlicka ask, "What are the outer limits of this potential scope for agency?"—and they respond, "It can only be answered by engaging in the process—expecting agency, looking for agency, and enabling agency."[54]

One may argue that the human expectation of animal agency merely anthropomorphizes animals as it projects what one wants to see upon what is actually there. The stakes are too high, though, to continue dismissing animal agency as a mere human projection. Recognizing and respecting an animal's ontology is at stake. The human (often inhumane) treatment of animals is at stake. The ethics of eating meat is at stake as is experimentation practices using animals. The place of animals in the polis is at stake as is an economics dependent upon animal subjugation.

For this argument, the process of making poetry is at stake, as is the expansion of the poetic tradition to include other animal makers.

Though I cannot provide proof, I contribute to a perspective that identifies and grapples with the agency of animals. Concerning human *poiesis*, I contend that the poets explored here do not project agency upon the animals that they attentively engaged. Rather, the experience of engaging an animal in all of his or

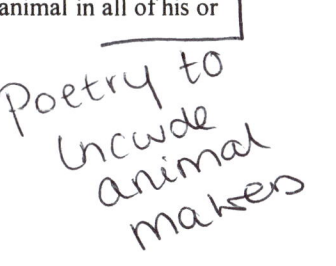

her agency provokes new ways-of-being in language and in relationship to the given animal—new ways of gesturing.

The Poetic Gestures of the Long-Twentieth Century

Poetry—more than any other written genre—thrives on the gesture. One can trace the evolution of poetics across the last 160 years, from Whitman to Hillman, by paying attention to each particular poet's poetics, that is, to their theories concerning the gestures of a poetic line. In the chapters to come, I provide an extensive look at Walt Whitman, E. E. Cummings, W. S. Merwin, and Brenda Hillman's poetics of the gesture, and I expose and explore how an attentiveness to animals contributes to each poet's makings. Here, though, I briefly survey the pervasive obsession with textual gestures in general across the long-twentieth century.

Gertrude Stein's "a rose is a rose is a rose" epitomizes her fascination with the gesture. Her poetics of repetition foreground the physicality of sounds, and the words gesture as she "make[s] it as it is made."[55] When Robert Frost discusses "The Figure a Poem Makes"—and I note his word choice, *figure*, suggesting *body*—he wants a poetic line, its form, its gesture, to become the "straight crookedness of a good walking stick."[56] The imagist Amy Lowell emphasizes the "manner of presentation" of a poem—its form—and she compares the illimitable possibilities of shifts in rhythm and movement enacted by a poetic line to the illimitable ways a person can walk around a circle: they may "dawdle," "run madly," "leap, and run, and skip, and linger in all sorts of ways."[57] Poetry, then, like the somatic motion of walking, reflects innumerable ways-of-being. In the poem "Add this to Rhetoric," Wallace Stevens wants the "figure" of a poem added to rhetoric.[58] William Carlos Williams sees "The Poem as a Field of Action," and he calls for "sweeping changes from top to bottom of the poetic structure. . . . to expand the structure, the basis, the actual making of the poem."[59] A poem from 1942 captures his obsession with the poetics of form:

> I am a writer
>   and I take
> great satisfaction
>   in it
>
> I like to time
>   my phrases
> balance them by
>   their sensual
>
> qualities and make
>   those express
> as much as
>   or more

> than the merely
>   literal
> burden of the thing
>   could ever tell

Williams' idiosyncratic indentations mark his commitment to the gestures of poetic form, and he suggests that these gestures accomplish just as much, or more, than the meanings of words. In his introduction to *The Wedge*, Williams emphasizes the material aspect of a poem: "It isn't what [the poet] *says* that counts as a work of art, it's what he makes." In a short work from *The Wedge* titled "The Poem," Williams articulates what I see as a seed for zoopoetics. A poem should be "made of / . . . wasps, / a gentian."[60] After Whitman's leaves, the trope of the plant pervades discussions of poetics. As "a gentian" encapsulates a family of flowering plants, Williams continues to explore the commonalities between the organic growth of plants and poems. Provocatively, though, for zoopoetics, the animal precedes the plant, and Williams' choice of animal suggests that poetic form can attain a waspish ferocity for those attentive to a wasp's way-of-being.

And one cannot overlook the valuable contribution of Jerome Rothenberg and Pierre Joris' hefty two-volume *Poems for the Millennium*. They provide a "mapping of the possibilities . . . that have continued to open up" the field of poetry.[61] From the Futurists, to the Dadaists, Beats, and technologically embodied Cyberpoetics, the somatic gestures perpetually create and sustain the avant-garde breakthroughs. Midway through the second volume, Steve McCaffery's manifesto articulates the poetic vision of many of the poets in the long-twentieth century to "return language to its somatic base" so that poetry becomes a "gift back to the body of those energy zones repressed.[62] McCaffery's language may remind us of how Charles Olson's "Projective Verse"—known for its emphasis on the body's breath shaping the poetic line—begins by claiming that "the poem itself must, at all points, be a high energy-construct and, at all points, an energy-discharge."[63] McCaffery and Olson's use of *energy* makes explicit the connection I tend toward. As poems gesture, they contain a material, somatic, and, to use Kennedy's phrase, rhetorical energy through the poetics of making. A poem's form, at times, functions as an unconscious gesticulation, and other times as an emblem gesture. It is the breaks, fissures, and blank space that makes room for textual gestures, and I suggest that one reason why people "don't get" poetry is that they neglect the body. In an epistemologically driven culture where Knowledge is Power, gestures are often regulated to the periphery. The main event is a word's content rather than its delivery. Many poets, though, push against such a mindset through foregrounding the gestures carrying language. Poets revel in ways-of-being—in ontology—rather than ways of knowing. More readily than philosophers, theorists, rhetoricians, and ethologists, poets recognize the profundity of gestures in language. Gestures already pervade the evolution of poetry and poetics across the long-twentieth century. Zoopoetics, though, extends the understanding of gestures in twentieth century poetry and poetics by exposing the places where the gestures of poetic form depend on, mime, or play with the gestures of animals. Poetry is not a monospecies event. Innumerable other animals have crept into the forms of many poems, much like the gestures of hands migrating across the body into the gestures of human speech. Zoopoetics names the process through which a poet creates a multispecies event by discovering innovative breakthroughs in form through an attentiveness toward animals. Such poems open up possibilities as they become rich borderlands of energy exchanges between poet and animal, animal and poem, poem and reader, animal and reader, and many more interactions.[64]

Attentiveness

An attentive disposition is crucial to zoopoetics, and I suggest that *attentiveness* is prior to Aristotle's "impulse to imitate." Though imitation generates innovations in form, an attentiveness to another's gestures precedes imitation. The Latin root *tendere*, meaning *stretch*, is nestled in *attentiveness*. When combined with *ad*, meaning *toward*, *attentiveness* suggests a *stretching toward* something else. It is a word suggesting an embodied action of the mind.

Paul Shepard and Donna Haraway further inform my use of *attentiveness*. In *Thinking Animals: Animals and the Development of Human Intelligence*, Shepard argues that human intelligence emerged through *minding animals*: "My thesis is that the mind and its organ, the brain, are in reality that part of us most dependent on the survival of animals. We are connected to animals . . . by sinews that link speech to rationality, insight, intuition, and consciousness." Part of this connection emerged through the "reciprocal spiral of consciousness with its constituents of stratagem and insight" shared by "hunter and hunted."[65] The fittest who survive, then, are those who can read tracks, scents, snarls, bristled hair—and respond accordingly. Though Shepard's argument focuses on human hunters who *minded animals*, he implies that the same "spiral of consciousness" occurs when any species engages in prey-predator dynamics. As one animal *stretches the mind* toward the bodily movements, gestures, and vocalizations of another, consciousness continues its "reciprocal spiral."

He also observes the host of animal infinitives still present in language that demonstrate how words have their origins in a zoopoetic process of an attentiveness to other species: *to bug, to hound, to bullshit, to outfox, to skunk, to badger, to parrot, to rat, to duck, to wolf your food, to worm your way, to clam up, to crow about, to horse around, to fish around, to leapfrog, and so forth.*[66] Today, animals infuse the process of a child's acquisition of language, from the many poses learned in toddler yoga—the lion, the dog, the flamingo, the snake, the cat—to the crudely anthropomorphized animals in children's books. Though animals are "present," for Shepard, such simulacra does not replace attuning oneself to wild animals: "Neither pets nor zoos, books nor films can replace [minding animals]; indeed, they are threats to it." Minding and miming animals, engaging animals, living in proximity and observing animals, attuning oneself to the motions of animals, and inviting such motions to enlarge one's concept of being all can impact, I suggest, a poet's process of making—and not in a superficial manner. As Shepard argues, "human intelligence," and I add poetic intelligence, is "bound to the presence of animals."[67] The more attentive the poet, the more bound his or her poetics are to the bodily *poiesis* of animals.

I extend Shepard's insight to include other cross-species activities, such as play. In *When Species Meet*, Haraway uses the trope of an "ecotone" to illuminate the surprising innovations that emerge when one species plays with another. The "edge effects" that emerge when one ecosystem merges with another likewise emerge when the spheres of two species meet. "Probabilities alter," she insists, "topologies morph." When Haraway and her companion species Cayenne undergo agility sports, an "ontological and semiotic invention" by *both species* occurs.[68]

But for this to happen, Haraway establishes a crucial prerequisite, one that is consanguineous with Shepard's "minding animals" and my use of attentiveness: curiosity. Early on, Haraway discusses Derrida's fundamental incuriosity of his cat whom he discusses in the beginning of *The Animal That Therefore I Am*. Haraway suggests,

> He came right to the edge of respect, of the move to *respecere*, but he was sidetracked by his textual canon of Western philosophy. . . . Derrida failed a simple obligation of companion species; he did not become curious about what the cat might actually be doing, feeling, thinking, or perhaps making available to him in looking back at him that morning.

She suggests that Derrida's echo of Bentham's question *can they suffer* is not the "decisive question," and she offers others: "how much more promise is in the questions, can animals play? Or work? And even, can I learn to play with *this* cat?"[69] Haraway also thought she might find an "ally for the tasks of companion species" in the work of Deleuze and Guattari's theory of "becoming animal" from *A Thousand Plateaus*. Instead, they "made [her] come as close as [she gets] to announcing 'Ladies and Gentlemen, behold the enemy!'" Haraway spends several paragraphs critiquing their work, out of which emerges a crucial insight: they exhibit a fundamental "incuriosity about animals." Like Derrida, they fail to be curious about an animal's way of being.[70]

To lend more weight to what could be a vapid notion of *curiosity* (curiosity killed the cat, Curious George), Haraway, integrates it with respect—*respecere, to look again*—which she defines as an "active looking" involving "many tones of regard/respect/seeing each other/looking back at/meeting/optic-haptic encounter" shared between species. Throughout *When Species Meet*, Haraway explores many instances of interspecies *respecere* that grows out of and sustains a profound curiosity.[71]

Haraway's *curiosity* and *respecere* combined with Shepard's *minding animals* inform an attentiveness that *stretches toward another*. Both Shepard and

'Attentiveness'

Mary Oliver

Haraway's distinct projects require, as a mandatory prerequisite, a patient, interested, and involved turning toward animals, again and again, whether to survive prey-predator dynamics or to play. For some poets, a similar attentiveness, mindfulness, and curiosity turns them toward animal spheres, whereupon they discover innovative breakthroughs in the makings of their poems.

The Makers

In what follows, I intersperse interludes amongst chapters, for they lend space to explore the bodily *poiesis* of animals. The interludes on the beluga whale and the elephant explore a bodily *poiesis* that emerged from their attentiveness toward . . . *humans*, which is a crucial aspect of this argument. The zoopoetic dynamic is not limited to the human sphere, nor is it one-sided. Through discussions of the bodily *poiesis* of other animal makers (and not just Whitman, Cummings, Merwin, and Hillman) I tangibly demonstrate how literary studies can integrate explorations of animal *poiesis* into what has been limited to human *poiesis*.

The chapters focus on human makers from the Euro-American tradition. Undoubtedly, one can trace facets of zoopoetics at work across the storytelling and *poiesis* of many peoples. Future work may benefit from juxtaposing the zoopoetics of multiple traditions, so long as the starting point involves how the maker discovers innovative breakthroughs in *form* through an attentiveness to another species' bodily *poiesis*. To be clear, zoopoetics helps us move beyond the ways the trope of the animal utterly pervades storytelling, for it emphasizes how animal *poiesis* is a catalyst for poetic intelligence. Within the Euro-American tradition, I omit extensive study of many poets' *oeuvres* in which zoopoetics is more than a minor event, such as the aforementioned Emily Dickinson. My hope is that an extensive study of four poets, ranging from 1855 through 2009, will establish a framework to see the zoopoetic dynamic in the work of many makers.

For many reasons, I begin with Whitman. Rothenberg and Joris commence their anthology with the epigraph, "Indeed, if it were not for you, what would I be? / What is the little I have done, except to arouse you?"—thereby attributing the surge of experimentation in twentieth century poetry and poetics to Whitman's work and vision.[72] In the second chapter, "Walt Whitman and the Origin of Poetry," I revisit Whitman's poetics of the body, but I do so with an eye on zoopoetics. When Whitman says that he and animals follow the *same old law*, his *oeuvre* suggests he means the *same old law* of bodily *poiesis*. And when *the body reappears in the best poems*, his *oeuvre* again suggests that he means animal bodies, too. I expose places where the gestures of many animals still endure within his lines, and I argue that he, in essence, presents a poetics consanguineous with Kennedy's understanding of a rhetorical energy shared by many animals.

Elsewhere, I have demonstrated how Cummings descends from Whitman in peculiar ways. Here, I further demonstrate how Cummings pushed Whitman's vision in radically new directions. Perhaps more than any other poet of the twentieth century, Cummings reveled in gestures. Animal gestures. Textual gestures. Cubist and Futurist gestures. Somatic possibilities. A host of animals permeate his work content-wise, but moreover, the radical forms of his poems often emerged out of an attentiveness toward the gestures of animals. In chapter 3, "'Whose poem is this?': E. E. Cummings' Zoopoetics," I expose and explore the multispecies event of Cummings' makings.

Five years separate Cummings' death (1962) and Merwin's publication of *The Lice* (1967), and it is astounding that Cummings' later work contains little trace of the ominous and angst ridden sense of loss pervading Merwin's *The Lice*. Merwin, like Cummings and Whitman, sees that poetry happens in many places other than the printed page, and moreover, a zoopoetics is at work within his craft. But unlike his predecessors, an anguish pervades his poetics. In the fourth chapter—"'learning my steps': Zoopoetics and Mass Extinction in W. S. Merwin's Poetry"—I trace how the bodily *poiesis* of whales, lizards, primates, butterflies, insects, snakes, swallows, and bats are present in and helped shape his poems, but I also explore the implications of a zoopoetics inextricably bound-up with an attentiveness toward the growing absence of animals.

Like Merwin, Brenda Hillman vociferates for animals through her poetry, especially in *Practical Water*, but she much more aggressively foregrounds an overt political sphere. Hillman reminds readers, though, of Shelley's claim that *poets are the unacknowledged legislators* in society. To be a poet is to be political. Hillman's innovations, like Cummings', daringly creates multispecies events, but she locates such events within the political sphere. The polis, poetry, and poetic form include animals. In the fifth chapter, "The Zoopoetics of a Multispecies Polis: Brenda Hillman's *Practical Water*," I demonstrate how Hillman's poetics extends a rich tradition. Like Whitman, she gravitates to elements, in this case *water*; like Cummings, she hesitates not to embrace daring poetic forms; like Merwin, anguish pervades the poems; and like all three poets, an attentiveness toward animals shapes some of her innovative breakthroughs in form. *Practical Water*, published in 2009, demonstrates what some of those tiny swirls Whitman breathed into the poetic atmosphere became a century and a half later.

Zoopoetics opens a space within the poetic tradition. This space, though, is not exclusively human. Rather it is a sphere where the old lines dividing humans and animals dissolve into fluid borderlands as one species discovers innovative breakthroughs in form through an attentiveness toward another species' bodily *poiesis*. Gestures dissolve the supposed divide between human *poiesis* and animal *poiesis*; between the gestures of speech, the gestures of the poetic page, and the gestures of the body. Gestures are what make imitation possible, and though Aristotle had in mind the imitation of actors on the stage, one readily sees the poems explored in the following chapters as actors on the poetic page. The imitation of animals is not a "one-to-one" or a linear growth, but rather, due to innovations, the imitations generate an exponential growth of creative break-through. As the poems mime, imitate, innovate upon, and play with the bodily *poiesis* of animals, the page becomes a multispecies event. I apply Shepard's insight to the Euro-American poetic tradition. Animals are not some nicety or some metaphorical convenience in poetry; rather, poetic intelligence is "bound to animals" profoundly, and necessarily so.

Notes

1. Simon Estok, "Theorizing in a Space of Ambivalent Openness: Ecocriticism and Ecophobia," *Interdisciplinary Studies in Literature and Environment* 16, no. 2 (2009): 208–209.

2. Ray Gonzalez, *Consideration of the Guitar: New and Selected Poems, 1986-2005* (Rochester: BOA Editions, 2005), 35.

3. Walt Whitman, *Leaves of Grass* in *The Walt Whitman Archive* (Lincoln: Center for Digital Research in the Humanities, University of Nebraska, 1995), 1891–92, 179; hereafter cited parenthetically as *LG*.

4. Wallace Stevens, *The Collected Poems* (New York: Vintage Books, 1982), 94.

5. David Abram, *The Spell of the Sensuous: Perception and Language in a More-than-Human World* (New York: Pantheon Books, 1996), 101.

6. Aristotle, *The Complete Works of Aristotle: The Revised Oxford Translation*, ed. Jonathan Barnes (Princeton: Princeton University Press, 1984), 2:2318.

7. Max Nänny, "Iconic Dimensions in Poetry," in *On Poetry and Poetics*, ed. Richard Waswo, Swiss Papers in English Language and Literature 2 (1985) (Tübingen: Gunter Narr Verglag, 1985), 111–135.

8. Richard Lanham, *The Electronic Word: Democracy, Technology, and the Arts* (Chicago: University of Chicago Press, 1993), 43; Brian Rotman, *Becoming Beside Ourselves: The Alphabet, Ghosts, and Distributed Human Being* (Durham: Duke University Press, 2008), 2.

9. Diane Davis, *Inessential Solidarity: Rhetoric and Foreigner Relations* (Pittsburgh: University of Pittsburgh Press, 2010), 155.

10. Debra Hawhee, "Toward a Bestial Rhetoric," *Philosophy and Rhetoric* 44, no. 1 (2011): 81.

11. George A. Kennedy, "A Hoot in the Dark: The Evolution of General Rhetoric," *Philosophy and Rhetoric* 25, no. 1 (1992): 6, 3, 1, 2.

12. Ibid., 4, 14.

13. Ibid., 4.

14. Ibid., 6 italics added, 7.

15. Paul Patton, "Language, Power, and the Training of Horses," in *Zoontologies: The Question of the Animal*, ed. Cary Wolfe (Minneapolis: University of Minnesota Press, 2003), 89; Debra Hawhee, "Language as Sensuous Action: Sir Richard Paget, Kenneth Burke, and Gesture-Speech Theory," *Quarterly Journal of Speech* 92, no. 4 (2006): 342–45; Donna Haraway, *When Species Meet* (Minneapolis: University of Minnesota Press, 2008), 206; Hawhee, "Bestial," 81–87; Diane Davis, "Creaturely Rhetorics," *Philosophy and Rhetoric* 44, no. 1 (2011): 88–94.

16. Jacques Derrida, *The Animal That Therefore I Am*, ed. Marie-Louise Mallet, trans. David Wills (New York: Fordham University Press, 2008), 6; Christopher T. White, "An-

imals, Technology, and the Zoopoetics of American Modernism," Dissertation (Pennsylvania State University, 2008).

17. Emily Dickinson, *The Poems of Emily Dickinson*, ed. Ralph William Franklin (Massachusetts: Harvard University Press, 1999), 333.

18. Colleen Glenney Boggs, "Emily Dickinson's Animal Pedagogies," *Publications of the Modern Language Association of America* 124, no. 2 (2009): qtd. in 538; 539.

19. "Whippoorwill," *Oxford Dictionary of English* (Oxford: Oxford University Press, 2010).

20. Boggs, "Animal Pedagogies," 539.

21. Hal Whitehead, "How Might We Study Culture?: A Perspective From the Ocean," in *The Question of Animal Culture*, ed. Kevin N. Laland and Bennett G. Galef (Cambridge: Harvard University Press, 2009), 126.

22. E. E. Cummings, *A Miscellany Revised*, ed. George J. Firmage (New York: October House, 1965), 174. This quote comes from the short piece "The Secret of the Zoo Exposed." Cummings, though, did not have a blind zeal for zoos. Zoos, Cummings argues, are Freudian mirrors, "a glass wherein we see revealed not only our powers, but our weaknesses, not only our docility but our cruelty and our will to crush" (176).

23. Ibid., 251.

24. Shelly R. Scott, "The Racehorse as Protagonist," 47.

25. Rotman, *Becoming*, 17–18.

26. Haraway, *Species*, 206.

27. See Frans B. M. De Waal and Kristin E. Bonnie, "In Tune with Others: The Social Side of Primate Culture," in *The Question of Animal Culture*, ed. Kevin N. Laland and Bennett G. Galef (Cambridge: Harvard University Press, 2009), 33.

28. Rotman, *Becoming*, 20, 23.

29. Sir Richard Paget, *Human Speech: Some Observations, Experiments, and Conclusions as to the Nature, Origin, Purpose and Possible Improvement of Human Speech* (New York: Harcourt Brace & Company, 1930), 132, 133.

30. Ibid., 140–45.

31. Ibid., 149, 150, 151, 153.

32. Ibid., 138.

33. Sir Richard Paget, *This English* (London: K. Paul , Trench, Trubner & Co., 1935), 69, 71, 80, 85.

34. William Blake, *The Complete Poetry and Prose of William Blake*, ed. David V. Erdman (Berkeley: University of California Press, 2008), 24.

35. E. E. Cummings, *Complete Poems, 1904-1962*, ed. George J. Firmage (New York: Liveright, 1991), 722; hereafter cited parenthetically as *CP*.

36. Hawhee, "Language," 336.

37. Paget, *Human Speech*, 126–130; Paget, *This English*, 26.

38. Cummings articulates his thoughts on gestures and prime numbers in notes found in the archives: bMS Am 1823.7 (25), folder 4 sheet 74, Houghton Library, Harvard University. I discuss Cummings' thoughts on gestures and prime numbers further in chapter 3.

39. Charles Darwin, *From so Simple a Beginning: The Four Great Books of Charles Darwin*, ed. Edward O. Wilson (New York: Norton, 2006), 802–05, 810, 1308–21.

40. Aristotle, *History of Animals, Books VII-X*, trans. and ed. D. M. Balme (Cambridge: Harvard University Press, 1991), 215.

41. I investigated Aristotle's usage of "sign" by using *Perseus Digital Library*, and I verified my findings through several email exchanges with Tim McGee from Rider University. McGee's background in classical rhetoric and in Greek helped ground the exploration of *semeion* in Aristotle's works.

42. Aristotle, *Animals*, 335, 347–51.

43. Alastair Fothergill, *Planet Earth* (BBC Worldwide Americas Inc., 2007).

44. Brooke L. Sargeant and Janet Mann, "From Social Learning to Culture: Intrapopulation Variation in Bottlenose Dolphins," in *The Question of Animal Culture*, ed. Kevin N. Laland and Bennett G. Galef (Cambridge: Harvard University Press, 2009), 161.

45. Cary Wolfe, *Zoontologies: The Question of the Animal* (Minneapolis: University of Minnesota Press, 2003), xi.

46. John Berger, *Why Look at Animals?* (London: Penguin, 2009), 14, 18, 20–21.

47. Chris Philo and Chris Wilbert, "Animal Spaces, Beastly Places: An Introduction," in *Animal Spaces, Beastly Places: New Geographies of Human-Animal Relations*, ed. Chris Philo and Chris Wilbert (New York: Routledge, 2000), 19–20, 5.

48. Greg Garrard, *Ecocriticism*, 2nd ed. (New York: Routledge, 2012), 154, 152–170.

49. Phillip Sipiora, "Introduction: The Ancient Concept of *Kairos*," in *Rhetoric and* Kairos: *Essays in History, Theory, and Praxis*, ed. Phillip Sipiora and James Baumlin (Albany: State University of New York Press, 2002), 1.

50. Carolyn R. Miller, "Foreword," in *Rhetoric and* Kairos: *Essays in History, Theory, and Praxis*, ed. Phillip Sipiora and James Baumlin (Albany: State University of New York Press, 2002), xii.

51. Haraway, *Species*, 230, 177.

52. Carolyn Eriksen Hill, "Changing Times in Composition Classes: *Kairos*, Resonance, and the Pythagorean Connection," in *Rhetoric and* Kairos: *Essays in History, Theory, and Praxis*, ed. Phillip Sipiora and James Baumlin (Albany: State University of New York Press, 2002), 218, 215.

53. Derrida, *Animal*, 31, 39–41.

54. Sue Donaldson and Will Kymlicka, *Zoopolis: A Political Theory of Animal Rights* (Oxford: Oxford University Press, 2011), 109, 110.

55. Gertrude Stein, "Composition as Explanation," in *Twentieth-Century American Poetics: Poets on the Art of Poetry*, ed. Dana Gioia, Meg Schoerke, and David Mason (Boston: McGraw-Hill, 2004), 20.

56. Robert Frost, "The Figure a Poem Makes," in *Twentieth-Century American Poetics: Poets on the Art of Poetry*, ed. Dana Gioia, Meg Schoerke, and David Mason (Boston: McGraw-Hill, 2004), 12.

57. Amy Lowell, "Preface to Some Imagist Poets," in *Twentieth-Century American Poetics: Poets on the Art of Poetry*, ed. David Mason, Meg Schoerke, and Dana Gioia (Boston: McGraw-Hill, 2004), 16.

58. Stevens, *Collected Poems*, 198–99.

59. William Carlos Williams, "The Poem as a Field of Action," in *Twentieth-Century American Poetics: Poets on the Art of Poetry*, ed. Dana Gioia, Meg Schoerke, and David Mason (Boston: McGraw-Hill, 2004), 51.

60. William Carlos Williams, *The Collected Poems of William Carlos Williams*, ed. Christopher MacGowan, 2 vols. (New York: New Directions, 1988), 2:44–45, 54, 74.

61. Jerome Rothenberg and Pierre Joris, eds., *Poems for the Millennium: The University of California Book of Modern and Postmodern Poetry*, 2 vols. (Berkeley: University of California Press, 1995), 2:13.

62. Ibid., 2:427.

63. Charles Olson, "Projective Verse," in *Twentieth-Century American Poetics: Poets on the Art of Poetry*, ed. Dana Gioia, Meg Schoerke, and David Mason (Boston: McGraw-Hill, 2004), 174.

64. William Rueckert's 1978 essay informed my thinking on the energy exchanges that occur when a group of people read and discuss a poetic text. Rueckert, though, limits the energy exchange to the human sphere. I suggest that the energy exchange extends to include the bodily *poiesis* of animals especially when a discussion foregrounds a zoopoetic dynamic in a text. See William Rueckert, "Literature and Ecology: An Experiment in Ecocriticism," in *The Ecocriticism Reader: Landmarks in Literary Ecology*, ed. Cheryll Glotfelty and Harold Fromm (Athens: University of Georgia Press, 1996), 105–123.

65. Paul Shepard, *Thinking Animals: Animals and the Development of Human Intelligence* (New York: Viking Press, 1978), 2, 6–7.

66. Ibid., 27.

67. Ibid., 249. Though Shepard may be right about how nothing replaces living in proximity with wild animals, he overstates his point. In *Why the Wild Things Are: Animals in the Lives of Children*, Gail Melson provides a balancing perspective. She explores the profound ways that animals utterly pervade the world of a child through pets, animal characters in stories, zoomorphized alphabetic letters, stuffed animals, imaginary animals (dragons, mermaids, monsters), extinct animals (dinosaurs), zoos, animals in children's television programming, and so forth. Early in her argument, Melson highlights how a child interacts with animals similar to how a parent interacts with a newborn, with "gesture and gaze" (2)—two aspects at work in zoopoetic dynamics. See L. Gail Melson, *Why the Wild Things Are: Animals in the Lives of Children* (Cambridge: Harvard University Press, 2001).

68. Haraway, *Species*, 217, 232.

69. Ibid., 20, 22.

70. Ibid., 27, 30. For Deleuze and Guattari, "a becoming-animal always involves a pack, a band, a population, a peopling, in short, a multiplicity" (239). They speak of the "pack or swarm" that has an "effectuation of a power . . . that throws the self into upheaval and makes it reel" (241, 240). The child who sees, at once, the assemblage of a street-horse-omnibus is in the midst of a becoming-animal (263). One of the many ways Deleuze and Guattari describe the rhizome is "when rats swarm over each other" (7). And so, "becoming-animal" has to do with understanding and experiencing the theory of a rhizome and an assemblage. Though the theory of the swarm can brilliantly illuminate, for instance, Cummings' swarm of letters in "r-o-p-h-e-s-s-a-g-r" (*CP* 396), Deleuze and Guattari are much less interested in actual species and the spaces where they meet. Gilles Deleuze and Félix Guattari, *A Thousand Plateaus: Capitalism and Schizophrenia* (Minneapolis: University of Minnesota Press, 1987).

71. Haraway, *Species*, 164. Barbra Smuts' work with baboons highlights one notable example. Haraway argues that "Smuts began adjusting what she did—and who she was— according to the baboons' social semiotics directed both to her and to one another. . . . Smuts defines a greeting ritual as a kind of embodied communication, which takes place in entwined, semiotic, overlapping, somatic patterning over time" (*Species*, 24, 26). Smuts' words evince a curiosity sustained by a looking and looking again: "In the process of gaining their trust, [I] changed almost everything about me, including the way I walked and sat, the way I held my body, and the way I used my eyes and voice. I was

learning a whole new way of being in the world—the way of the baboon. . . . I was responding to the cues the baboons used to indicate their emotions, motivations and intentions to one another, and I was gradually learning to send such signals back to them" (qtd. in Haraway, *Species*, 24). For Smuts, interspecies communication hinges on an attentiveness toward the bodily *poiesis* of the baboons.

   72. Rothenberg and Joris, *Poems for the Millennium*, 1:xxviii.

Interlude
Mimic Octopi

These creatures, *Thaumoctopus mimicus*, are *makers*. Unlike human makers whose bodily *poiesis* evolved within the element of air, mimic octopi's *poiesis* evolved within the element of water. Eight buoyant arms swaying in currents of ocean. Eight buoyant arms ready to flare into new forms, including venomous sea snakes, toxic flatfish, flounders, and more.[1] It is no wonder Cary Wolfe discusses the mischievous and curious disposition of cephalopods to undermine the assumption that only mammals—or vertebrates even—possess "higher" cognitive traits. He emphasizes how the existence of these spineless creatures is a "scandal" as they disrupt what people may think they know about animals.[2]

With some degree of agency, mimic octopi discovered an innovative bodily *poiesis* through an attentiveness to the ways other sea creatures move through liquid. They are zoopoetic to the extreme. They exhibit innovative emblem gestures. They are Proteus incarnate—the maker of all makers who morphs into innumerable species including a lion, snake, leopard, and boar.[3] They manifest an Aristotelian impulse to innovatively imitate as they craft numerous ways to suggest *float back*.

Every time, the morphing is utterly sudden and utterly complete. It is difficult not to be jealous of this creature's Protean *poiesis* buoyant, awash in the sea.

And I think many poets would be jealous. To be a poet is to play with Proteus. Karen Gordon, for instance, argues that "words are more Protean than Procrustean."[4] Instead of being forced into prescribed forms, words want to morph, in any language. I recall a former math student who could reduce complex mathematical expressions involving radicals and exponents with lightness and ease—effervescently. Suddenly, the cubed root of 512 all squared, divided by the fourth root of 256 all cubed, morphed through several forms until it became 1. I should have turned to the math student and said, "You, like Menelaus, succeeded. You held on brilliantly."

But holding onto Protean morphings in mathematics or in poetry or in online videos of mimic octopi—no matter how material, how embodied—pales in comparison to diving into the ocean, swimming past a rock, and being startled by a face-to-face encounter with a creature who instantly becomes a venomous sea snake. Dickinson's "Zero at the Bone" only hints at the chill in one's psyche.[5] One would be mad to even think of holding on.

Notes

1. Christine L. Huffard et al., "The Evolution of Conspicuous Facultative Mimicry in Octopuses: An Example of Secondary Adaptation?," *Biological Journal of the Linnaean Society* 101, no. 1 (2010): 68.

2. Cary Wolfe, *Before the Law: Humans and Other Animals in a Biopolitical Frame* (Chicago: University of Chicago Press, 2013), 71–72.

3. Homer, *The Odyssey*, trans. Robert Fitzgerald (New York: Vintage Books, 1989), IV. 487–89.

4. Karen Elizabeth Gordon, *The Deluxe Transitive Vampire: The Ultimate Handbook of Grammar for the Innocent, the Eager, and the Doomed* (New York: Pantheon Books, 1993), 8.

5. Dickinson, *Poems*, 1096.

Chapter 2
Walt Whitman and the Origin of Poetry

The place of origins included
dust that spoke, the particle spirits,
a hawk with its droplet of blood,
an armored toad.

Brenda Hillman
from *Practical Water*

Julia Kristeva, one of the well-known French literary theorists, explores how the revolution in poetic language involves a "deluge of the signifier." She suggests that *"reading* means giving up the lexical, syntactic, and semantic operation of deciphering, and instead retracing the path of their production." "How many readers can do this?" she asks. "We read signifiers, weave traces, reproduce narratives, systems, and driftings, but never the dangerous and violent crucible of which these texts are only the evidence."[1]

Kristeva presents ideas similar to those explored in the introduction, but with a twist. Kennedy gravitates toward that "genus" of the rhetorical energy of a body, while Kristeva gravitates to what could be called the "genus" of the *poetic energy* of the body. She speaks of the "discrete quantities of energy [that] move through the body . . . [which are] always already involved in a semiotic process." She calls this energy the *semiotic chora*, a "modality of significance in which the linguistic sign is not yet articulated." The *chora* is the energy of the body, the concrete operations that "precede the acquisition of language" and carve out a "preverbal semiotic space." Indeed, Kristeva does not locate this energy within rhetoric *per se*, but within "poetic animality." She would probably argue that *poetic animality* precedes rhetoric, and though rhetorical energy is a crucial place to begin, I prefer *poetic energy* as it foregrounds the agency necessary to be a *maker*. The revolution occurs in poetry when a "deluge of the signi-fier" contributes to "cracking the socio-symbolic order, splitting it open, chang-ing vocabulary, syntax, the word itself."[2]

Though Kristeva focuses on the European tradition, what she says aptly describes the revolution of poetics in the American tradition. I cannot read, for instance, the last quote without thinking of Cummings who *split open language, changed vocabulary*, etc. Kristeva encourages readers to "break through the sign, dissolve it . . . , tearing the veil of representation to find the material signifying process"—a process that possesses a "violent rhythm." And I cannot read these words without thinking of Cummings' predecessor, Walt Whitman. In later sec-tions of this chapter, Kristeva's theory helps identify and explore a "deluge of the signifier" that draws on the energy of animal *poiesis*.

Whitman intersperses his theory of the origin of poems throughout his *oeu-vre*, but before exploring it, I establish the work of two other influential thinkers in the nineteenth century: Charles Kraitsir and Ralph Waldo Emerson. Charles Kraitsir's work helps contextualize Whitman's "original energy" of language—an energy that is elemental, organic, and animistic. I do not claim that Kraitsir directly influenced Whitman; however, and as Michael West exposes in "Charles Kraitsir's Influence upon Thoreau's Theory of Language," Kraitsir's ideas of language circulated amongst Whitman's peers.[3] Kraitsir, a Hungarian philologist, published two instrumental books that Thoreau owned, the second of which he made notes in, suggesting an attentive reading: *Significance of the Al-phabet* (1846) and *Glossology: Being a Treatise on the Nature of Language and on the Language of Nature* (1852). Emerson, too, owned *Glossology*,[4] and though we cannot say whether Whitman read either book, his readings of Tho-reau and Emerson would have provided adequate exposure. Perhaps, though, Whitman discovered similar lines of thought independently.

Regardless of direct influence, Kraitsir's ideas resonate with Whitman's vision. Kraitsir marvels at the "organic energy contained in language" and he claims "language is a living organism." He saw "the principle of motion" as something that "presided at the birth of language."[5] In *Significance of the Al-phabet*, Kraitsir sees humans as "plunged into a material universe"—a necessary prerequisite for the rise of language. He divides alphabets into categories that correspond to the material universe including linguals that "express movement"; labials that "express all that the lips signify"; gutturals that "express what re-sembles the throat physically, the dimensions of *heighth* [*sic*] or *depth*"; and the dentals that "*name* the *teeth*, and express all that the teeth signify." The word "gorge," therefore, requires a guttural dimension, for the location of the source of the sound in the throat resonates with the depth of an actual gorge. Likewise, Kraitsir sees the letter *R*, as a lingual, as a "symbol of *rough* and *original move-ment*," and he observes how an *R* occurs in roots of words like "*trembling*" and "*vibration*." The earth, therefore, becomes the "raw material of natural language," and as letters incite the mouth to perform in all of its physicality, alphabets come to "represent" the materiality of the earth.[6] Kraitsir, then, provides a prototype of Sir Paget's gesture-speech theory (see introduction), for he emphasizes the importance of the body already "plunged into a material universe"—and he glimpses the mouth's correspondence to that material universe—but he does not make the leap to the body's gestures and to how those gestures migrated to the mouth.

For Kraitsir, the English language, having lost many of its guttural sounds, is impoverished, and he works so that "the English language" may "recover its creative energy." To do so, he argues that we must "treat it in a totally different way," one that does not lose "sight of the signification of elementary sounds."[7] Whitman, surely, treated poetry in a "totally different way." As Muriel Rukeyser says, Whitman "remembered his body as other poets of his time remembered English verse." She continues, "Out of his own Body, and its relation to itself and the sea, he drew his basic rhythms." His poetics emerged "not out of English prosody but the fluids of organism."[8] Just as Kraitsir saw language, the body, and the earth to be necessarily interdependent, Whitman saw the origin of all poetry to be, in part, founded in a body's engagement with the material universe.

However, Whitman extends Kraitsir's ideas. Kraitsir recognizes that the "cries of animals have their meaning," but sees these as merely "voices of the instincts"—a typical perspective in a culture that largely saw a sharp divide between humans and animals.[9] For Whitman, *all poems* includes the bodily poetics of other species. Another, more direct influence contained a possible seed for this idea. It is well known that Whitman read Emerson's "The Poet" and set out to answer the call. In the essay, Emerson urges poets to find "not metres, but a metre-making argument . . . a thought so passionate and alive that like the spirit of a plant *or an animal* it has an architecture of its own."[10] Scholars have readily explored how *Leaves of Grass* plays on the trope of the organic, sexual, and cosmological blade of grass; how Whitman hand-stamped the title into leather so that *Leaves of Grass* morphs into vines and leaves; how grass and poetry partake in a continual process of decomposition and composition to form its innovative architectures; how Whitman's "This Compost" becomes the master trope of Jed Rasula's "wreading" of poetry in *This Compost*—and yet, Emerson said "like a plant [. . .] *or an animal*."[11]

In comparison to the numerous works on human *poiesis* and Whitman's poetics, only a small handful of scattered essays touch on the importance of animal *poiesis*. A brief survey of them helps identify the need for a more thorough exploration. In the 1963 *PMLA* article "Whitman's Debt to Animal Magnetism," Edmund Reiss begins this work as he traces the trope of the "universal fluid which saturate[s] all bodies" in Whitman's work. The body is electric, that is, because of the "vital force" of a "physical fluid." Reiss focuses on human bodies in his work, but regardless, no one extended his ideas.[12] In 2011, Garrison observes how *Leaves of Grass* "achieves expansive community through communion at a primordial, nonlinguistic, animal level"—but his aim is to show how Whitman influenced John Dewey's philosophy.[13] In the 2010 "'As if the beasts spoke'," M. Jimmie Killingsworth discusses how early readers of Whitman often revolted at the pervasive animality in *Leaves of Grass*. The idea that "Song of Myself" is a "poem of recovery, a poem about gathering energy from animal life" was not lost upon them. Killingsworth suggests that Whitman "clearly places the poet in the category of the other, the nonhuman animal."[14] The essay begins to address the absence of animals in Killingsworth's earlier book, *Whitman's Poetry of the Body*, that focuses on the bodies of humans. Thomas Gannon also explores the animals in Whitman's works, but he doubts "Whitman ever actually gets beyond his own androcentric poetics and point of view in his adoption of another animal's 'barbaric yawp.'"[15] Gannon sees animals functioning merely as tropes and does not suspect Whitman is concerned with the actual animals of the earth living outside of his poetic vision.

Something is missing in these discussions of Whitman's animals, namely, a perspective that sees animal *poiesis* to be much more central to Whitman's poetry and poetics. In what follows, I retrace well-trodden steps in Whitman scholarship: the poetics of the human body. I do so to re-establish the overwhelming emphasis Whitman placed on the body, but with a slant. Whitman does not elevate human *poiesis* over the *poiesis* of other animals, and as such, it is helpful to contextualize the human within the overarching *zoopoetics* shared by many animals. After discussing human bodies, I shift to the animal bodies permeating Whitman's works. Some of Whitman's innovative breakthroughs in form emerged from an attentiveness to the bodily *poiesis* of locusts, spiders, eagles, and more. The exploration highlights how, for Whitman, the origin of poetry is found not only in the forces of the human body and the elemental forces of the earth, but also, and necessarily so, in the forces of other animal makers.

The Human Body and the Origin of Poetry

In what became "Song of Myself," Whitman urges his readers to pause and reflect upon what might be gained from reading his poetry: "Stop this day and night with me and you shall possess the origin of all poems" (*LG* 1855, 14). This phrase captures one of the dominant, driving forces of Whitman's poetic vision. Time and time again, Whitman gravitates to the origin of poems that is found in the body, in the body's interaction with other bodies, and in the body's embeddedness within the material, elemental forces of the earth. I suggest that Whitman gravitates toward what George Kennedy calls "rhetorical energy":

> Rhetoric in the most general sense may perhaps be identified with the energy inherent in communication: the emotional energy that impels the speaker to speak, the physical energy expended in the utterance, the energy level coded in the message, and the energy experienced by the recipient in decoding the message.

Later in "A Hoot in the Dark . . . ," Kennedy locates the source of the energy to be in the body's "physical actions, facial expressions, gestures"—and, for Kennedy, rhetorical energy describes a phenomenon that crosses species lines. Kennedy establishes an evolutionary framework to support his claims. He sees the myriad vocalizations and languages to be similar to the taxonomic category of individual species, and the energy generated by the body to be a common *genus* shared by many animals.[16]

Likewise, Whitman embeds "the origin of all poems" within an evolutionary framework. Later in his career, he wrote the prose-piece "Darwinism—(Then Furthermore)." He sees the "advent of Darwinism" as crucial so that the "world of erudition, both moral and physical" will be "eventually better'd and broaden'ed in its speculations."[17] For Whitman, the "advent of Darwinism" puts pressure on the poet, and midway through the piece, he shifts to discuss the implications that arise for the poet in Darwin's wake: "What is finally to be done by priest or poet . . . amid all the stupendous and dazzling novelties of our century . . . remains just as indispensable," and he calls on poets to "recast the old metal, the already achiev'd material, into and through new moulds, current forms" (*CPW* 1892, 326–27). He is very Emersonian, echoing the mandate from "The Poet" to create the "metre-making argument . . . [that] has an architecture of its own." Poetic form, then, must evolve.[18]

More astonishing is the fact that Whitman establishes an evolutionary perspective in his 1855 *Leaves of Grass*—which he published four years before Darwin's *On the Origin of Species*. In what became "I Sing the Body Electric," Whitman locates the presence of a human body within cosmological space and time: "For him the globe lay preparing quintillions of years without one animal or plant, / For him the revolving cycles truly and steadily rolled" (*LG* 1855, 81). Likewise, "Song of Myself" locates "a leaf of grass," a "pismire," "grain of sand," an "egg of the wren," a "tree-toad," a "blackberry," the "narrowest hinge in [his] hand," a "cow crunching with depressed head," a "mouse," and "the farmer's girl boiling her iron tea-kettle and backing shortcake" all to be "no less than the journeywork of the stars" (*LG* 1855, 34). For Whitman, the organic poem, like a leaf of grass, also emerges from the "journeywork of the stars." That is to say, the poem's origin—the origin of language—has its roots in the "quintillions of years" it took for material life to emerge.[19]

And yet, scholars have not fully explored what Whitman means by "the origin of all poems."[20] The oversight emerges, in part, from a (mis)reading that assumes a transcendental origin of words. Whitman's insistence upon the inseparable unity of body and soul, the material and the immaterial, the earthly and the divine, seemingly supports such a read; however, the notion of a transcendental origin of words, separate from the body, creates a blindspot. In "The Pregnant Muse: Language and Birth in 'A Song of the Rolling Earth,'" for instance, James Griffin sees Whitman advocating for a transcendental origin of language: "Even as the poem begins, Whitman sets out his first definition, a crucial distinction between words and Words." In a note, Griffin emphasizes the distinction further as he articulates his commitment to use "uppercase to distinguish the metaphysical use from the conventional one." Griffin discusses how the Word/word dichotomy "stems from Greek philosophy" and the gospel of John where the Word—"the self-revealing thought and will of God"—becomes flesh.[21] As a result, he sees phrases such as "human bodies are words, myriads of

words" as meaning "human bodies are the incarnation of metaphysical *Words*."
Though one cannot discount the fusion of the body and soul in Whitman's work,
I suggest that such readings obscure Whitman's emphasis upon the material
origin of words.

Rather than establishing a separation between Word/word, the opening lines
of the "A Song of the Rolling Earth" establish the material origin of language:

> A SONG of the rolling earth, and of words according,
> Were you thinking that those were the words, those upright lines?
>   those curves, angles, dots?
> No, those are not the words, the substantial words are in the
>   ground and sea,
> They are in the air, they are in you.

Here, Whitman pushes against the bias prevalent in cultures that use alphabetic
systems of language. The words printed on the page, with their uncanny shapes,
are not the "substantial words." Rather, the "substantial words" are found in the
forces of the "ground and sea" and in the forces of the "air" and in hu-
man/animal bodies. Later in the poem, he foregrounds the four elements, "Air,
soil, water, fire—those are words," and when he says "human bodies are words,
myriads of words," he tends toward a poetics founded upon bodily *poiesis* (*LG*
1891–92, 176). Readers familiar with Whitman's preface to *Leaves of Grass*
readily notice the echo. There he writes, "your very flesh shall be a great poem
and have the richest fluency not only in its words but in the silent lines of its lips
and face and between the lashes of your eyes and in every motion and joint of
your body" (*LG* 1855, vi). Circling back to the opening lines of the "A Song of
the Rolling Earth," Whitman distinguishes not between words and the "ancient
tradition of The Word as a cosmic reason" as Griffin suggests, but rather between the seemingly disembodied print marks on a page and a body who is embedded within the elemental forces of the earth.

The third section of the poem clarifies the distinction further:

> I swear I begin to see little or nothing in audible words,
> All merges toward the presentation of the unspoken meanings
>   of the earth,
> Toward him who sings the songs of the body and of the truths
>   of the earth,
> Toward him who makes the dictionaries of words that print can-
>   not touch. (*LG* 1891–92, 179)

The beginning of the poem shuns alphabetic words, and here, Whitman dispar-
ages even "audible words." They are not enough. He pushes *words* back out of
the mouth, returning them to the "songs of the body" and to the elemental
"truths of the earth." That is to say, he pushes words back toward what Kristeva
calls the pre-linguistic energy of the *semiotic chora* and what Kennedy calls the
"rhetorical energy" of the body.

Though the body and the soul, the material and the immaterial, are insepa-rable in Whitman's vision, he nonetheless begins with the body. The material precedes the immaterial. He makes this clear in "Starting from Paumanok": "I will make the poems of materials, for I think they are to be the most spiritual poems, / And I will make poems of my body and of mortality, / For I think I shall then supply myself with the poems of my soul and of immortality" (*LG* 1891–92, 21). "Vocalism" further establishes Whitman's commitment to starting with a body who is embedded in the elemental forces of the earth (*LG* 1891–92, 297). The first line defines vocalism as "measure, concentration, determination, and the divine power to speak words," but Whitman follows the definition with several questions that challenge the reader:

> Are you full-lung'd and limber-lipp'd from long trial? from vigor-
> ous practice? from physique?
> Do you move in these broad lands as broad as they?
> Come duly to the divine power to speak words?

The following sentence, spanning eight long lines, explicates what a speaker needs to undergo in order to attain the "divine power to speak words." She or he finds this power "only at last after many years, after chastity, friendship, procre-ation, prudence, and nakedness, / After treading ground and breasting river and lake, / After a loosen'd throat. . . ." That divine power comes from existing with-in the forces of soil, rivers, lakes—and though this poem does not mention the other two elements, I infer that fire and air likewise shape the human tongue. In the 1860 edition of *Leaves of Grass*, Whitman adds two stanzas that eventually find their way into "Song of Myself."[22] The first further highlights the tongue's connection to the elements: "My tongue . . . form'd from this soil, this air." He has attained the divine power to speak words and makes this explicit in the end of the second added stanza: "I permit to speak, / Nature, without check, with *original energy*" (*LG* 1860, 8, italics added). *Original* resonates with two mean-ings. His poetry and poetics are clearly innovative—that is, original—but they draw upon and transmit an originary, primal, physical energy. What is more, and what has often been overlooked, is that Whitman's *oeuvre* extends *original en-ergy* beyond the human species. Other animals participate within and generate this energy. While Kennedy argues that many animals "share a 'deep,' universal rhetoric," Whitman's poetics suggests that many animals share a deep, universal *poetics*. Many animals, as makers who are embedded within the elemental forc-es of the earth, generate poetic energy.

The "same old law": Animals & the Origin of Poetry

In "(De)composing Whitman," Paul Outka observes how "Whitman's texts are embodied and his bodies are textualized"—but such an insight must expand to include the bodies of animals. Though he further contributes to a more thorough understanding of Whitman's ecological vision, he nonetheless does not pursue the implications of the textualized *animal* body. Rather, he suggests Whitman sees animals from the entrenched perspective of division. "Whitman," states Outka, "often expresses deep admiration for the *unselfconscious* existence of animals." [23] Such thinking perpetuates the long history of Western philosophy and religion that casts animals as agency-less, instinct-driven machines. In what follows, I present evidence to suggest Whitman saw animals as possessing agency. (The eagles in "The Dalliance of the Eagles," discussed later, seem quite conscious of their play.) Exploring the implications of the textualized animal body must not turn the body and the text into merely tropes. He textualizes the body because the body is, through its material existence within the elemental forces of the earth, the origin of all poems. The body *is* the poem, not a metaphor *for* the poem. The oxen written about in "Song of Myself" exemplify the textualized body of an animal:

> Oxen that rattle the yoke and chain or halt in the leafy shade,
> > what is that you express in your eyes?
> It seems to me more than all the print I have read in my life. (*LG* 1891–92, 38)

Whitman's "My Canary Bird" likewise casts the vocalizations and gestures of birds as something on par with human texts:

> Did we count great, O soul, to penetrate the themes of mighty
> > books,
> Absorbing deep and full from thoughts, plays, speculations?
> But now from thee to me, caged bird, to feel thy joyous warble,
> Filling the air, the lonesome room, the long forenoon,
> Is it not just as great, O soul? (*LG* 1891–92, 386)

Ambiguity leaves room for two readings. The soul Whitman addresses could be his, or it could be the bird's. To discount that birds feel emotions—and to assume that they are unconscious of their expressions of those emotions—fails to recognize the complex social rituals such calls create and sustain. Whitman's textualization of oxen and a canary points toward the poetic energy of animals.

Recalling the first foci of zoopoetics from the introduction, Whitman celebrates how animals are makers. Furthermore, Whitman sees a similarity between the bodily *poiesis* of animals and that of humans. Section fourteen of "Song of Myself" begins with a list of the gestures and vocalizations of several animals:

> The wild gander leads his flock through the cool night,
> *Ya-honk* he says, and sounds it down to me like an invitation,
> The pert may suppose it meaningless, but I listening close,
> Find its purpose and place up there toward the wintry sky.
> The sharp-hoof'd moose of the north, the cat on the house-sill,
> > the chickadee, the prairie-dog,

> The litter of the grunting sow as they tug at her teats,
> The brood of the turkey-hen and she with her half-spread wings, . . .

. . . but then Whitman, like Kennedy many years later, merges the human and animal spheres: "I see in them and myself *the same old law*" (*LG* 1891–92, 38–39). These two stanzas, with slight revision, appear in each iteration of what became "Song of Myself" from the 1855 edition to the final draft of 1891–92, and it demonstrates how, for Whitman, animals exhibit agency and purpose in their bodily *poiesis*. As Whitman "listen[s] close" to the sounding of the gander, he makes explicit his *attentiveness* to the bodily *poiesis* of other species. Only then does he "find its purpose and place." The passage quoted above shows Whitman gravitating toward what Rotman calls "emblem gestures" (discussed in the introduction). For instance, the emblem gesture of the "half-spread wings" of the turkey-hen means something to her brood and to those who know how to interact with such gestures. Whitman's language suggests the turkey-hen has agency in the way she carries herself amongst her hatchlings.

Zoopoetics helps illuminate a question to which Whitman draws attention. Near the end of his career, Whitman provided "A Backward Glance o'er Travel'd Roads"—an essay that reflects upon his poetic and cultural achievement. Perhaps surprisingly, Whitman includes animality as one of the driving sources of his songs, but with a cryptic qualifier: "'Leaves of Grass' is avowedly the song of Sex and Amativeness, and even Animality—though meanings that do not usually go along with those words are behind all, and will duly emerge; and all are sought to be lifted into a different light and atmosphere" (*LG* 1891–92, 436). *Animality*, normally read in the negative light of human carnality, suggests something ineffable, something different, something more encompassing. Whitman casts Animality (like Sex and Amativeness) as a positive force. He blurs the distinction between humans and other animals, but he leaves the meaning un-explicated. He leaves the work of "lift[ing]" animality "into a different light and atmosphere" to his readers. His poetry casts Animality as none other than "the same old law" shared between many animals. As I explore later in a discussion of "The Dalliance of the Eagles," Whitman's Animality is unrelentingly *sexual*, but it is, at the same time, very similar to Kristeva's notion of the *semiotic chora*. The "deluge of the signifier" in Whitman's poetry and poetics is, to use Kristeva's wording, a "poetic animality."[24] What Whitman does, though, is he takes seriously, listens to, and is affected by the energy of other species' "pre-verbal" bodily *poiesis*. Like Kennedy argued nearly a century and a half later, Whitman demonstrates how many animals share a universal rhetorical/poetic energy. As a maker, he opens himself up to the makings of other species, which, in turn, shape his poetry. That is to say, Whitman sets forth a vision that assumes the origin of all poems is one shared by many animals.

Concrete examples substantiate these claims. In the already discussed "Song of the Rolling Earth," Whitman includes the "open countenances of animals," highlighting how facial expressions of animals contribute to the "dictionaries of words that print cannot touch" (*LG* 1891–92, 179). Such gestures are, like Cummings suggests later, prime numbers, irreducibly so. Like the faces of humans, these countenances have been shaped by beings who are embedded within the earth's elements. More to the point, the first section of "Starting from the Paumanok" emphasizes how animals shape Whitman's poetic vision. One long sentence stretches across fourteen lines, showing a continuity and a synthesis of many contributing influences. Symbolically, the first line emphasizes Whitman's animal origins: "Starting from *fish-shape* Paumanok where I was born" (italics added). The metaphor establishes the origin of the elements of the earth (the water of the river) as well as the origin of animality (the fish). As the sentence continues to unfold, other animals further contribute. He "strike[s] up for a New World" only after increasing his "Aware[ness] of the buffalo herds grazing the plains, the hirsute and strong-breasted bull" and after "Having studied the mocking-bird's tones and the flight of the mountain-hawk, / And heard at dawn the unrivall'd one, the hermit thrush from the swamp-cedars" (*LG* 1891–92, 18–19). His word choice of *awareness* and *studied* resonates with the etymological roots of *attentiveness*—a *stretching toward*, in this case, animals.

Animals populate *Specimen Days*: bees, hornets, wasps, blackbirds, crows, ravens, thrush, swallows, robins, hogs, horses, quail, snakes, and many more. Often, the prose-pieces on animals expose Whitman's conscious attentiveness toward their bodily *poiesis*. For instance, on August 22, 1876, he writes about his time spent listening to the "reedy monotones of locust." I include a long quotation from the entry as it demonstrates how Whitman's attentiveness manifests itself through his writings. The symphonic metaphors he uses to describe the locust-song could easily be applied to the way his language gains momentum, crescendos, breaks, and begins anew:

> A single locust is now heard near noon from a tree two hundred feet off, as I write—a long whirring continued, quite loud noise graded in distinct whirls, or swinging circles, increasing in strength and rapidity up to a certain point, and then a fluttering, quietly tapering fall. Each strain is continued from one to two minutes. The locust-song is very appropriate to the scene—gushes, has meaning, is masculine, is like some fine old wine, not sweet, but far better than sweet. . . .

> . . . Let me say more about the song of the locust, even to repetition; a long, chromatic, tremulous crescendo, like a brass disk whirling round and round, emitting wave after wave of notes, beginning with a certain moderate beat or measure, rapidly increasing in speed and significance, and then quickly and gracefully dropping down and out. Not the melody of the signing-bird—far from it; the common musician might think without melody, but surely having to the finer ear a harmony of its own; monotonous—but what a swing there is in that brassy drone, round and round, cymballine—or like the whirling of brass quoits. (*CPW* 1892, 89)

While the "pert" may find the locust-song as meaningless as the wild gander's "Ya-honk," Whitman "listens closer" (*LG* 1855, 21). As he listens to the locust-song—a song that "gushes, has meaning" where "each strain is continued from one to two minutes"—Whitman listens as a poet listens to another maker. Many of Whitman's poetic sentences continue for "one to two minutes . . . increasing in strength and rapidity up to a certain point" before a "fluttering, quietly tapering fall." Even here, the sentence structure of his prose harmonizes with the locust-song. Long sentences emerge, like "swinging circles," and the many verbful adjectives—*swinging, increasing, fluttering, whirling, emitting, dropping*—add energy to the passage's "long, chromatic, tremulous crescendo." The architecture of Whitman's sentences emerges from his attentive listening to another species' song, epitomizing the zoopoetic process.

Another instance further exposes the zoopoetic dynamic in Whitman's *oeuvre*, "A Noiseless Patient Spider":

> A NOISELESS patient spider,
> I mark'd where on a little promontory it stood isolated,
> Mark'd how to explore the vacant vast surrounding,
> It launch'd forth filament, filament, filament, out of itself,
> Ever unreeling them, ever tirelessly speeding them.
>
> And you O my soul where you stand,
> Surrounded, detached, in measureless oceans of space,
> Ceaselessly musing, venturing, throwing, seeking the spheres to
>   connect them,
> Till the bridge you will need be form'd, till the ductile anchor
>   hold,
> Till the gossamer thread you fling catch somewhere, O my soul. (*LG* 1891–92,
> 343)

Rather than seeing the spider merely as a trope for Whitman's soul, I suggest that the impetus for the poem emerged from Whitman's attentiveness toward a spider undergoing her own act of bodily *poiesis:* web-making. From this perspective, the poem hinges not on the turn to the soul in the second stanza, but rather on the line "It launch'd forth filament, filament, filament, out of itself." The spider's *poiesis* animates the poem on several layers of iconicity. Most obvious, perhaps, is the onomatopoetic effect of the five *f* sounds, the *ffffffff* of the thread launched into the "vacant vast surrounding." A more involved reader, though, begins to mime this launching of the thread—mime, therefore, the bodily *poiesis* of the spider—gesturing with one's arm and hand out toward the "vacant vast surrounding" in front of him or her. This insight leads to a third level of iconicity: the spatial/temporal dynamic both on the poetic page and in the empty space around the spider/reader. Because the line pulses with a dactylic beat (IT launched forth FILament, FILament, FILament, OUT of itSELF)—one expects the two soft beats following SELF. A patient reader pauses not only because of the line break, but because of the stillness generated by the absence of the soft beats. One then sees the last *f* trailing off in this temporal pause into the "vacant vast surrounding" of the spatial poetic page at the end of the line break, and this coincides with the empty space around the spider/reader who launches (or mimes launching) the filaments. The audio/visual/bodily/spatial/temporal iconicity allows the reader to experience vestiges of the *poiesis* of the spiders Whitman attentively engaged.[25] Moreover, the several layers of iconicity extend Kristeva's "deluge of the signifier," for it is not only a deluge caused by a human body, but by the energy of an animal's bodily *poiesis*. The poem's accomplishment is found not merely in its content, but the gestures of its form.

But that is not all. The dactylic pulses from "filament, filament, filament" augment throughout the poem. Much like the *whirling, swinging, emitting* energy of the locust-song, the dactylic energy of *filament, filament, filament* gives shape to harmonious iambic/dactylic/anapestic rhythms of three stresses in "the vacant vast surrounding" (iambic); "measureless oceans of space" (dactylic); "Till the bridge you will need be form'd" (anapestic); "till the ductile anchor hold" (anapestic); "Till the gossamer thread you fling" (anapestic). This rhythm of threes (filament occurs three times; filament has three syllables; each phrase quoted has three strong beats; there are three till's), manifests itself in the title and first line's iambic trimeter "A Noiseless Patient Spider." Whitman could have said "thread, thread, thread" or "silk, silk, silk"—but he selected *filament, filament, filament*. That constellation of repeated words becomes the starting point that shapes the rhythms throughout the entire poem, and I suggest that he chose that word, in part, through minding an actual spider who launched more than one or two threads. Consequently, this poem transcends the alphabetic system it begins in and becomes an ideogrammatic, material architecture where the bodily poiesis of another species emerges through the poetic gestures of human language. Moving beyond seeing the spider as a trope for the soul places emphasis on how Whitman's attentiveness toward spiders enabled him to achieve significant breakthroughs in poetic form, especially the interrelated constellations of iambs, dactyls, and anapests that all gyrate out of the iconic *fffff* of a spider launching a filament. "A Noiseless Patient Spider" is one of the "best poems," for in it, the body of a spider "re-appears" (*LG* 1891–92, 176).

"A Noiseless Patient Spider" approaches that which precedes Aristotle's "general origin of poetry": imitation. Though it imitates the launching of the filament, it foregrounds the crucial prerequisite: *attentiveness*. As established in the introduction, the Latin roots of *attentiveness* suggest a *stretching toward*. Whitman not only expresses a desire to "stretch toward" the earth through the trope of a spider/soul who is "ceaselessly musing, venturing, throwing, [and] seeking spheres [of connection]"—but he moreover stretches toward a specific spider through the *material gestures* of the poem itself. It is a stretching toward embodied in the form of the poem, and it is this kind of exquisite attentiveness that provides impetus for the imitation found in *filament, filament, filament, out of itself*. Whitman and the spider, indeed, follow the *same old law*.

Spiders in a Posthuman World

Do spiders have agency in the creation of their web? Is there conscious intention, problem solving, or something akin to the imagination at work when a spider looks for, finds, and creates a web? How much of the process is genetically coded? Do spiders navigate the timing of any of their movements? If I claim that spiders possess a degree of agency, am I simply anthropomorphizing them? Is a spider really a *maker* who undergoes *poiesis*?

Before continuing an exploration of Whitman's zoopoetics, I further address the issue of anthropomorphism and agency. It is much easier to recognize the agency of a dolphin, or elephant, or chimpanzee, or even of an eagle over a spider's—or to say that mammals share the *same old law*—but arachnids? Arachnids aside, animal agency is, for some, circumspect. Despite Donna Haraway's observation that in scientific culture in the late-twentieth century, "the boundary between human and animal is thoroughly breached," and that the "last beachheads of uniqueness [language, tool use, social behavior, mental events] have been polluted if not turned into amusement parks"; despite the ecocritics call for a multiculturalism that includes animals; despite the work of ethologists, such as the many in Laland and Galef's 2009 collection *The Question of Animal Culture*, who argue that animals are social beings who cultivate a sense of belonging through clear gestures and vocalizations—that is, they cultivate culture consciously and intentionally for no other reason than to belong; despite the known fact that many animals possess mirror neurons that "scientifically proves" their capacity to empathize; and despite the innumerable personal anecdotes regarding human experiences within what Haraway calls the interspecies "contact zone" where humans and animals invent while they play; despite the fact that literary figures such as Edgar Allan Poe, among others, have argued that "the line which demarcates the instinct of the brute creation from the boasted reason of man, is, beyond doubt, of the most shadowy and unsatisfactory character—a boundary line far more difficult to settle than even the North-Eastern or the Oregon"; despite the growing awareness of how speciesism erroneously limits cognitive abilities to the higher mammals—despite this work and these interdisciplinary perspectives, a common response I often receive when discussing zoopoetics with colleagues is, "aren't you anthropomorphizing here?"[26] Given the length and energy of Derrida's attempt in *The Animal that Therefore I Am* to deconstruct the HUMAN/animal divide perpetuated throughout Western thought, it is a fair question.

In their introduction to *Animal Agency*, Sarah McFarland and Ryan Hediger identify two prevailing viewpoints concerning humans and animals that can help navigate the issue of anthropomorphism. One viewpoint "emphasizes continuity" between humans and animals "and has Darwin as its familiar champion." The other viewpoint "emphasizes the discontinuities" between humans and all other animals "and has traditional western monotheistic religion and much of the western philosophic tradition as it strongest supports."[27] McFarland, Hediger, and the authors in the collection see continuity between animals and humans. Anthropomorphism—as well as zoomorphism, or attributing animal traits to humans—if "guarded" and "critical" can illuminate that continuity.[28]

Despite the overwhelming work in ethology that supports continuity, McFarland and Hediger still feel pressed to address the two viewpoints in 2009. Moreover, they begin the introduction by reminding readers what happened at the San Francisco Zoo on December 25th, 2007. Tatiana, the Siberian Tiger, "escaped . . . and killed a man who may have been taunting her."[29] Is this an inter-species hate-crime? A retaliation? The tiger did not kill the man to satisfy basic needs, for she passed over many other "meals" while she tracked the man down. One cannot say the tiger murdered the man, a heterocide so to speak, for "murder" is a term too saturated with human agency to attribute to an animal, but the tiger, nonetheless, possessed a degree of conscious intention in the carrying out of her actions.

It is much easier, though, to recognize how tigers, chimpanzees, orca, and other large animals possess agency, and much more difficult to see a spider, spinning her web, as a being who acts with degrees of agency. The perspective that sees continuity between animals helps. I see the spider—like many animals—to be genetically coded and yet to also have a degree of agency to act, as I mention in the introduction, at the right time. Not as much as tigers or humans, but some. Darwin nor God (nor Darwin and God—whatever one's perspective is) did not turn agency on for the mammals and off for other animals. Anthropomorphism is only a fallacy when stark divide, rather than continuity, shapes an understanding of ANIMAL↔HUMAN spheres. There are differences between humans and other animals, but they are differences in degree.

Crying "fallacy" at all anthropomorphisms and zoomorphisms fails to account for the posthumanist perspective. Traditional definitions of *being human* are upset for the posthumanist as the technological and the animal transgress boundaries. It is no longer adequate to define *human* as *not-animal* and *not-machine*. Rather, as Haraway and Wolfe (among others) have suggested, to be *human* is to be hybrid, acknowledging, in part, one's physical, material, animal and/or technological body. Posthumanist figures have always been with us: the zoomorphisms at play in Medusa, centaurs, and the Minotaur; and Odysseus becomes an unsuspecting hybrid figure as the technology of his tools (to make his raft; his bow) become extensions of himself, contributing to his august ontology.

Though others disagree, I see Whitman as a proto-posthumanist.[30] Ed Folsom foregrounds Whitman's intimate and organic connection with the print setting technology of his time in the article with a telling title, "Whitman Making Books/Books Making Whitman." Whitman *was* a printer. He set his own type. He held the heft of the steel blocks as part of his making as a poet. He stamped out the letters morphing into leaves on the cover of the 1855 *Leaves of Grass*. Folsom suggests that Whitman "probably never composed a line of poetry without, in his mind's eye, putting it on a composing stick."[31] Along with his technological hybridity, Whitman's poetics blurs the boundary between humans and animals. For Whitman to see the *poiesis* of a spider on par with the *poiesis* of a poet suggests that, long before the term "posthuman," Whitman celebrated the continuity shared across ANIMAL↔HUMAN spheres.

Derrida, in *The Animal that Therefore I Am*, provides yet another way of thinking about spiders. As he deconstructs the Western philosophic tradition that perpetuates a divide between humans and animals (Decartes, Kant, Hegel, Heidegger, Levinas, and Lacan), he articulates his vision:

> *Limitrophy* is therefore my subject. Not just because it will concern what sprouts or grows at the limit, around the limit, by maintaining the limit, but also what *feeds the limit*, generates it, raises it, and complicates it. Everything I'll say will consist, certainly not in effacing the limit, but in multiplying its figures, in complicating, thickening, delinearizing, folding, and dividing the line precisely by making it increase and multiply.

The process of *limitrophy* complicates the divide between the abyss of the human and the abyss of the animal—and, what is more, for Derrida, the *limit* itself becomes its own abyss. "As with every bottomless gaze, as with the eyes of the other," he says, "the gaze called 'animal' offers to my sight the abyssal limit of the human: the inhuman or the ahuman, the ends of man, that is to say, the bordercrossing." When a human enters the limit and gazes into the abyss of the animal other, she or he can, according to Derrida, experience vertigo.[32] Other senses, too, may draw attention to the abyss of the animal other. For Whitman, the tactile superiority of the spider—not her or his eyes—became the catalyst that ushered Whitman into a vertiginous state of being.

I cannot offer more than a perspective that identifies the agency of spiders, but for far too long assumptions that dismiss the possibility of agency have limited human understanding of animals. A leaf falls through the air differently than a spider. Some may limit the spider's fall to a "mindless reaction." How much more wonder is there, though, in the phrase, "a spider's well-timed response." Then one reels at the abyss.

I Sing the Eagle Electric

Repeatedly, Whitman senses the abyss of the animal not through their eyes but through the animal's bodily *poiesis*. His understanding that the "great poem" resides in "every motion and joint" of a body (*LG* 1855, vi) extends to animal bodies. Whitman does this work, but the *same old law* of a poetic Animality shared by many animals has yet to "duly emerge" in conversations surrounding Whitman (*LG* 1891–92, 436). Perhaps this is due to a hesitancy to make the obvious connection between "The Dalliance of the Eagles" and "I Sing the Body Electric." Granted, Whitman carves out nine sections to explore the dalliance of the human body and only one stanza for the electricity of eagles; his emphasis, therefore, *is* upon the human. Nonetheless, in the context of *the same old law* shared by many animals and his claim that Sex, Amativeness, and Animality infuse *Leaves of Grass*, I suggest that Whitman is concerned less with hierarchy and much more with a continuity between species.

No other poem brings to fruition the poetics of the human body than "I Sing the Body Electric." The second section reestablishes the bodily *poiesis* of humans:

> The expression of the face balks account,
> But the expression of a well-made man appears not only in his
>   face,
> It is in his limbs and joints also, it is curiously in the joints of his
>   hips and wrists,
> It is in his walk, the carriage of his neck, the flex of his waist and
>   knees, dress does not hide him,
> The strong sweet quality he has strikes through the cotton and
>   broadcloth,
> To see him pass conveys as much as the best poem, perhaps more,
> You linger to see his back, and the back of his neck and shoul-
>   der-side. (*LG* 1891–92, 81–82)

Here, Whitman emphasizes how the movement of the *human* body "conveys as much as the best poem," and the poem delves into both the male and female body. The final sentence, in Whitmanian fashion, spans the ninth section's thirty-six lines, and as it progresses through a host of individual parts of the body, the form reinforces the body's unity. Each part is a whole and each whole contains multitudes of parts.

However, "I Sing the Body Electric" ought to be contextualized within a greater Animality. The movement of the *animal body*, for Whitman, also "conveys as much as the best poem." "The Dalliance of the Eagles" revisits the three-fold, interrelated themes of Sex, Amativeness, and Animality Whitman explored. The eagles undergo an "amorous contact high in space together," and though some may cry "anthropomorphism," these creatures that mate for life are not emotionless. I am drawn to the context of the love-making. Like the noiseless patient spider, the pair of eagles enter the atmosphere's "measureless oceans of space" and "vacant vast surrounding." It is a context that encourages a body to create, and it is no mistake that Whitman's language conjures images of the formless void of empty space prior to one myth's creation story. In this empty space—and to use language from "I Sing the Body Electric"—the eagles' "mad filaments"; "[beak]-hinges"; "Ribs, belly, backbone, joints of the backbone"; "lung-sponges" participate in the joint creation of the poem, and the eagles generate their own type of "voice, articulation, language, whispering, shouting aloud" throughout their feat:[33]

> Skirting the river road, (my forenoon walk, my rest,)
> Skyward in air a sudden muffled sound, the dalliance of the eagles,
> The rushing amorous contact high in space together,

> The clinching interlocking claws, a living, fierce, gyrating wheel,
> Four beating wings, two beaks, a swirling mass tight grappling,
> In tumbling turning clustering loops, straight downward falling,
> Till o'er the river pois'd, the twain yet one, a moment's lull,
> A motionless still balance in the air, then parting, talons loosing,
> Upward again on slow-firm pinions slanting, their separate diverse
>   flight,
> She hers, he his, pursuing. (*LG* 1891–92, 216)

Like the ninth section of "I Sing the Body Electric," one sentence spans many lines of "The Dalliance of the Eagles." All the motion, and each individual moment of that motion, contributes to a unified whole. Sounds of the union linger in the musicality of "clinching interlocking claws." The alliterated *k* sounds, of course, echo the talons clashing and in this context, the *ch* sound midway through *clinching* echoes the softer sound of feathered flesh coming together. Whitman follows no strict line length, but the lines emit an iambic beat throughout. He does, though, return to the same language used to express the locust-song. The poem of these eagles—their bodily *poiesis*—creates a "gyrating wheel" and a "swirling mass" that, like the locust-song, moves through the atmosphere. Likewise, Whitman uses a host of verbful adjectives to lend an every increasing crescendo of energy throughout the poem—*skirting, rushing, clinching, interlocking, gyrating, beating, swirling, grappling, tumbling, turning, parting, loosing, slanting, pursuing*—until the poem undergoes the post-spasm "tapering fall" in the final line's three short beats, "She hers, he his, pursuing."

Whitman's "The Dalliance of the Eagles," "The Noiseless Patient Spider," and his prose piece on the locust-song are all multi-species events. Readers do not readily see such poems in this light, and I suggest that one reason lies in what Cary Wolfe calls the "unexamined framework of speciesism" within the humanities, the "fundamental repression" of "nonhuman subjectivity"—a speciesism that "take[s] it for granted that the subject is always already human."[34] Point in case, the trope of "energy" is familiar in the field of poetry and poetics—but this energy is often defined as a solely and uniquely *human* energy. Muriel Rukeyser sees poems as sources of "human energy": "Exchange is creation. . . . In poetry, the exchange is one of energy. Human energy is transferred, and from the poem it reaches the reader."[35] Charles Olson in his influential "Projective Verse," focuses on the "*kinetics*" of the poem, how it is a "high energy-construct and, at all points, an energy-discharge." Olson recognizes the energy comes from many places outside of the poet, from "several causations," but by leaving the causations implicit, the energy of the animal remains in the background.[36] In another influential essay, "Literature and Ecology: An Experiment in Ecocriticism," William Rueckert echoes Gary Snyder's viewpoint that the poem is "stored energy, a formal turbulence, a living thing." Rueckert's essay is the first formal use of the term *ecocriticism*, and it is telling that Rueckert uses the ecological trope of energy transfers to illuminate the dynamics of a classroom:

> Coming together in the classroom, in the lecture hall, in the seminar room (any-
> where, really) to discuss or read or study literature, is to gather energy centers
> around a matrix of stored poetic/verbal energy. In some ways, this is the true
> interactive field because the energy flow is not just a two-way flow from poem
> to person as it would be in reading; the flow is along many energy pathways
> from poem to person, from person to person. The process is triangulated,
> quadrangulated, multiangulated.[37]

Though I could not agree more that a multiangulated energy transfer best articulates the "interactive field" of the classroom, Rueckert's work, nonetheless,
demonstrates the unexamined speciesism to which Wolfe draws attention. Prior
to the work of Rukeyser, Olson, and Rueckert, Whitman set forth a vision of
"original energy," one that necessarily includes the energy exchanges between
many species. Zoopoetics encapsulates the energy exchanges across species as
the bodily *poiesis* of numerous animals contribute to Whitman's makings of
poems.

Toward Whitman's Descendants

In "A Song of the Rolling Earth," Whitman claims that "in the best poems re-
appears the body" (*LG* 1891–92, 176). In light of his *oeuvre*, this claim extends
to include the bodies of many different species that reappear in the material architecture of the poem. Indeed, Whitman demonstrates that many animals participate in "original energy," a *poiesis* of a body embedded in the elemental forces
of the earth. He locates his poetics within an evolutionary framework that does
not exclude other species from this energy, but rather exposes continuity. Many
animals partake in the "same old law." Moreover, as Whitman attentively engaged the *poiesis* of many species—including oxen, canary birds, turkey-hens,
locusts, spiders, eagles—the animal *poiesis* contributed to the architecture of his
own poems. "A Noiseless Patient Spider," "The Dalliance of the Eagles," and
his prose piece on the locust-song would not exist if Whitman did not attentively
observe and study such animals. He performed, though, what is now called a
close-reading of these animals' *poiesis*, and his reading contributed to some of
his innovative breakthroughs in form. Animals inextricably entangle themselves
in Whitman's poetics. His creations are not a purely human affair, but rather
bend to, sway with, and progress alongside the makings of other animals.

   And it just so happens that Whitman contributes a tremendous amount of
energy to the evolution of American poetry. Though plants and the elemental
forces of the earth contribute energy to Whitman's forms, so do locusts, eagles
and other flocks of birds, spiders, oxen, mice, ants, and many other species. The
bodily, material energy that becomes the "deluge," overwhelming the signifier,
is an animality shared across species lines—something E. E. Cummings knew
all too well.

Notes

1. Julia Kristeva, *Revolution in Poetic Language*, trans. Margaret Waller (New York: Columbia University Press, 1984), 79, 102–103.

2. Ibid., 25, 26, 27, 79.

3. In an email exchange with the Whitman scholar Ken Price, I learned that a comprehensive list of Whitman's library is underway. Price verified that neither of Kraitsir's books have yet been identified within Whitman's library.

4. Michael West, "Charles Kraitsir's Influence Upon Thoreau's Theory of Language," *ESQ: A Journal of the American Renaissance* 19, no. 4 (1973): 262.

5. Charles V. Kraitsir, *Glossology: Being a Treatise on the Nature of Language, and on the Language of Nature* (New York: George Putnam, 1852), 19, 22, 214.

6. Charles V. Kraitsir, *Significance of the Alphabet* (Boston: Peabody, 1846), 3, 15, 16.

7. Ibid., 19, 18.

8. Muriel Rukeyser, *The Life of Poetry* (New York: Kraus, 1968), 79, 80.

9. Kraitsir, *Alphabet*, 4.

10. Ralph Waldo Emerson, *The Essential Writings of Ralph Waldo Emerson*, ed. Brooks Atkinson (New York: Modern Library, 2000), 290, italics added.

11. M. Jimmie Killingsworth, "Whitman's Physical Eloquence," in *Walt Whitman: The Centennial Essays*, ed. Ed Folsom (Iowa City: University of Iowa Press, 1994), 70; Ed Folsom, "Whitman Making Books/Books Making Whitman: A Catalog and Commentary," *The Walt Whitman Archive* (Lincoln: Center for Digital Research in the Humanities, University of Nebraska, 2005); Paul Outka, "(De)composing Whitman," *Interdisciplinary Studies in Literature and Environment* 12, no. 1 (2005): 45–48; Jed Rasula, *This Compost: Ecological Imperatives in American Poetry* (Athens: University of Georgia Press, 2002), 84–85.

12. Edmund Reiss, "Whitman's Debt to Animal Magnetism," *Publications of the Modern Language Association of America* 78, no. 1 (1963): 80, 81. In light of Akira Lippit's *Electric Animal: Toward a Rhetoric of Wildlife* (Minneapolis: University of Minnesota Press, 2000), Edmund Reiss' work on fluids, bodies, and magnetism may yet impact the field.

13. Jim Garrison, "Walt Whitman, John Dewey, and Primordial Artistic Communication," *Transactions of the Charles S. Peirce Society: A Quarterly Journal in American Philosophy* 47, no. 3 (2011): 302, 316.

14. M. Jimmie Killingsworth, "'As if the beasts spoke': The Animal / Animist / Animated Walt Whitman," *Walt Whitman Quarterly Review* 28, no. 1–2 (2010): 19, 23, 20.

15. Thomas C. Gannon, "Complaints from the Spotted Hawk: Flights and Feathers in Whitman's 1855 *Leaves of Grass*," in *Leaves of Grass: The Sesquicentennial Essays*, ed. Susan Belasco, Kenneth M. Price, and Ed Folsom (Lincoln: University of Nebraska Press, 2007), 143.

16. Kennedy, "Hoot," 2, 4, 1.

17. Walt Whitman, *Complete Prose Works* in the *Walt Whitman Archive* (Lincoln: Center for Digital Research in the Humanities, University of Nebraska, 1995), 1892, 326; hereafter cited parenthetically as *CPW*.

18. In "A Backward Glance O'er Travel'd Roads," Whitman provides another explicit acknowledgement of evolutionary thinking. He suggests his poems "grow of circumstances, and are evolutionary" (*LG* 1891–92, 429).

19. Aside from the blackberry, animals pervade the list, and in the context of this argument, the list implicitly suggests a connection between the making of a poem ("leaf of grass") and the presence of these animals.

20. When Killingsworth, for instance, discusses Whitman's belief that humans and animals share "the same old law," he only goes as far to suggest Whitman refused to reinforce the Great Chain of Being. He does not venture into an exploration concerning how the "same old law" relates to the origin of poetry ("As if the beasts spoke" 22).

21. James Griffin, "The Pregnant Muse: Language and Birth in 'A Song of the Rolling Earth,'" *Walt Whitman Quarterly Review* 1, no. 1 (1983): 1, 7, 1–2.

22. They begin in a 1860 "proto-leaf," and in the 1867 *Leaves of Grass*, Whitman places the stanzas in "Starting from Paumanok." In the 1881–82 *Leaves of Grass*, he moves the stanzas to the first section of "Song of Myself."

23. Outka, "(De)composing Whitman," 48, 50 italics added. Outka further contributes to ecocritical explorations of Whitman's "This Compost" as he argues that "This Compost" demonstrates a "proto-toxic consciousness" (56), and that it sets forth a poetics charged with the process of (de)composing. Though his contribution is valuable, his subargument perpetuates a deeply rooted bias against the consciousness of animals. Other recent ecocritical work on Whitman's vegetation include the following: Jed Rasula, in his performative exploration of the "trope as poetry's composting medium," draws on Whitman for the book's title, *This Compost* (9); and in *Walt Whitman and the Earth: A Study in Ecopoetics* (Iowa City: University of Iowa Press, 2004), Killingsworth sees "This Compost" as "Whitman's greatest contribution to the literature of ecology" (11).

24. Kristeva, *Revolution in Poetic Language*, 79.

25. Though I do not discount the influence of Jonathan Edwards' essay on flying spiders upon Whitman's "A Noiseless Patient Spider," I also do not discount that Whitman had ample opportunities to watch spiders prior to, during, and/or after his reading of Edwards' essay. Edwards attentiveness toward spiders contagiously affected Whitman's, and, as my argument suggestions, Edwards' essay alone does not account for the several layers of iconicity found in Whitman's poem. Edwards, for instance, did not use the term "filament" but rather "string" and "thread." Jonathan Edwards, *Puritan Sage: Collected Writings of Jonathan Edwards*, ed. Vergilius Ferm (New York: Library Publishers, 1953), 2, 3.

26. Donna Haraway, *Simians, Cyborgs, and Women: The Reinvention of Nature* (New York: Routledge, 1991), 151–52; Helena Feder, "Rethinking Multiculturalism: Theory and Nonhuman Cultures," *Interdisciplinary Studies in Literature and Environment* 17, no. 4 (2010): 775–777; Kevin N. Laland and Bennett G. Galef, eds., *The Question of Animal Culture* (Cambridge: Harvard University Press, 2009); Haraway, *Species*, 205–248; Edgar Allan Poe, *Collected Works of Edgar Allan Poe, Tales and Sketches, 1831-1842*, ed. T. O. Mabbott, vol. 2 (Cambridge: Harvard University Press, 1978), 477–78. Poe's comparison of the borderline between humans and animals to political maps reminds us that such mappings impose artificial boundaries for convenience and for power.

27. Sarah E. McFarland and Ryan Hediger, "Approaching the Agency of Other Animals: An Introduction," in *Animals and Agency: An Interdisciplinary Exploration* (Boston: Brill, 2009), 4.

28. See the introduction for discussion on Garrard's term "critical anthropomorphism" and Philo and Wilbert's term "guarded anthropomorphism."

29. McFarland and Hediger, "Introduction," 1.

30. In "Complaints from the Spotted Hawk," Thomas Gannon, for instance, explicitly charges Whitman for a failure to get beyond a humanist mindset (see "Complaints," 143, 167).

31. Folsom, "Making Books."

32. Derrida, *Animal*, 29, 30, 12, 66. I suggest, though, that the direction of the gaze can be reversed. The gaze called "human," likewise, offers to the sight of animals *their* abyssal limit.

33. "Mad filaments" comes from section five, line six, and the remaining phrases are from section nine of "I Sing the Body Electric" (*LG* 1891–92, 84, 86–88).

34. Cary Wolfe, *Animal Rites: American Culture, the Discourse of Species, and Posthumanist Theory* (Chicago: University of Chicago Press, 2003), 1.

35. Rukeyser, *Life*, 185.

36. Olson, "Projective," 174.

37. Rueckert, "Literature and Ecology," 108, 110.

Interlude
Cats

Cats are makers. They create and sustain a sense of belonging through nuzzling, purring, kneading, licking, gazing, and meowing themselves into the social fabric of a home. Much is at stake, though, concerning whether or not humans learn to respond to the *poiesis* of cats. I have to agree with Haraway who suggests that Derrida, perplexed in front of his cat, failed to respond in that moment to his cat's material-semiotics.[1] The more attentively I watch my cat, the more I recognize her constant bodily *poiesis* as she meanders through her day, and how many times I too, in the past, neglected to respond.

I would love to see Haraway and Derrida joined by Edgar Allan Poe and E. E. Cummings so they could all talk about cats. Poe could discuss both the black cat of his tale as well as the cat whom he saw innovatively open a door. "The black cat," Poe marvels, "in doing what she did, must have made use of all the perceptive and reflective faculties which we are in the habit of supposing the prescriptive qualities of reason alone." Poe then argues that the line separating the "instinct" of animals from the "reason" of humans is of a "shadowy and unsatisfactory character—a boundary line far more difficult to settle than even the North-Eastern or the Oregon."[2]

But Cummings' story would soon take center stage. He could recount his letter to Mr. Ishibashi who was working on a Japanese translation of "(im)c-a-t(mo)" from *XAIPE*. As Cummings "explains" the poem, he exposes his complete bewilderment at the cat's acrobatics and following gesture:

I am looking at a relaxed "c-a-t";a creature motionlessly alive—
"(im)(mo)b,i;l:e"

suddenly,for no apparent reason,the animal executes a series of crazily acrobatic antics—"Fall(-)leAps!flOat(-)tumblIsh?-drIft(-)whirlF(Ul)(lY) &&&"

after which,he wanders away looking exactly as if nothing had ever happened . . . whereas,for me,the whole universe has turned upside-down in a few moments.[3]

It is not only the difficult, acrobatic maneuvers the cat performs to land on his feet, but moreover the bodily *poiesis* of "wander[ing] away looking exactly as if nothing had ever happened" that made Cummings reel. The gesture of carefree nonchalance . . . of saving face . . . of *that whole thing you saw there was planned.*

Cummings, Poe, Derrida, and Haraway could discuss how the acrobatic cat concealed his trace of losing control; how the cat invented a material gesture in that ecotone of innovative space when and where species meet; how Cummings, too, invented a material response through the gestures of "(im)c-a-t(mo)"; and how a line dividing humans from animals is often much more about power just like the lines of a political map—such as the North-Eastern or the Oregon that Poe mentions—that arbitrarily divide bioregions.

Notes

1. Haraway, *Species*, 20–22; Derrida, *Animal*, 1–10.
2. Poe, *Works*, 2:479, 477–78.
3. E. E. Cummings, *Selected Letters of E. E. Cummings*, ed. F. W. Dupee and George Stade (New York: Harcourt, 1969), 231.

Chapter 3
"Whose poem is this?": E. E. Cummings' Zoopoetics[1]

Were you thinking that those were the words, those upright lines?
those curves, angles, dots?

Walt Whitman
from "A Song of the Rolling Earth"

When Whitman draws attention to the actual print marks on the page, he foregrounds the background. Readers may fumble as the marks of print suddenly become strange until re-focusing the gaze around the totality of the familiar word.[2] Though Whitman pushes his readers off the page and toward the "substantial words" of the earth and the body, chapter 2 demonstrates how Whitman nonetheless plays with the substantiality of printed text. Indeed, the lines and curve of an *f* attain an iconic, material, substantial force: *filament, filament, filament, out of itself. . . .*

However, I still imagine Cummings' response to the opening questions of "A Song of the Rolling Earth" to be, "In fact, yes: the curve of an *O*, the squiggles of an *&*, the angles of a *K*, the dot above the *i* and beneath the *!* all can become 'substantial words' not unlike the air, soil, water, and fire of the earth, nor unlike the poetics of a body."

Critics often trace other influences upon Cummings than Whitman including Stein, Duchamp's *Nude Descending a Staircase*, Freud, Futurism, Cubism, Taoism, English Romantic poets, Burlesque Theatre, Circuses, Coney Island, and other "high" and "low" cultural sources. Admittedly, Whitman is often seen as an influence of other twentieth century poets (such as Ginsberg) rather than a major factor in the growth of Cummings. However, archival evidence suggests

Cummings, at one point, gave Whitman much more than a cursory read. Moreover, directly or indirectly, Cummings revisits and expands many of the themes central to Whitman's *Leaves of Grass*: sex, amativeness, animality, the earth, plants, animals, and the dynamics between an individual and a community.

Like Whitman, Cummings exhibits an attentiveness toward animals, but the interdependence between such attentiveness and Cummings' poetics is even more explicit than his predecessor. Near the end of "The Adult, the Artist, and the Circus," Cummings conflates the material and the immaterial in a way very reminiscent of Whitman: "the fluent technique of seals and of sea lions comprises certain untranslatable idioms, certain innate flexions, which astonishingly resemble the spiritual essence of poetry."[3] One may expect Cummings to say that the bodily movements of these creatures resemble the *forms* of poetry—and they do, at least for Cummings. Cummings' work casts, like Whitman's, the body/soul duality to be a unified whole, but his starting point, also like Whitman, is the material body. I am interested, though, in how Cummings' discussion of sea mammals also extends Emerson's theory that a poet ought to seek "a metre-making argument . . . a thought so passionate and alive that like a spirit of . . . an animal it has an architecture of its own."[4] Like the "fluent technique" of a seal's bodily *poiesis*, a poem's form moves. It gestures on its own with an organic architecture that is *alive*. And the gestures become "untranslatable idioms" so powerful in all avant-garde poetics.

A sheet from the Cummings archive provocatively reveals how Cummings studied Whitman during his early (pre-1920's) experimentation with poetic form (see Fig. 3.1.).[5] Cummings typographically recasts Whitman's lines from "Song of the Open Road," "By Blue Ontario's Shore," and "Song of Myself," readily exposing his play with interrelated aural and spatial poetics. He counts the pulses of Whitman's lines, capitalizes stresses, and repeats lines in new arrangements as if to listen again. He experiments with indentation, stepped lines, and blank space. Thematically, Cummings gravitates to passages that resonate with his own poetic vision: the individual's place within the universe. Elsewhere, I have argued that, like Whitman, Cummings cultivated an "ecological *i*"—a self who becomes enormous through his or her dynamic interconnections to all other parts within the whole.[6] More astonishingly, though, Cummings' innovative poetics—at this point in time—emerged out of a conflation of sound and space, the ear and the eye. Cummings arrives at such initial insights through playing with Whitman's lines.

But Cummings is difficult. People often do not know what to do with him. Anthologies readily include him, but introductions to his work often suggest he is a "break" from Modernism.[7] In the 1930's, the critic R. P. Blackmur lambasted Cummings' poetics as "a kind of baby talk." He did not know what to do with even Cummings' tamer experiments. Blackmur recognized that the "textual scholarship of the future" may be able to do something with Cummings, but he saw "little importance" in the "excessive hyphenation of single words, the use of lower case 'i,' the breaking of lines, the insertion of punctuation between letters of a word, and so on."[8] Given, though, Kristeva's argument that the poetic revolution of the twentieth century involves the "deluge of the signifier" by "pre-verbal gestures," calling Cummings' work "baby talk" may actually be a pro-found insight.[9]

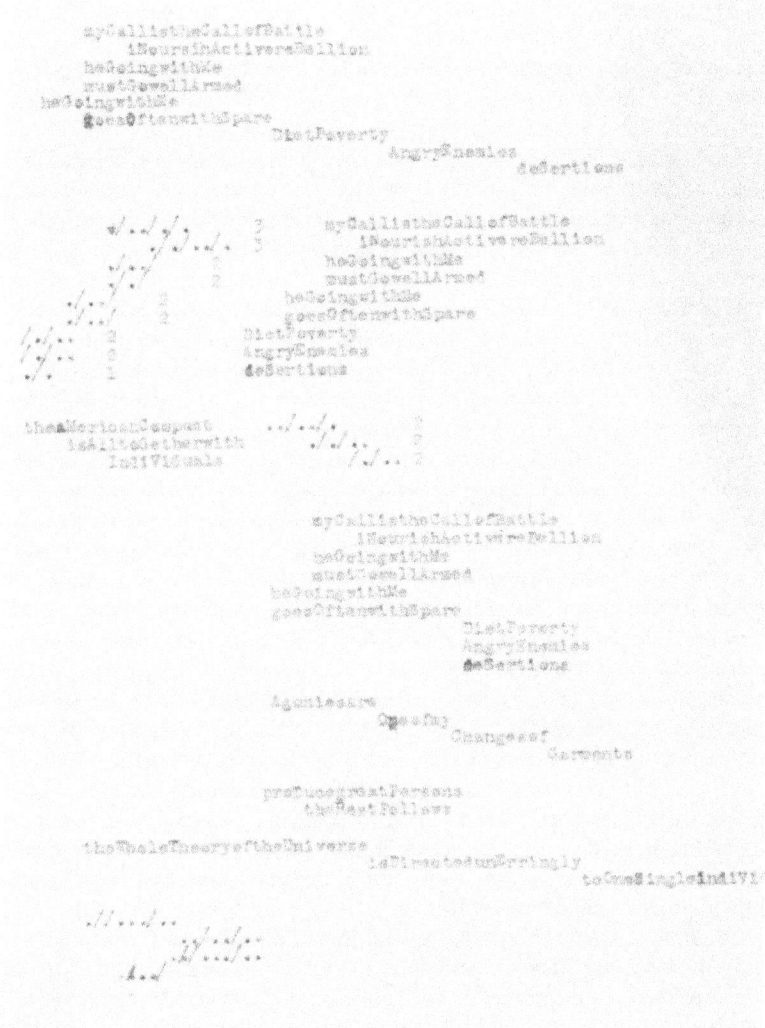

Figure 3.1. Cummings' scansion and typographical arrangement of Whitman's lines. bMS Am 1892.5 (369), Houghton Library, Harvard University.

Ironically, Blackmur had the potential to understand Cummings' textual gestures, for his infamous essay on Cummings appears in his book, *Language as Gesture*. He gravitates to the poetic gestures of other modernist poets, and in the introduction, he foregrounds the importance of the gesture to understanding modern poetry. His thesis is that the gesture is of great "structural importance in poetry"; he sees gestures to be "made of language beneath or beyond or alongside the language of words"; gestures, for Blackmur, come "before [language] in a still richer sense"; and he draws on Othello to make us point: "I understand a fury in your words / But not the words." If any poet allows a "fury" to override "words," it is Cummings. Blackmur, though, limits the gesture to sounds, repetition, alliteration, meter, rhyme, and refrain.[10] He was ready to read the material gestures of some modernist poetry, but not the visual/aural gestures of Cummings.

Another reason why Cummings is difficult involves Whitman's question: "Were you thinking that those were the words, those upright lines? those curves, angles, dots?" (*LG* 1891–92, 176). Alphabetic systems tend to efface the body as they are supposedly "gesture-less." Readers entrenched in alphabetic systems of language are not used to looking at the gestures of the print-marks on the page. As discussed in the introduction, Brian Rotman articulates the bias of alphabeticism, and he provides the three categories of gestures that are crucial to my project—especially the theory of emblem gestures. However, I disagree with his claim that alphabetic systems are completely devoid of gestures. Rotman sees alphabetic systems as effacing all iconic mimicry of the extratextual world: "Not only are letters in no way iconic, their visual form having no relation to that of the body or to how sounds produced by the body's organs of speech are received by those hearing them, but the sounds which the letters notate are meaningless monads, minimal hearable fragments of speech absent any trace of the sense-making apparatus of the body producing them."[11] Rotman fails to consider the ways that the gestures of the hands migrated to the gestures of the mouth. The body is hardly "absent" from the "minimal hearable fragments of speech." As chapter 2 explored, the poetics of the body permeates the form and content of Whitman's *oeuvre*. Likewise, human and animal bodies re-appear in many of Cummings' best poems. The pre-linguistic energy of the gesture overwhelms the sign; the letters, profoundly so, gesture. Rotman's argument that alphabetic language is in "no way iconic" indirectly emphasizes Cummings' ability to accomplish the impossible.

Cummings is not without precedent. When the form of Cummings' letters and poems resemble "fluent techniques" of another species, he revisits the origin of the alphabet. As mentioned in the introduction, David Abram uncovers how an attentiveness to animals contributed to the innovative breakthroughs of some letters. Though it may seem that an *A* and a *Q* are "in no way iconic," a vestige of animal ways-of-being remains. The Hebrew word for the letter *Aleph*, which became *A*, is the same Hebrew word for *ox*. Likewise, the Hebrew word for the letter *Qoph*, which became *Q*, is the same Hebrew word for monkey. Turn the *A* upside down reveals an ox's head and two horns, and I can no longer look at a *Q* without seeing monkey's tail swinging to and fro—especially in italicized Garamond: Q.[12] Cummings morphs the A into a leaping cat and a leaping grasshopper—or rather, an attentiveness toward a leaping cat and a leaping grasshopper contribute to Cummings' breakthroughs in iconicity. The letter A possesses Protean possibilities in its origin and in Cummings' use of it, morphing from ox, to cat, to grasshopper. By creating a poetics where letters innovatively imitate the gestures of animals, Cummings keeps alive an attentiveness toward animals crucial to the very origin of the alphabet.

Nothing epitomizes zoopoetics more than such moments of innovation: innovative breakthroughs in form emerge from an attentiveness to another species' bodily *poiesis*. Le Guin has it right. "Whose poem is this?" she asks at the end of a poem on cats. The poem emerged out of her attentiveness toward her cats, who likewise attentively watched the *poiesis* of birds: "The cat is aware of the writing / of swallows / on the white sky."[13] Le Guin feels an ethical dilemma. She is not the sole author of the poem. Her cats are too, as are the swallows. Her awareness *and* her cat's awareness contributed to the making of the poem. How should humans acknowledge multispecies, co-authorships? Often, when a poet bases a poem on another poet's poetry/poetics, they acknowledge the source either with a dedication, a note at the end of the book, or they make the homage explicit as the poem unfolds. Le Guin draws attention to the fact that other animals, too, could be, ought to be, acknowledged for their role in the making of the poem.[14]

In this chapter, I explore the crucial role of the gesture in Cummings' zoopoetics. Perhaps more than any other avant-garde modernist poet, Cummings pushed textual gestures to the extreme. I establish passages where Cummings develops his theory of gestures, and then I explore several instances of his theory at work, including a few poems out of his flock of birds, his cat poem, and his grasshopper poem. I see Cummings as a poet who revisits what Whitman called "original energy"—and like Whitman, Cummings sees a kinship between himself and other animals as they all participate in the *same old law* of *poiesis*.

Gestures and Cummings' Poetics

Around 1921, Cummings jotted down several thoughts on gestures and words—thoughts that now, in retrospect, provide glimpses into the early formation of his poetic vision. These notes are held in the Houghton library, and one folder contains a sustained exploration of Cummings' theory of gestures. Cummings defines gestures as "music," as a "painting which does not suggest or inspire recognizable shapes," and as "language when i do not understand it . . . where the alphabet is incomprehensible." He continues, "The difference between a spoken language and a written language is the difference between a gesture and words. There is no such thing as the spoken word. To read is words. We speak a gesture."[15] Like Whitman, Cummings differentiates between the embodied language of Speech and the disembodied language at work in alphabetic systems;

however, his thoughts, in retrospect, seem to establish traction to rebel against alphabetic systems, to turn letters into Speech, to make them embodied.

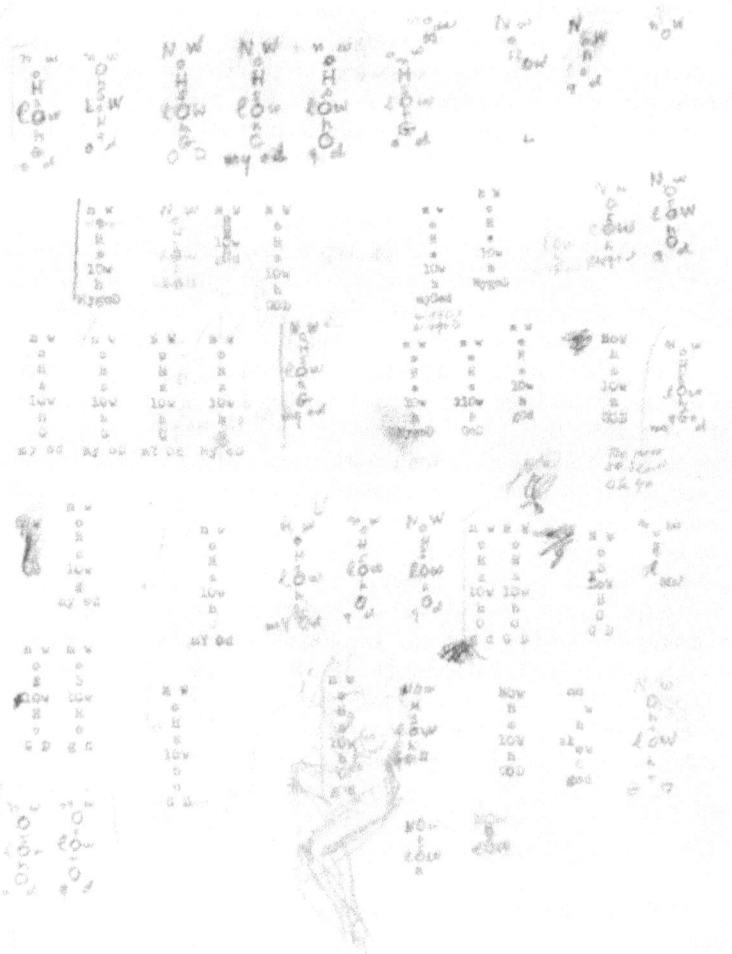

Figure 3.2. One page of Cummings' drafts of "n w" typed and handwritten, accompanied by a drawing of lovers. The archive holds two additional sheets with sixteen further full-poem drafts, five drafts of the final lines, and one draft of the first lines. bMS Am 1892.5 (371), Houghton Library, Harvard University. (For the final draft, see *CP* 1031).

Later in the same series of jottings, Cummings aligns the gesture to what becomes his driving ontology of IS, and he shifts to a manifesto-like tone: "Whatever be the kind of creation,it [the gesture] must Occur." He sees disembodied "words" to be the "antithesis to gesture, the IS. . . . 'Words' are like 2 x 6 or 3 x 4." They can be reduced. He pushes his thought further by equating "the completeness of gesture" to a "prime number": "A gesture is like 11 or 13."[16] The mathematical trope ushers us back to the theory of the "original energy" of the gesture, the "prime movements" out of which poetry emerges. To put it another way, Cummings' poetics gravitates to the textual gestures that cannot be further reduced. Eleven, thirteen, and the gestures of humans, animals, and some poems contain an irreducible, primal, original energy. Later in his notes, Cummings makes this more explicit, theorizing about the "imitative origin" of words where "1st—signs were 'roots' . . . in their entirety,not divisible(into parts)." He continues, "look,gesture,grunt / holophrastic g or uttered sign—beckoning."[17] In language acquisition, holophrasis refers to the process of condensing complex ideas into a single word. (A toddler says "block" meaning "can you hand me that block.") Cummings, though, condenses the holophrastic utterance into the gesture of a single letter, *g*.

Cummings, like Whitman, gravitates to the body. The recent publication of Cummings' erotic poems and drawings makes public many of Cummings' nude sketches. He celebrated the human body, *singing the body electric*. Critics, including myself, though, have mixed responses to *Erotic Poems*. On one hand, it raises further awareness of Cummings' work, but on the other, it eradicates poems and drawings from their rich and nuanced context. There is no foreword, introduction, or clarification of the purpose of the edition, and it therefore seems to be nothing more than a cheap effort to generate revenue.[18]

Nonetheless, *Erotic Poems* captures Cummings' fascination with the gestures of the human body, not unlike Whitman who saw the body as the supreme poem. A sheet from the archive further demonstrates how Cummings' imaginative process dynamically oscillates between the gestures of text and the gestures of drawing. An erotic sketch of a couple's lovemaking accompanies the forty-plus drafts—some typed, some handwritten—of what became the graphically eroticized "n w" (see Fig. 3.2.). In the context of Cummings' *oeuvre*, the poem revisits the pervasive motif of "now"—here, that moment when the woman ("n w") envelopes the tip of the man ("O"). As the first line settles around the second, the assonance of sex—*oh, sLoW*—commences, and the gestures of the letters accentuate the rhythm of lovemaking. The text epitomizes the *body electric*.

The highly eroticized "n w" is not the only time Cummings sketched during the making of poems. Blotches of paint can be found on the sheets of notes and drafts in the archives at Houghton, suggesting Cummings often wrote when he painted and painted when he wrote allowing the gestures of text and of paintings/drawings to dynamically impact the imaginative process. In two of the earliest known drafts of "r-p-o-p-h-e-s-s-a-g-r" (*CP* 396), Cummings sketched two boxers (see Fig. 3.3.).[19] A leaping grasshopper and two boxers may seem to have little in common until one recognizes that the grasshopper's leap, the textual leaps of the poem, and the two boxers all emanate a tremendous amount of en-

ergy through their material movements. The energy of human and animal bodies
coexist on the page.

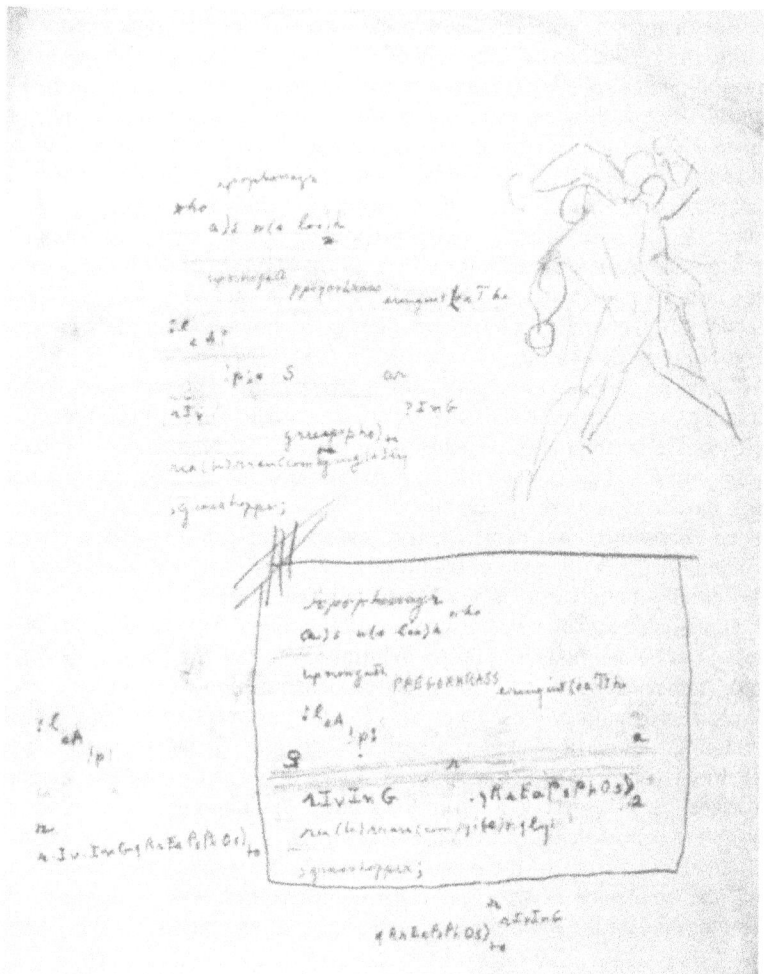

Figure 3.3. Early drafts of "r-p-o-p-h-e-s-s-a-g-r" accompanied by drawing of two boxers. bMS Am 1892.5 (475), Houghton Library, Harvard University.

Like Whitman, more than the human body permeates Cummings' *oeuvre*.
Animals are not only abundant, but moreover an attentiveness to the bodily
poiesis of other species contributed to some of Cummings innovative breakthroughs in poetic form. Cummings exhibits a curiosity about animals in

Haraway's sense of *looking again.*[20] He demonstrates Paul Shepard's argument that human intelligence necessarily depends upon *minding animals*—but with specification.[21] Cummings' poetics is bound up with the ontology of existing in The Verb, in IS, in AM. The *poiesis* of animals epitomizes this ontology, and as he attentively *minds* the *poiesis* of birds, cats, grasshoppers, and bats (to name only a few), he discovers breakthroughs in his own makings to such a degree that his poems move beyond purely human creations. They are multispecies events, at the least, being co-authored by other "citi / zens of / (hush" (*CP* 600).

Cummings' attentiveness to the *poiesis* of other animals is not a passing phase but recurs throughout his *oeuvre*. In an early poem, published in the *Dial Papers* (1919–1920), Cummings deftly challenges the underlying assumption within Western philosophy and epistemology that animals are nothing more than instinct driven machines, having no more sense of *being-in-the-world* than a stone (to echo Descartes and Heidegger).[22] For Cummings, though, the green bird makes something:

> in front of your house i
>
> stopped for a second in the
> rain,in the Spring.
> At the window
>   only your hands
>
>   beautifully,
>   were
>
> (and the green bird perched carefully upon
>   a gesture
> knew me.)   (*CP* 982)

The green bird could have been perched upon a post, or a mailbox, or a gutter, or a branch, but Cummings has the bird "perched carefully upon / a gesture." The line break and blank space of the indentation generates suspense and energy. The poem, like the bird, *gestures*, and it puts pressure on the words "a gesture." Drawing on Rotman's category of "emblem gestures" discussed in the introduction, the line break (and indentation) and the bird's bodily movement carry weight, and they mean something more than the energy of gesticulations. They are a rich and nuanced action much like a wink, a squeeze on a shoulder, or a smirk. Like the "fluent techniques" of seals, they exhibit "untranslatable idioms." The innovative line break and indentation emerged from an attentiveness toward the green bird (who likewise attentively engaged the poem's speaker), and in this way, the poem epitomizes zoopoetics. Moreover, the gesture of the bird let Cummings know she or he *knew* him (italics added), recognized him, was aware of Cummings' *being-in-the-world*. John Berger in *Why Look at Animals?* observes that "animals are always the observed" and the "fact that they can observe us has lost all significance"—but not for Cummings.[23] This is a poem about a *bird* who is *minding humans*. Donna Haraway would call this moment an interspecies "ecotone" and an "ontological and semiotic invention" of both human and bird.[24] Cummings' poem suggests that both species underwent their own epistemological and ontological processes of acknowledging each other's existence. He unabashedly casts the bird as one who possesses the agency to craft a clear (emblem) gesture for the human audience. In light of Cummings' theory of gestures, the holophrastic bird condenses his or her epistemological process of knowing into an articulate sign.

Like many punctuation marks in Cummings' *oeuvre*, parentheses are Protean. Here, they further juxtapose two rarified moments: the hands at the window and the green bird perched on a gesture. Parentheses normally diminish the contents therein, but here they magnify the gesture of the green bird in all of his or her hushed silence. Moving outside the parentheses, the reader revisits the gesture of the hands in a process of their own movements—movements that likewise shaped the breaks and spaces of the third and fourth stanzas leaving a square of white space reminiscent of a square window. The hands and the bird both shaped the poem, merging the ANIMAL↔HUMAN spheres.

Flock of Birds

Throughout Cummings' *oeuvre*, he revisited the bodily *poiesis* of birds time and time again. Often, an attentiveness to the gestures and vocalizations of birds pushed Cummings to discover innovative breakthroughs in poetic form, as demonstrated by *the green bird* discussed above. My intent, though, is not to simply provide a survey of bird poems *per se*. Marjorie Perloff's approach of placing a poem in a series of "frames"—the poem, the surrounding poems, the section, the book, the poet's life's work, the poetic tradition, the larger cultural and historical contexts, and so forth—must be taken into account so a poem is not eradicated from the interrelations surrounding it.[25] The etymology of *anthology* (*anthologia*, "flower-gathering") highlights why reading a poem in isolation so often disrupts the poet's accomplishment. Anthologies attempt to gather and re-plant poems, but each poem must then find a new way of relating to the new surroundings in order to become fit. In this section, I trace the zoopoetics at work in several of Cummings' bird poems, but I keep an eye on surrounding poems as well as some of the overall thematic interests of the book in which the poem appears. Such an approach could quickly become unwieldy, for just as any dynamic system, the complexity becomes infinite. What may have been seen as parts become their own infinite wholes on every scale of Cummings' interrelated makings.

In *95 Poems* (1958), Cummings wrote several bird poems, two of which I explore below. The book begins with the highly anthologized leaf poem, "l(a" (*CP* 673). Along with the haiku-esque mediation that merges *loneliness* with a solitary *falling leaf*; along with the myriad repetitions of ONE (*l*'s look like a number one, the poem looks like a number one, "one" stands out as a readable word, there is one leaf, in the middle of the poem are two ones, and so forth); along with the iconic flipping of the leaf "af / fa"; along with the paradox of an ordered disorder (the upheaval of language occurs across a pattern of 1-3-1-3-1 lines per stanza)—the poem also descends into the ontology of *i-ness*, the state of being *i*. The notion of *i-ness* is one of Cummings' master tropes, and it epitomizes the individual who exists in the verb, in the now, and in humility. The poem that follows "l(a" continues the thematic exploration of loneliness as the first line emphasizes the speaker "stand[s](alone)." It is autumn, and he "breath[es] a fatal / stillness." In this context, he discovers a "creature" that may be a bird. He sees the creature's activity as "enormous"—a word that echoes the title *The Enormous Room*. Cummings gravitates to "how" the creature "puts always on by always // dream." The *dream*, for Cummings, often recurs as the place of *poiesis*, of making, of creating, of existing in The Verb (*CP* 674). To put it another way (inferior to the poem), to stand in the "autumnal afternoon" and witness the activity of creatures—perhaps birds—is to taste unimaginable mysteries. Cast in another light, this poem emphasizes Cummings' continual attentiveness toward animals who, like humans, have the potential to exist in a state of *i-ness*.

Later in *95 Poems*, Cummings includes two poems clearly shaped by his attentiveness to the *poiesis* of birds. The onomatopoeia of the first, coupled with the explosions of capital letters, resonate with the darting flight of hummingbirds. Poetic form as well as the flight pattern of hummingbirds move beyond the unconscious material movement of gesticulations to the conscious crafting of emblem gestures. Reading the poem, then, becomes an act of seeing the emblem gestures emerge from the energy of gesticulations. The moment of emblem gestures occurs in the final moments of the poem. Cummings scrambles three words, *cries, noise,* and *hi* into "chino / ise // r(!)i(?)e(.)s" (*CP* 747)—an *untranslatable idiom*. Some might see the activity of hummingbirds to be no more than "buzzsqueaking" *noise*, but Cummings identifies at least four distinct categories of *cries* that transgress the supposed border between humans and other animals—cries that are consanguineous with the general categories, or rather the general gestures, of all human sentences. These birds exclaim "(!)"; interrogate "(?)"; declare and command "(.)"; they punctuate through their bodily *poiesis*. The speaker also identifies a "hi"—perhaps between the hummingbirds, perhaps directed toward him—and this "hi" could be expressed, through the poetic energy of the birds, as exclamatory, inquisitive, or declarative. Through an attentiveness toward the hummingbirds' way of being alive, Cummings made a breakthrough in his form. He scrambled human language, turned it into a seemingly unconscious garble, but then, in this flux, allowed the fundamentals of any language to emerge.

A couple of poems later, Cummings includes a seemingly simple poem about a whippoorwill. Cummings often jumbles syntax, but here, something more is at work. If Cummings followed the conventions of grammar, the first three stanzas ought to read *this whippoorwill tosses hello into moonday (big with unthings)*. But he didn't. However, tracing the poem with a finger while reading

this whippoorwill tosses hello into moonday (big with unthings) reveals a coun-
ter-clockwise spiral "whirling" into the page:

> whippoorwill this
>
> moonday into
> (big with unthings)
>
> tosses hello
>
>
> whirling whose rhyme
>
> (spilling his rings)
> threeing alive
>
> pasture and hills (CP 751)

He speaks of the whippoorwills as *makers*, for they have a "rhyme." Moreover,
they are "alive"—that is, existing within the ontology of *i-ness* and The Verb.
As their "toss[ing of] hello" shapes the form of Cummings' poem, the poem
becomes a multi-species event. I am not aware of another poem—by Cummings
or another poet—in which the words create a hidden spiral. Cummings discovered this innovative breakthrough through an attentiveness to the *poiesis* of another animal that, like the hummingbirds, exists in a state of *i-ness* through their
own bodily *poiesis*.

In "t,h;r:u;s,h;e:s" (from *73 Poems*, 1963), Cummings further explored a
bird's *poiesis*, but in order to contextualize the poem within Cummings' larger
body of work, I begin with "rainsweet" from *Etcetera: The Unpublished Poems
of E. E. Cummings*. The editors place "rainsweet" in the "Late Poems" ranging
from 1930–1962, a period they describe as his "mature years" where the "linguistic play [is] more fully developed and controlled than in the earlier years."
The editors highlight Cummings' "extension of the semantic [and I add material]
possibilities of words that he chooses to stretch, squeeze, or intensify by typographical acrobatics or grammatical innovations."[26] The poem "rainsweet" epitomizes such innovations as Cummings explicitly elevates the birdsong of a
thrush to be a *voice*, and as the emblem gestures of the final lines preserve the
uncanny moment of the presence of absent sound (*CP* 1045):

> rainsweet
>
> s
> tillnes
> s
>
> &

farnearf
uling
a thrush

's

v
oi
c

e

In terms of taxonomic ranks, the family "Thrush" contains myriad species, so it is difficult to know exactly what species Cummings engaged. That said, the musical phrase of the hermit thrush (*Catharus guttatus*) lasts roughly 1.5 seconds. Silent pauses punctuate the phrases of music, and these pauses last roughly two seconds.[27] Cummings' poem foregrounds such silences. Not only do the *s's* hover in their own *stillness*, the silent "e" of *voice* does as well. If read aloud, the sound ceases after "v / oi / c"—but then readers experience the long pause of a stanza break, only to stare at the silent "e." When the final moments of the poem are heard and seen through careful reading, the pregnant silence after a bird song becomes palpably present in that silent *e*. Nothing is there save the strange letter. In *Ecology without Nature*, Timothy Morton discusses the ambient poetics of "in between." The final moments of "rainsweet" place us in the ambient space "in between" the sound of the thrush and yet the following silence. The poem also places the reader "in between" hearing the poem and yet seeing the strange letter in isolation. As the silent *e* encompasses many paradoxes, it draws attention to the material environment of the letters/words on the materiality of a page. Morton discusses a similar dynamic in M. C. Escher's work: "On the first level, we perceive a breakdown of our normal distinction between background and foreground, but on the second, this distinction is preserved. In order for the first level to be effective, the second level must also be effective. What is given with one gesture is paradoxically taken away with another. Term x dissolves into term y, but retains the form of term x."[28] The silent *e* rushes to the foreground to be its own emblem gesture of absence, and the uncanny moment of listening to thrush reappears in an uncanny moment of hearing/seeing the absence of sound on the page.

To push this thought further, the mark of the "e" epitomizes how ambient poetics troubles any easy reading:

[Ambient poetics unsettles the] differences between, for example, graphic mark/sign, noise/sound, noise/silence, foreground/background. . . . there is nothing in between; literally nothing, not even space, since space is also subject to these distinctions. Something is either a noise or it is sound. (The ideological fantasy of ecomimesis and especially ambience, seems to suggest that something could be both.)[29]

The "e" may begin as just a mark on the printed page, hovering in the background of the reading process. When one hears its silence in Cummings' poem, though, it rushes to the foreground as a clear, material sign. Perhaps the best way to approach the conundrum is through Wallace Stevens' "The Snow Man," for the silent *e* is a material sign for the nothingness that is simultaneously present and absent.[30]

Another poem, from *73 Poems*, revisits the same idea, but Cummings adds another layer of complexity.[31] Though I agree with Terblanche that the punctuation of the first line becomes iconic for the thrushes who remain hidden and shadowy within vegetation, something else is also at work.[32] Protean-like, Cummings often uses variations of the cyclic pattern ", ; : . : ; ," in new and exciting ways. (For instance, the last three endmarks of *EIMI*—a book whose first word is "SHUT" and last word is "OPEN"—are a colon, a semi-colon, and a comma.)[33] Often, the comma represents something that exists in a "more open" state while a period suggests a "more closed" state. The colon and semi-colon can be seen as nuanced gradients between openness and closeness. Here, the punctuation begins with a comma, proceeds to a colon, returns to a comma, proceeds to a colon, and two stanzas later, arrives at the period. The birds, then, begin with singing, proceed to silence, but return to singing, proceed to silence . . . which prompts Cummings to conclude *they are silent now*, followed by a stanza break of waiting for another note, and as there is silence, the period can then begin the next line. One of the main events of the poem, then, occurs in the ambient space between stanzas:

> t,h;r:u;s,h;e:s
>
> are
> silent
> now
>
> .in silverly
>
> notqu
> -it-
> eness
>
> dre(is)ams
>
> a
> the
> o
>
> f moon (*CP* 820)

The silence between the word "now" and the period suggests a long pause of waiting—will they begin another 1.5 second musical phrase? Like "rainsweet," the gesture draws attention to the materiality of the blank page that emerges between the print marks. The line breaks that follow suggest many iterations/readings: the state of *not quite-ness* is one of the uncanny not-quite-silent nor not-quite-sound; such a state, "it" is a dream; the dream is the epitome of "(is)" as well as one of many expressions of "ams" or ways of being alive; this dream state, full of creative potential is *a moon, the moon,* and is *of the moon*; and the stanza break that breaks *of* into "o // f" allows the *o* to be an iconic representation of a *"f moon"* or *full moon*. The gestures ensure that the poem dwells in the same space as the thrushes: a dreamful and verbful state of between-nesses.

Crucially, in the sonnet following "t,h;r:u;s,h;e:s" Cummings explicitly expresses his gratitude toward the "twilight voice[s]" that, when finished, create that rarified "silence of each bird." Cummings turns to the "undaunted guest[s] of dark" and asks that they "receive . . . the more than thanks of always merest me" (*CP* 821). Though admittedly conjecture, I suggest that Cummings felt compelled to thank the thrush because of the exhilarating thrill it must have been to make "t,h;r:u;s,h;e:s"—so much so that he must acknowledge the other species' roll in the discoveries of his innovative breakthroughs. It is not just his poem, to answer Le Guin. This sonnet of gratitude provides further evidence of Cummings' awareness of the role of animals in the makings of his poetry. It is an explicit "nod" to individuals of another species; Cummings defers sole authorship. Like any poet who draws on the *poiesis* of others, Cummings points readers to the source that prompted his innovative breakthrough.

A Cat

Along with birds, other species contributed to Cummings' poetic breakthroughs. And though it can be fatuous to claim that one poem is greater than another (for "greatness" is really a matter of perspective), in terms of complexity, the cat poem surpasses what has been discussed so far. I define complexity as the number of interacting layers of patterns within the poem. I see "t,h;r:u;s,h;e:s" containing at least four layers of interacting patterns including word breaks, line breaks, stanza breaks, and the pattern of punctuation, while "(im)c-a-t(mo) exhibits at least nine: word breaks, line breaks, stanza breaks, the pattern of punctuation, poem flips, stanza flips, line flips, punctuation flips, and the pattern of balanced "two's" at both sides of many lines. Cummings published the poem in *XAIPE*, the Greek word for *rejoice*, and biographers readily comment on how the book coincides with Cummings' reunion with his daughter, Nancy.[34] *XAIPE* includes many other poems exploring the verb-ful ontology of animals, such as the nocturnal creatures of "hush)" (*CP* 600); a sonnet that speaks of other species as "incredible / unanimal mankind" (*CP* 620); "nine birds(rising" who become "a / manying / one" (*CP* 627); and a poem that celebrates the birth of a foal: the "gro // Wing)silence,who; / is:somE // oNe. [N-E-W]" (*CP* 657). *XAIPE* also includes a short poem about how the pieces of a broken mirror are "each . . . whole with sky" (*CP* 623), and as I have suggested elsewhere, the poem draws attention to Cummings' fractal poetics.[35] The fragments of language often reflect a whole. Such is the case with the cat poem (*CP* 655):

    (im)c-a-t(mo)
    b,i;l:e

    FallleA
    ps!fl
    OattumblI

    sh?dr
    IftwhirlF
    (Ul)(lY)
    &&&

    away wanders:exact
    ly;as if
    not
    hing had,ever happ
    ene

    D

Unless the reader flips the poem around and around, the cat will land on his head, the "D." I recognize that readers unfamiliar with Cummings may think such interpretations are nothing more than "cloud gazing," but many readers who read slow may, at one point, wonder something like, "why are there two longer lines near the end?"—or "why is the 'D' isolated at the end?—strange." Such inquiries often lead to epiphanies if readers continue to linger in them. Flipping the poem around exposes a silhouette of a cat, facing to the left, reaching out his front legs toward the "ground." I see the middle stanza as the cat's belly. The next stanza to the right can be the hind legs tucked in, and the line "(im)c-a-t(mo)" becomes the tail. An online search of images on "falling cats" helps clarify the silhouette:

Though readers may be skeptical, Cummings made similar moves on the microscale of individual lines and punctuation marks. Because words break across lines, a portion of "leA / ps" and a portion of "fl / Oat" occupy the fourth line. Flipping the line and the exclamation mark highlights Cummings' attention to the flipping motif in the minutiae of his poems:

> ps!fl
> fl!ps
> flips

Thematically, the exclamation mark that establishes the expression of the alive individual who exists in The Verb becomes the lower case *i*. As noted above, *95 Poems* begins with a statement of *i-ness*, but here, as I have said elsewhere, *i-ness* merges with what could be called *!-ness*.[36] The cat—as well as the foal, the birds, and the nocturnal creatures included in *95 Poems*—exist within what Cummings sees as the epitome of creative dwelling: a bodily motion that becomes a "fluent technique . . . compris[ing] certain untranslatable idioms, certain innate flexions, which astonishingly resemble the spiritual essence of poetry."[37]

A portion of *drift, whirl,* and *fully* occupy the same line—"IftwhirlF"—thereby creating several iterations of expression. Two *if's* balance the line, keeping in step with the many other balanced pairs at both ends of a line, and they reinforce the possibilities of the cat's bodily *poiesis* as well as the linguistic *poiesis* of the poem. *Whirl* also becomes *twhirl* or rather *twirl*, leading us to read *if the cat twirls if the cat whirls* (he won't land on his head). Two lines later, Cummings reinforces the whirling, twirling, flipping path of the cat through the air—"&&&"—suggesting the cat performed three continuous, somersaulting twists. Like the *!* turning to an *i*, the ampersands are no long disembodied signs; rather, they become more like sensuous ideographs full of gesture, texture, and materiality. And one cannot overlook John Pollock's observation of how the poem's sounds merge the ANIMAL↔HUMAN spheres:

> I expect a cat so rudely awakened might experience much the same sensations a human being would under similar circumstances: an immediate sense of disorientation followed by an instinctual flailing about of arms and legs in an attempt to re-establish some feeling of order and control. Like a cat, a person falling through the air, trying to right himself or herself, might make involuntary sounds such as "ps!" or "sh."[38]

Cummings may have (un)intentionally placed the "sh?" in the poem, or he may have been, like Pollock, surprised by it. This is a poet, though, who placed the ass-end of a grasshopper at the end of a line "PPEGORHRASS" (*CP* 396). The cat vocalizes something akin to "sh?" that is, *oh shit!—I'm screwed*—a sensation felt by many species the moment one loses control.

And the cat does fall unexpectedly. Earlier, I suggested the poem contains myriad patterns that dynamically interrelate. The first two lines, when the cat falls, epitomizes such dynamism. A former student observed that the "c-a-t" falls into the word *immobile*, breaking the *immobile* state of being. Cummings, in his letter, hints at how the broken words create a new phrase: "I am looking at a relaxed "c-a-t"; a creature motionlessly alive—'(im)(mo)b,i;l:e'."[39] *I am mo-bile. I am in a state of motion.* The poem begins *in medias res* with the cat hav-ing already fallen into the state of mobility. When the cat "leA / ps!"—and its noteworthy to emphasize how the exclamatory flip of the *!* to an *i* coincides with the *leap*—he is already in midair. A difficult feat for any gymnast. The iconic *A* leaps from the end of the line into the open space of the page—but again, the leap occurs after the cat has already fallen. This notion is further reinforced by the pattern of lines per stanza, which begins already-having-started: 2-3-4-5-1. (Starting with two lines provides opportunity for Cummings to end the poem with the solitary "D," or head, of the cat.) The first line also establishes the pat-tern of two pairs of balanced letters that occur at both ends of several lines. Cummings scholars will also readily note how the outer edge of the first line introduces the "i" and the "o"—two recurrent and crucial tropes throughout Cummings' life work.[40] Here, I see the "i" as the alive individual and the "o" suggesting the open possibilities of an acrobatic, verbful ontology. These two letters gyrate across the first couple of stanzas and become flipped and capital-ized at the end of the second stanza:

    (im)c-a-t(mo)
    b,i;l:e

    FallleA
    ps!fl
    OattumblI

The last pattern I see at work in the first stanza is that of punctuation. The com-ma crescendos to a semi-colon and then a colon. Readers attuned to the pattern may expect a period soon, but Cummings modifies the pattern by progressing later in the poem toward an exclamation mark, then a question mark, before re-turning to the colon, semi-colon, and comma. I see the comma, then, as the "creature motionlessly alive"—the creature, full of potential energy, at rest, who, through the fall, progresses into the state of *i-ness* and *!-ness*, and into a state of perplexity (sh?) before returning to the relaxed state of a comma. Looking at just the first two stanzas reveals a bewildering concentration of overlapping and in-teracting patterns.

With complex poems such as "(im)c-a-t(mo)," it is difficult to step back from the acrobatic language, and respect (to look again at) the fact that Cum-mings attentively marveled at the well-timed acrobatics of an actual cat, and it is not only the acrobatics of a cat that Cummings found captivating. He shares in his letter to Mr. Ishibashi, his Japanese translator, that the cat's falling and *walk-ing away as if nothing had ever happened* "turned [his whole universe] upside-down in a few moments."[41] Though the cat's marvelous ability to leap off of air in order to flip and land on his feet is undeniably stupendous, the cat's ability to craft an emblem gesture, at the end of the fall, is as well. To save face. To pre-tend he maintained control the entire time. This, I suggest, also turned Cummings' universe "upside-down." What makes this poem is not only the agency in the cat's imaginative response to the sudden losing of control—acting in that *kairotic* moment to recall this book's introduction—but moreover his ability to enter instantly a rhetorical situation: to craft an emblem gesture for a human audience while sauntering off.

A Grasshopper

Like the cat poem, Cummings' grasshopper poem exhibits several layers of interacting patterns (perhaps even more). To introduce the zoopoetics of "r-p-o-p-h-e-s-s-a-g-r," I turn to Cummings' juxtaposition of children and prisoners:

> There are two types of human beings children and prisoners. Prisoners are inhabited by formulae. Children inhabit forms. A formula is something to get out of oneself, to rid oneself of—an arbitrary emphasis. . . . A form is something to wander in, to loose oneself in—a new largeness.[42]

Perhaps no other modernist poet "wander[ed] in" poetic form to the extent of Cummings, ever "loos[ing]" (a great pun on "losing") himself and discovering a "new largeness" of the diminutive *i*. As the poems explored above demonstrate, the process of attentively engaging animals contributes to the wandering in poetic form and to creating a new largeness. This occurs, too, when Cummings wanders in poetic form *with* a grasshopper.

The highly anthologized poem has generated much discussion amongst Cummings scholars at conferences, in publications, and in email exchanges. In the presentation "How to Plot a Grasshopper," Michael Webster suggests that the poem "looks like a sonnet that has been shot full of holes." He continues, "if one removes line ten, whose two letters are outside the right and left margins, then one gets 14 lines within the 'square' of the poem—and thus a kind of parody sonnet."[43] His insight advances Max Nänny's suggestion that the last line of the poem could be its title, and if it is so, then only 14 lines remain: "The very title of the poem, "grasshopper," has leapt to the last line so that a fourteen-line poem or sort of 'sonnet' remains."[44] In the earlier essay "Iconic Dimensions in Poetry," Nänny is more confident in the poem's sonnet status, for he speaks of its "genre as a titled sonnet" due to how the "title" of the last line "disguis[es] the fact that the poem has the fourteen lines of a sonnet."[45] If Cummings titled his poems, Nänny's argument would be more tenable. However, Webster's perspective that the tenth line exists outside the poem encourages readers to "loo)k" at the poem's potential sonnet status again.

In "How to Plot a Grasshopper," Webster also uncovers archival material that shows Cummings plotting poems on graph paper.[46] The grasshopper poem, then, has 15 rows and 39 columns. Cummings' precision is not readily apparent, though, in today's re-typings of the poem, for many of today's fonts make thin letters such as an *i* or an *l* that take up less space than wide letters such as an *m* or a *w*. On Cummings' typewriter, even the commas, colons, exclamation marks, hyphens, take up the same space as anything else. The differences are drastic.

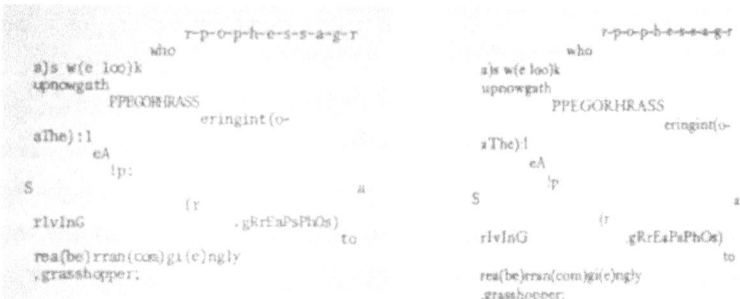

Figure 3.4. Two published versions of "r-p-o-p-h-e-s-s-a-g-r." The version from *No Thanks*, Typescript Edition on the left preserves the original font and spacing of the poem; the version on the right, though published in *The Complete Poems*, significantly alters the typography. The sixth line—"eringint(o-"—exposes the drastic difference. On the right, it almost reaches the right margin while on the left, it sits closer to the center-line.

To accentuate the differences, I juxtapose an image of the typescript edition that preserves the look of Cummings' typed poems next to an image of *The Complete Poems*. The difference can be summarized by paying attention to the sixth line, for in the typescript edition, the sixth line only reaches the thirty-first space, leaving eight more spaces between the hyphen and the right margin (on the left).[47] In *The Complete Poemss* the sixth line almost reaches the right margin (see Fig. 3.4.).The significance of this observation can be found in Cummings' deliberate crafting of the margins. Gillian Huang-Tiller recently uncovered a page proof Cummings sent to his printer, Jacobs, so Jacobs could set the poem for the 1935 publication, and she circulated an unpublished essay about it amongst Cummings scholars: "One Art: Intuition and Typography in E. E. Cummings' Original Analysis of 'r-p-o-p-h-e-s-s-a-g-r' (1935)." The manuscript, preserved at the Special Collections of the University of Virginia Library, grants a profound glimpse as to how Cummings saw the poem. For instance, he sees "lines 1, 2, 3" as "establishing . . . 2 margins right&left." He also highlights how "line 10 consists of two outside-the-frame units" and "line 11 consists of two centered-in-the-poem units."[48] These two lines refer respectively to the provocative "S . . . a" and the "(r":[49]

S   a
                              (r

Cummings' comments suggest that the poem hinges upon how a line either establishes a margin, exists at the center of the margins, or exists outside of the margins. Eight lines establish the margins, for there are six lines establishing the left margin plus two lines establishing the right margin. This leaves six lines that "float" between the margins, and one line, of course, that exists outside of the margins (see Fig. 3.5.). It is difficult to dismiss the observation that a sonneteer, who wrote hundreds of sonnets across his career—and who plotted this poem on graph paper in its early drafts—allows the numbers 8 (an octet) and 6 (a sestet) to emerge in the grasshopper poem. Indeed, the poem is placed in a book that exhibits a highly wrought, overarching "V-schema": a descent from the moon down to the earth and back up to the stars. Eighteen sonnets are deliberately placed throughout this schema in a clear pattern. The grasshopper poem exists in the middle of two sonnets: (sonnet, poem, "r-p-o-p-h-e-s-s-a-g-r," poem, sonnet)—perhaps pointing toward the poem's state being "in-between" a sonnet and open form.

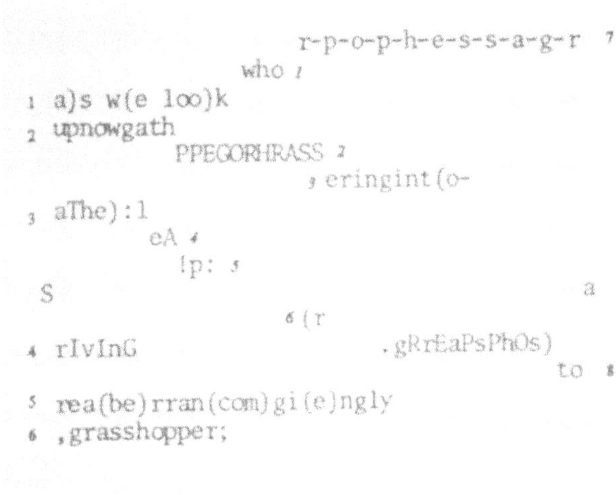

$$r\text{-}p\text{-}o\text{-}p\text{-}h\text{-}e\text{-}s\text{-}s\text{-}a\text{-}g\text{-}r \quad 7$$

who $_1$

$_1$ a)s w(e loo)k

$_2$ upnowgath

PPEGORHRASS $_2$

$_3$ eringint(o-

$_3$ aThe):l

eA $_4$

!p: $_5$

S   a

$_6$(r

$_4$ rIvInG   .gRrEaPsPhOs)

to $_8$

$_5$ rea(be)rran(com)gi(e)ngly

$_6$,grasshopper;

Figure 3.5. Eight lines establish the margins (six for the left and two for the right); Six lines "float" margin-less within the box of the poem; and one line—the uncounted "S . . . a"—extends beyond the margins.

   If the poem is indeed a sonnet, it epitomizes the zoopoetic process of discovering one's most innovative breakthroughs in poetic form through an attentiveness toward animals. The poem's sonnet-status is controversial, namely because it is fifteen lines. However, in "The Iconic Meta-Sonnet, Manhood, and Cultural Crisis in *No Thanks*," Huang-Tiller argues "nowhere is the sonnet metaform more prominently manifested than in Cummings' collection of poetry *No Thanks*." She discusses how the eighteen sonnets of the book structure the "V-scheme" of descent and ascent, and she observes that "Cummings' fourteenliners bear resemblance to the sonnet, yet depart from it in their open typographic form, as if commenting on the genre's iconic status." "r-p-o-p-h-e-s-s-a-g-r" may be one of the most intense iconic meta-sonnets, for the poem pushes against the sonnet tradition while still pointing toward the age-old gestures of the form.[50]

Along with the observation that eight lines establish the margins, six lines float between the margins, and one line exists outside of the margins, the poem can be grouped visually in the inverted pattern, "sestet/octet." The first six lines (sestet) form a pattern of three steps from the right to the left, and three steps from the left to the right. Provocatively, Cummings experimented with this "stepping" pattern in his scansion of Whitman's lines, discussed earlier in this chapter. In the 1935 proof of the poem, Cummings speaks of these steps as either a "(reverse) fall" or a "(regular) fall."[51] The last eight lines (octet) consist of the shape of the grasshopper that leaps out of the poem as well as the poem's resolution (see Fig. 3.6.). Many sonnets end with a paradox, and here, the poem "ends" by pointing readers to the theme of *becoming* a legible ",grasshopper;" of the last line through *rearranging*—but the semi-colon suggests an ending that will begin again. In a conference presentation, Vakrilen Kilyovski suggests that the poem can be read from the bottom up, beginning with clarity and entering into the dynamism of leaps.[52] The paradox, then, is that the "resolution" is to begin again, to leap again, and to continue the process of looking and rearranging.

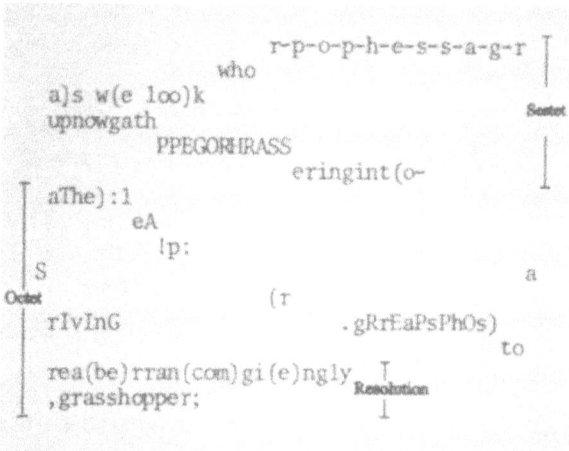

Figure 3.6. The content suggests an inverted sonnet, with a sestet establishing potential energy and an octet unleashing kinetic energy that leads to the paradoxical "resolution" of a ",grasshopper;" poised on a semi-colon to leap again.

Perhaps one of the more crucial characteristics of a sonnet is that they include a turn, a *volta*, between the octet and the sestet. The sestet here establishes a tremendous amount of potential energy (the "gath . . . eringinto-"), but a clear break indicated by the hyphen at the end of "into-" suggests the question, *into what?* The poem turns into the dizzying array of kinetic energy displayed by the leap, but as this leap occurs in what I see as the octet of the poem, the break between the sestet and the octet comes further into focus. The poem exhibits a clear *volta* from potential energy into kinetic energy that coincides with the break from the sestet toward the octet.

Elsewhere, I have argued that the poem exhibits a fractal dynamics, for the leap of the grasshopper occurs on several scales:[53]

  o   microscale of individual letters: the *A* leaps explosively out of the word ":l / eA / !p:";
  o   larger scale of words: the "hOPPER" hops out of the lowercase word "grass" in ".gRrEaPsPhOs";[54]
  o   and the even larger scale of several lines: the silhouette of a grasshopper leaps out of the poem, as Max Nänny highlights (see Fig. 3.7.).[55]

But these leaps all occur within the octet of the poem, further establishing the difference between the initial six lines of the poem. As the leaps of the grasshopper shape the fractal poetics of the poem's form, "r-p-o-p-h-e-s-s-a-g-r" epitomizes zoopoetics—the process of making innovative forms of poetry shaped by a very attentive engagement with another species' way-of-being.

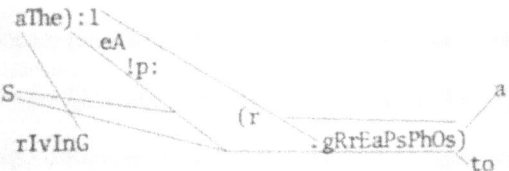

Figure 3.7. In "Iconic Dimensions in Poetry," Max Nänny exposed the otherwise overlooked shape of the grasshopper by drawing a few choice lines.

The poem reenacts the grasshopper's *poiesis* through not only the poem's textual leaps, but also the poem's material sounds. Terblanche observes that the poem contains onomatopoetic clusters of sound reminiscent of the sounds of leaping grasshoppers:

> Various whirring and clicking sounds of the leap, familiar to anyone who has been surprised by it as has the speaker in this instance, are onomatopoetically suggested by the creative rearrangement of letters on the page: examples include "r-p", "s-s", "g-r", "RHR", "SS", "Ph", "rr", and "gRr."[56]

Though Cummings is often known for being a visual poet, he also experimented with sounds throughout his career, as he does here.[57] Just as Whitman's attentiveness toward the locust-song shaped his writing, so Cummings shaped aspects of "r-p-o-p-h-e-s-s-a-g-r" to highlight the sounds emanating from an animal body in a moment of the animal's way-of-being.

Cummings' attentiveness to the grasshopper's leap led to innovative break-throughs in poetic form. The breakthroughs are worthy in their own right, even if readers see the poem as free-verse experimentation. However, if the poem is seen as a sonnet, the zoopoetic dynamic intensifies. Cummings often gravitates toward traditional forms (sonnet) or self-created forms in order to achieve his innovative moves. "(im)c-a-t(mo)" for instance, has a clear pattern of 2-3-4-5-1 lines per stanza that could be seen as restraints, but they are restraints that para-doxically generate much freedom. I suggest that "r-p-o-p-h-e-s-s-a-g-r" achieves its radical freedom due to the pressure placed upon it (consciously or uncon-sciously) by the sonnet tradition.

When Cummings sees form as something to "wander in" and to "loose" oneself in, thereby achieving a "new largeness," he means it. The discussion above demonstrates, though, that he wanders not alone. Grasshoppers, cats, whippoorwills, hummingbirds, thrush, and many more species wander in that space with him, pushing him to discover new ways to make readers *l!ook*.[58]

"jam on the shelf"

Like Whitman before him, Cummings continues the Emersonian poetics of dis-covering a "thought so passionate and alive that like the spirit of . . . an animal it has an architecture of its own."[59] Some of Cummings' most innovative architec-tures emerge from an attentiveness to the bodily *poiesis* of many species, and for Cummings, each of these ways-of-being is worth celebrating. In "The Secret of the Zoo Exposed," Cummings explores the Greek root of *zoo*, reminding us that it "originates in that most beautiful of all verbs, *zoo*, 'I am alive.'" And though his essay explores the darker side of zoos as well, he nonetheless sees zoos as containing "*a number of ways of being alive*." The architecture of his poems, shaped by the process of zoopoetics, reflect the many different ways of "being alive," of participating in a bodily *poiesis* that, for Cummings, encapsulates the "spiritual essence of poetry."[60]

One poem in particular highlights Cummings' conscious recognition of the importance of stretching toward animals: "i'd think 'wonder'" from his 1931 book *W[ViVa]*. This poem's publication predates many of Cummings' zoopoetic creations and may have been written around the same time as the early drafts of the grasshopper poem.[61] Its typographical gestures coincide with the temporal pauses, expectations, and brief sightings of a bat flitting through the night air. The poem also unites nature, the city, love, humans, and animals, but it is the parenthetical aside spanning the fifth, sixth, and seventh stanzas that crystallizes a zoopoetic mindset:

and here's my
hotel this is the
door(opening it i

think things
which
were supposed to
be out of my
reach
              ,they are like
jam on the shelf everybody guessed

was too high) (*CP* 354)

Through attentively looking at a bat, Cummings "thinks things / which / were supposed to / be out of [his] reach." He follows the statement with an epic simile that compares his innovative poetics to reaching the "jam on the shelf everybody guessed // was too high." As Paul Shepard argues, "human intelligence is bound to the presence of animals" so much so that humans are "connected to animals . . . by sinews that link speech to rationality, insight, intuition, and consciousness."[62] Zoopoetics expands Shepard's insight, for poetic form, poetic intelligence, is likewise linked to an attentiveness toward animals, directing poets like Cummings to "think things" that otherwise would be out of reach.

Though so often cast as an anomaly to or a break from the more serious modernist poets such as Pound and Eliot, Cummings is central to the evolution of zoopoetics.[63] He raises Whitman's poetics of the animal body to the next exponent through the innovative and material gestures of poetic form. Whitman's iconicity is very sparse compared with Cummings, but in both cases, the animal body "re-appears" in Cummings' "best poems," to echo Whitman (*LG* 1891–92, 176), through the iconicity of alphabetic language.

Notes

1. Inevitably, people wonder why EEC and not eec? Norman Friedman made two compelling arguments. In the first, Friedman points to Cummings' signature, discussions with Marion Moorehouse (Cummings' wife), and to the fact that, despite rumors, Cummings never changed his name. See Norman Friedman, "Not 'e. e. cummings,'" *Spring: The Journal of the E. E. Cummings Society* no. 1 (1992): 114–121. In the second, he cites an exchange of letters between Cummings and a French editor working on a translation of Cummings' work. The editor asked Cummings directly, "are you E.E. Cummings, ee cummings, or what?" Cummings replied "E.E. Cummings, unless your printer prefers E. E. Cummings"—the only difference the space between the initials. See Norman Friedman, "Not 'e. e. cummings' Revisited," *Spring: The Journal of the E. E. Cummings Society* no. 5 (1996): 41–43. But I think the most compelling reason returns to his signature—and the context of a particular signature—where Cummings chooses EEC. Upon delivering *i: six nonlectures* at Harvard in 1952–1953, late in his career, Cummings signed 350

copies. I happen to own number 279. It is an exquisite autograph. Simple. Sparse. Elegant. Something we would hope for from a poet-painter (see Fig. 3.8.). Point in case, Cummings signed this as a poet, after speaking at Harvard about being a poet. He *did* lowercase the personal pronoun in the event's title: *i: six nonlectures*. He also pushed against the establishment by calling his presentations "nonlectures." Had Cummings wanted to also lowercase his name, to be known as eec, this would have been the moment to make that happen. He didn't.

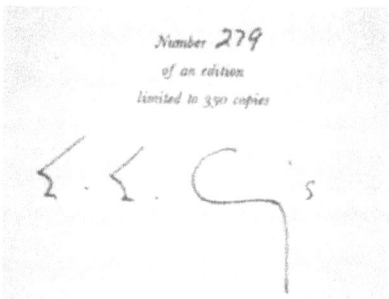

Figure 3.8. E. E. Cummings' Capitalized Signature from 1953.

    2.   Timothy Morton's "ambient poetics" are behind my discussion of the print marks on the page, for Whitman "highlights the page on which the words were written." "Ambience," writes Morton, "denotes a sense of a circumambient, or surrounding, *world*." He continues, "Ambience, that which surrounds on both sides, can refer to the margins of a page, the silence before and after music, the frame and walls around a picture," and so forth. And though ambient poetics occur "either at the level of content or at the level of form," it is the latter that pervades Cummings' craft. Timothy Morton, *Ecology Without Nature: Rethinking Environmental Aesthetics* (Cambridge: Harvard University Press, 2007), 37, 33, 34.

    3.   Cummings, *Miscellany*, 114.

    4.   Emerson, *Essential Writings*, 290.

    5.   In email exchange, Michael Webster suggests that Cummings wrote the sheet in 1916. Cummings may have gravitated toward Whitman during WWI. As Whitman worked with the wounded in the Civil War, so Cummings, as an ambulance driver, worked with the wounded in WWI. Provocatively, the sheet includes the line "The whole theory of the universe is directed unerringly to one single individual." Preceding this line, Whitman states "The American compact is altogether with individuals, / The only government is that which makes minute of individuals." Cummings includes the line "The American compact" on the sheet, but the second line makes explicit the tension between the individual and the government. Such tension becomes crucial to Cummings' *The Enormous Room.* The sheet suggests that Whitman's lines from "By Blue Ontario's Shore" may have contributed to the genesis of Cummings' WWI protest.

    6.   See Aaron Moe, "Cummings' Urban Ecology: An Exploration of *EIMI, No Thanks*, & the Cultivation of the Ecological Self," *Interdisciplinary Studies in Literature and Environment* 18, no. 4 (2011): 737–762.

7. For instance, Dana Gioia, David Mason, and Meg Schoerke suggest that Cummings was the "least jaded of modern poets"; that he "was less concerned with ideas than most other Modernists"; and that "we cannot read him in quite the same way as we might read Frost or Eliot" (289). Though such introductions may seem benign, they cast Cummings—a Harvard graduate—as an jejune anomaly to the poetic tradition. And yet, the aforementioned editors misprint the grasshopper's left and right borders (the "S . . . a" does not extend out of the "box"), and they also include a period at the end of "next to of course god america i" (294, 291). Such blatant typos suggest a superficial reading (and perhaps hasty dismissal) of Cummings' work. Cummings' very playful-yet-serious ideas are found precisely where a period is missing, or where letters break out of a boundary, that is, in the places the editor's typos conceal. See Dana Gioia, David Mason, and Meg Schoerke, eds., *Twentieth-Century American Poetry* (Boston: McGraw Hill, 2004).

8. R. P. Blackmur, *Language as Gesture: Essays in Poetry* (New York: Harcourt Brace & Company, 1952), 340, 320.

9. Kristeva, *Revolution in Poetic Language*, 79, 122.

10. Blackmur, *Language*, 6, 3, 5, 4, 20–21.

11. Rotman, *Becoming*, 3.

12. Abram, *Spell*, 101.

13. Ursula K. Le Guin, *Buffalo Gals and Other Animal Presences* (Santa Barbara: Capra Press, 1987), 154.

14. For more on Le Guin's perspective of animals and human language, see "She Unnames Them" (*Buffalo Gals*, 194–96). The distance human language creates between a human and another animal unravels, until the human and the animal achieve an understanding through an exchange of bodily *poiesis*.

15. bMS Am 1823.7 (25), folder 3 sheet 69; folder 4 sheet 74, Houghton Library, Harvard University.

16. bMS Am 1823.7 (25), folder 4 sheet 74, Houghton Library, Harvard University.

17. bMS Am 1823.7 (25) folder 4 sheet 77, Houghton Library, Harvard University.

18. For reviews of *Erotic Poems*, see Gillian Huang-Tiller, "Review of E. E. Cummings' Erotic Poems," *Spring: The Journal of the E. E. Cummings Society* 18 (2011): 167–171; and Eva Maria Gómez Jiménez, "Review of E. E. Cummings' Erotic Poems," *Spring: The Journal of the E. E. Cummings Society* 18 (2011): 164–66.

19. Concerning the date of this draft, Michael Webster shared the following in a group email exchange on "r-p-o-p-h-e-s-s-a-g-r": "It appears to be a very early draft, perhaps made before any typescript. Certainly it was composed before EEC first published the poem in the inaugural issue of William Carlos Williams' revival of the little magazine *Contact: An American Quarterly Review* (1.1, Feb. 1932)."

20. Haraway, *Species*, 164. As I have argued, Cummings "l!ook" pervades his ecopoetics. See Aaron Moe, "Two Converging Motifs: E. E. Cummings' *l!ook*," *Spring: The Journal of the E. E. Cummings Society* 18 (2011): 118–133.

21. For further discussion on Shepard's "minding animals" and Haraway's curiosity, see the introduction.

22. See Garrard, *Ecocriticism*, 147–48, 34.

23. Berger, *Why*, 27.

24. Haraway, *Species*, 217, 232.

25. Marjorie Perloff, *Differentials: Poetry, Poetics, Pedagogy* (Tuscaloosa: University of Alabama Press, 2004), 247. In "Poemgroups in *No Thanks*," Michael Webster demonstrates the importance of seeing Cummings' individual poems within the frame of

interrelated (rather than isolated) groups. For instance, in *No Thanks*, the sheer velocity of the grasshopper poem is followed by the stillness of the burial of a dead mouse. Michael Webster, "Poemgroups in No Thanks," *Spring: The Journal of the E. E. Cummings Society* 11 (2002): 19, 33.

26. E. E Cummings, *Etcetera: The Unpublished Poems of E. E. Cummings*, ed. George J. Firmage and Richard Kennedy (New York: Liveright, 1983), 117.

27. The Cornell Lab of Ornithology contains a wealth of resources for the birdwatcher: taxonomic breakdowns, identification, life history, sounds, videos, live web cams, and more. Recordings of the hermit thrush's voice can be found on the following page: www.allaboutbirds.org/guide/Hermit_Thrush/sounds.

28. Morton, *Ecology Without Nature*, 67, 69.

29. Ibid., 144.

30. Stevens, *Collected Poems*, 10.

31. Though there is not space to provide discussion on the zoopoetics in *73 Poems* as a whole, it nonetheless begins with the poem "O the sun comes up-up-up in the opening" (*CP* 773), which, as it unfolds, is a textual exploration of a rooster's vocalizations.

32. In an informal discussion at a conference, Etienne Terblanche provided a passing read on the punctuation of the title. He also suggested that "t,h;r:u;s,h;e:s" pushes us to consider the same question Wallace Stevens explored in the fifth section of "Thirteen Ways of Looking at a Blackbird" concerning the song of the blackbird or the silence "just after" (Stevens, *Collected Poems*, 93). In the context of the silent *e* of "rainsweet," Cummings seems to be mesmerized more silence thereafter.

33. E. E. Cummings, *EIMI: A Journey through Soviet Russia*, ed. George J. Firmage (New York: Liveright, 2007), 1, 452.

34. See Richard Kennedy, *Dreams in the Mirror: A Biography of E. E. Cummings* (New York: Liveright, 1980), 419, 431.

35. See Aaron Moe, "Chaos & the 'New' Nature Poem: A Look at E. E. Cummings' Poetry," *CT Review* 32, no. 1 (2010): 11–24.

36. See Aaron Moe, "Autopoiesis and Cummings' Cat," *Rupkatha Journal: On Interdisciplinary Studies in Humanities* 3, no. 1 (2011):110–120.

37. Cummings, *Miscellany*, 114.

38. John Pollock, "Appreciating Cummings' '(im)c-a-t(mo),'" *Spring: The Journal of the E. E. Cummings Society* 10 (2001): 45.

39. Cummings, *Letters*, 231.

40. For an excellent discussion of the ideogrammatic implications of both the *i* and the *O*, see Terblanche's *E. E. Cummings: Poetry and Ecology* (Amsterdam: Rodopi, 2012), 22, 72, 131.

41. Cummings, *Letters*, 231.

42. Qtd. in Kennedy, *Dreams*, 319.

43. Michael Webster, "How to Plot a Grasshopper: Reading E. E. Cummings' 'r-p-o-p-h-e-s-s-a-g-r' [to David Hendrickson, April 26, 1954-Feb. 15, 2012]" (presented at the American Literature Association Conference, San Francisco, 2012), 5.

44. Max Nänny, "Iconic Features in E. E. Cummings' Poetry," in *The Idea and the Thing in Modernist American Poetry*, ed. Cristina Giorcelli (Palermo: ILA Palma, 2001), 230. Nänny's move to place the title and therefore the beginning of the poem at the last line harmonizes with Cummings' poetics. Often, his poems begin again after they "end" (see *CP* 600, 657, 722), and the semi-colon at the end of "r-p-o-p-h-e-s-s-a-g-r" suggests something else must yet happen. Interestingly, Nänny observes how the scrambled words

for grasshopper progress from confusion to clarity reading from the top down ("Iconic Features" 231)—but if we start at the last line and read up, we leap back into the poem's (paradoxical) patterned chaos. In the conference presentation "The Nude, the Grasshopper, and the Poet Painter," Vakrilen Kilyovski argues for this ground-up reading of the poem. Vakrilen Kilyovski, "The Nude, the Grasshopper and the Poet-Painter: A Reading of E. E. Cummings' 'r-p-o-p-h-e-s-s-a-g-r'" (Presented at a conference in Sofia, Bulgaria 2009).

45. Nänny, "Iconic Dimensions," 135, 134.

46. Webster, "Plot," 5.

47. E. E. Cummings, *No Thanks*, ed. George J. Firmage, Typescript ed. (New York: Liveright, 1978), 13.

48. Qtd. in Gillian Huang-Tiller, "One Art: Intuition and Typography in E. E. Cummings' Original Analysis of 'r-p-o-p-h-e-s-s-a-g-r' (1935)," 2012.

49. For an excellent read on the Taoist and ecological implications of the line "S . . . a" see Terblanche's *E. E. Cummings: Poetry and Ecology* (49–52).

50. Gillian Huang-Tiller, "The Iconic Meta-Sonnet, Manhood and Cultural Crisis in No Thanks," in *Words into Pictures: E. E. Cummings' Art Across Borders*, ed. Jiří Flajšar and Zénó Vernyik, (Newcastle: Cambridge Scholars Publishing, 2007), 29, 28. To be clear, Huang-Tiller argues against seeing "r-p-o-p-h-e-s-s-a-g-r" as a sonnet. In an email exchange, I asked, "Do you see 'r-p-o-p-h-e-s-s-a-g-r' as an iconic meta-sonnet? If so, on what basis? Do you see it fitting within the V-schema? I have looked for a 'mirror' sonnet on the 'ascension side' of the V, but cannot find one." She replied:

> You can make a case for it if the poem is taken in isolation. For me, this poem embedded in Cummings' deliberate sonnet schema is not intended as "another" sonnet (experimental as it is) or a meta-sonnet in the way I analyze it to reflect on genre and culture simultaneously. Cummings' own analysis also discourages me from seeing the poem as a sonnet. My study is based on the V schema as a whole, so it is hard for me to see the poemgroups in isolation. Cummings' own note in his final schema also made a point about the last poem (#71) in fifteen lines as a sonnet (cited in my article p. 31). To embed the 3 poems between the sonnets seems to indicate that the poems set between the sonnets should probably not read as sonnets. Perhaps there is a Cummings note out there waiting to be found that might explain it.

In the same email exchange, Webster agrees with Huang-Tiller, but leaves room for readers to play with the implications of the sonnet patterns:

> Basically, I think Gillian is right, in the sense that EEC did not consciously intend the poem as a sonnet. But I do think that it is a kind of "accidental" sonnet—he writes so many sonnets that some of his poems tend to gravitate toward that form. Think of "Paris,this April sunset" for example—or even "poets yeggs and thirsties" which is in 14 lines but doesn't seem like much of a sonnet otherwise.

I agree that one cannot argue that the poem is an intentional sonnet, unless Cummings reveled in playing with the form of the sonnet surreptitiously, leaving no notes on the V-schema that could suggest it is a sonnet. The fact that several Cummings scholars use phrases such as "'accidental' sonnet," or "unconscious sonnet," or "parody sonnet," or "sort-of sonnet" nonetheless suggests that, intentionally or unintentionally, the patterns of the sonnet haunt the making (and reading) of the poem.

51. Qtd. in Huang-Tiller, "One Art."

52. Kilyovski, "The Nude."

53. See Moe, "Chaos."

54. Michael Webster, "E. E. Cummings: The New Nature Poetry and the Old," *Spring: The Journal of the E. E. Cummings Society* no. 9 (2000): 111.

55. Nänny, "Iconic Dimensions," 135.

56. Etienne Terblanche, "That 'Incredible Unanimal/Mankind': Jacques Derrida, E. E. Cummings and a Grasshopper," *Journal of Literary Studies* 20, no. 3–4 (2004): 16.

57. The poem "ygUDuh" exemplifies Cummings' acute experimentation with a poetics of sound (*CP* 547), where "ygUDuh" reads *ya gotta*, as does his poem "!" about the round moon rising discussed in this book's introduction.

58. For a discussion on the recurring motifs of Cummings' exclamation mark and the imperative to look, see my essay "Two Converging Motifs: E. E. Cummings' *l!ook.*"

59. Emerson, *Essential Writings*, 290.

60. Cummings, *Miscellany*, 174, 114.

61. "r-p-o-p-h-e-s-s-a-g-r" was first published in William Carlos Williams' magazine *Contact: An American Quarterly Review* in 1932. The early drafts of the grasshopper poem may have overlapped with the drafts of "i'd think 'wonder" (*CP* 354).

62. Shepard, *Thinking Animals*, 249, 2.

63. For an argument on Cummings' crucial place in modernist studies—one that refreshingly reads Eliot and Pound *through* Cummings poetry and poetics—see Terblanche's *E. E. Cummings: Poetry and Ecology.*

Part 2 Implications

Interlude
Beluga Whales

One aspect of zoopoetics focuses on how a human's attentiveness toward animals leads to innovative breakthroughs in the material forms of poems on a page. But this human emphasis must be balanced. Other animals experience innovative breakthroughs in their own makings through an attentiveness toward *humans*. Shepard speaks of the "reciprocal spiral of consciousness" amidst prey-predator relationships and argues that human intelligence is bound up with "minding animals," but as Donna Haraway demonstrates in the eighth chapter of *When Species Meets*, the same reciprocal spiral develops when two species play with one another.[1] In both theorists' arguments, intelligence increases for all parties involved (rather than just the human's).

A recent study highlights how the vocal range of a beluga whale increased through *minding humans*—and not out of a prey-predator relationship, nor solely out of playing with humans. Though speculative, I suggest the beluga whale's attentiveness toward humans stemmed from an effort to extend his social sphere—from a cultural agency to initiate interspecies interactions. Regardless, the study demonstrates how a beluga whale figured out how to mimic the frequency and cadences of human speech.

Known as the canary of the sea, the beluga whale is one of the most versatile vocalists among cetaceans. If they were human, they could write sonnets, haiku, and free verse with the same ease as composing graphic novels and an obituary. In a 2012 analysis of beluga vocalizations that mimic the frequency, rhythms, and cadences of human speech, the scientists recount the day a diver surfaced and asked, "Who told me to get out?" No human had. The team soon realized that a beluga whale, named Noc, had mimicked a sound resembling *out out out*. The scientists proceeded to study the bodily changes necessary to produce the new sound:

> Unlike echolocation clicks, ordinary pulse bursts, and whistle-like sounds, the production of speech-like sounds involved marked inflation of first one and then the other vestibular sac. This was readily observed on the surface of the whale's head and may have been necessary to emphasize lower frequencies of the speech-like sounds. In usual white whale sounds, such extreme inflation of these sacs is not evident.[2]

The study suggestions, therefore, that the beluga whale underwent an innovative, physiological change in order to achieve the "extreme inflation" necessary to replicate the lower frequencies of human speech, and I suggest that the innovation emerged out of the whale's Aristotelian impulse to imitate another species, this time, *homo sapiens*.

Like the poet who discovers new forms of poetry through an attentiveness toward other animals, the beluga whale discovered a new way to manipulate his vestibular sacs. These forms enrich his repertoire of bodily *poiesis*. Minding the rhythms, cadences, and frequencies of human speech patterns became a catalyst for a beluga whale to extend the range of his vocalizations.

I infer, then, that prior to this study, beluga whales expanded the range of their vocalizations through an attentiveness to conspecifics and to other marine species including, perhaps, dolphins, humpback whales, and seals. The fact that beluga whales have also *minded humans* is bittersweet. Captivity is a high price for new songs of the sea. And while the captive whales extend the range of their vocalizations—thereby demonstrating to humans, yet again, the amazing capabilities of animals—beluga communities in the ocean face the coming extinction.

Notes

1. Shepard, *Thinking Animals*, 6–7, 249; see, for instance, Haraway, *Species*, 232.
2. Sam Ridgway et al., "Spontaneous Human Speech Mimicry by a Cetacean," *Current Biology* 22, no. 20 (2012): 860–61.

Chapter 4
"learning my steps": Zoopoetics and Mass Extinction in W. S. Merwin's Poetry

Henry David Thoreau certainly raised walking to another exponent as he suggests that the walk is nothing less than an art: "I have met with but one or two persons in the course of my life who understood the art of Walking, that is, of taking walks, who had a genius, so to speak, for *sauntering*."[1] W. S. Merwin is one poet who had such a genius.

Merwin, like Cummings and Whitman before him, saw poetry as something much larger than words on a page. His statements on poetry and poetics reminds readers that poetry includes the printed page, but is not limited to it. In "On Open Form," Merwin sets forth a definition that preserves possibility: "A poetic form: the setting down of a way of hearing how poetry happens in words."[2] He does not define *the* poetic form, but rather, *a* poetic form, and his definition emphasizes the fact that poetry happens in other places than words, too. He also emphasizes that poetic form relates to one's ability to hear, and therefore to *listen*. Other senses permeate Merwin's *oeuvre* too, but *listening* becomes most crucial, for it directs readers to where the first stirrings of *poiesis* begin.

One of the reasons why Merwin stopped using punctuation midway through *The Moving Target* (1963) rarely to use it again in his published poems involves listening.[3] In the interview "'Fact Has Two Faces,'" Merwin discusses how the absence of punctuation encourages both the poet and the reader to listen more attentively:

> You have to pay attention to things. . . . Punctuation is there as a kind of manners in prose, articulating prose meaning, but it doesn't necessarily articulate the meaning of this kind of verse. I saw that if I could use the movement of the verse itself and the movement of the line—*the actual weight of the language as it moved*—to do the punctuation, I would both strengthen the texture of the experience of the poem and also make clear its distinction from other kinds of writing. One would be paying attention to it in those terms.[4]

The absence of punctuation pushes the reader to become less an observer and more of a participant in the poetic moment, for she or he must read more with the body, attentively *stretching toward* the language's weight. For Merwin, this weight is marked by "movement"—not unlike the bodies of humans and animals. Like Whitman, the body "re-appears" in some of Merwin's "best poems," experienced when the reader's body engages the physical heft of a line.[5] Later in the interview, Merwin discusses, at length, the need for a thorough wrestling with what, after all, a poetic line is. Merwin sees many emergent yet talented writers who still have a "very shaky sense of what a line is." In a workshop, he encouraged students to spend a moment to "figure out what a line of verse is." "After two hours," Merwin shares, "we hadn't got very far." He continues:

> We left it with my saying, "I think this is what you have to think about the next time you stop a line somewhere. At the risk of losing a great deal of spontaneity for awhile, you need to look closely, to figure out what in hell you think you're doing: why you stop it after three syllables, why you stop it after two beats, or why you stop it where you do—what are you doing? . . ." [We came] to realize that a line was a unit of something. What it was a unit of was something they couldn't agree on.[6]

Ed Folsom and Cary Nelson push Merwin further, asking if he thinks the line relates to [Olson's] theory of the breath. Merwin suggests it can, but that there is something more: "I think of stopping at a given point as a rhythmical gesture, and also as a gesture of meaning—because where you stop, if the rhythm is working, is going to have an effect on the meaning, particularly if you're not punctuating."[7] At the time of this interview (early 1980's), Merwin's understanding of a poetic line is inextricably bound up with the materiality of gestures. In a 2006 interview, Merwin emphasizes how the line is a "unit of energy" that "has to do, finally, with the *physical.*"[8] Cummings' theory on gestures discussed in the third chapter provides explanatory power. A gesture of a line is inscrutable, in part, because it is like a prime number, and one cannot explain a prime number or a prime gesture without the noise of other numbers, gestures, or words. Though less extreme than Cummings and much more quiet than Whitman, Merwin cultivates a poetics of the body. As will be demonstrated, his "listening" is both an auditory and haptic event. Readers listen to the *weight of the language as it moves* with more than just the ears.

And as both poet and reader enter a posture of listening to the weight of a line, a line break, and a stanza break, Merwin cultivates an ecopoetics.[9] The listening to language can direct the reader to the place where poetry happens outside of words. In this way, Merwin descends from Whitman—but with much more silence and circumspection. Throughout Merwin's *oeuvre*, the stirrings of *poiesis* begin through listening to the elemental forces of the earth, the organic growth of plants, and the bodily *poiesis* of animals—as demonstrated by "The Cold Before the Moonrise" (from *The Lice*):

> It is too simple to turn to the sound
> Of frost stirring among its
> Stars like an animal asleep
> In the winter night
> And say I was born far from home
> If there is a place where this is the language may
> It be my country[10]

Merwin's speaker turns to the elemental force of frost "stirring" in the cold night before the moonrise. The emphasis on the frost's "stars" establishes the cold, cosmological scope of Merwin's poetic vision, something that the critic J. Scott Bryson calls a "space-consciousness." Instead of seeing space/place as opposites, Bryson suggests a "place-space synergy" in Merwin's poetics. "What is necessary," Bryson argues, "is a space-conscious 'awe' combined with and resulting from a place-centered commitment to the world itself."[11] The turn toward the stirring of the elemental force of crystallizing water cultivates a sense of place, but this occurs within vast cosmological distances.

As later sections of this chapter explore, Merwin listens to the motions and movements of many species. This fact informs his comparison of the stirring frost to the "animal asleep / in the winter night." As he turns to the elemental forces of the earth, he animates those stirrings with the bodily *poiesis* of a sleeping and perhaps dreaming animal. The scene of the stirring frost will become further intensified when the moon actually does rise, flooding the poem with moonlight and moon-shadows, but in the context of vast cosmological distances—and in the context of the darkness of *The Lice* in which the poem appears— the sense of place is fragile.

Readers who turn toward the poem and listen can hear the stirring of the language through the onomatopoetic *s's* in the first three lines and can therefore experience vestiges of the language of the earth and another place where poetry happens. It happens in the stirrings of frost, the stirrings of animals, the stirrings of human poetry, and in the stirrings of the organic growth of plants. Though "The Cold Before the Moonrise" contains no explicit mentions of the organic growth of plants, it is implicit. Merwin, who has planted innumerable trees over three decades on what was once a pineapple plantation in Hawaii, is, indeed, a poet-planter. As will be discussed later in this chapter, planting informs his poetic posture. "The Cold Before the Moonrise" is the planting of a *poem*, and it is part of the "journeywork of the stars" (*LG* 1855, 34). In the poem's final lines, Merwin's poetics of planting emerges. He plants the "seed" of a bioregional identity that usurps one's national identity: the "place" where the "language" of the earth becomes one's "country."

"The Cold Before the Moonrise" establishes some of the crucial aspects of Merwin's poetry and poetics. Merwin turns, listens, plants, and cultivates a "place-space synergy." In this chapter, I focus primarily upon his turning toward animals, and crucially, toward their absence. Like Whitman and Cummings before him, Merwin makes poetic breakthroughs through an attentiveness to another species' bodily *poiesis*; however, when Merwin turns toward the animals, they are often not there. Juxtaposing his earlier "Leviathan" (1956) with a few poems from *The Lice* (1967) demonstrates how an attentiveness to the absence of animals contributed, in part, to breakthroughs in form. However, Merwin's poetry after *The Lice* often cultivates a connection to animals who are still present, but the shadow of *The Lice* and the ongoing mass extinction infuses Merwin's zoopoetics with anguish and with a sense of fragility amidst such moments. Butterflies, insects, lizards, foxes, monkeys, snakes, mice, and many more species populate his poetry after *The Lice*, demonstrating Merwin's continual return toward that most crucial posture of zoopoetics: an attentiveness to the bodily *poiesis* of another species. Unlike Cummings, Merwin's poetic breakthroughs have much less to do with an iconicity where the poetic form plays with the bodily *poiesis* of a particular animal; however, his attentiveness to animals still shapes the form of the poem. In *The Vixen*, I argue that Merwin's attentiveness toward animals—pervasive throughout many of his books—comes to clear focus, shaping and sustaining the book's innovative form of a *saunter*.

Attentiveness Toward the Absence of Animals

Biological and linguistic extinction generate a feedback loop in Merwin's poetics—a dynamic established in *The Lice*. Its epigraph from Heraclitus cryptically introduces the coming extinction:

> All men are deceived by the appearances of things, even Homer himself, who was the wisest man in Greece; for he was deceived by boys catching lice: they said to him, "What we have caught and what we have killed we have left behind, but what has escaped us we bring with us." (*P* 1:265)

Jarold Ramsey interprets the epigraph in terms of the "continuity of the self." He sees the lice that escapes as Merwin's "unresolved alternatives, the frustrated purposes, the guilt, the missed chances, and unwritten poems of his discontinuous lives."[12] I respectfully suggest that focusing on the growth of the self eclipses the ecological import of the epigraph as it relates to *The Lice* and to Merwin's anguish over extinction. The epigraph encapsulates the state of the planet in 1967 and today. All the species that humans have caught and killed—all the whales humans have driven to extinction—are left behind; humans only bring with us species that escape domination and exploitation.

In "The Animals" which is the first poem of *The Lice*, Merwin's speaker turns to the animals in a Whitmanian moment, only to find their absence:[13]

> All these years behind windows
> With blind crosses sweeping the tables

> And myself tracking over empty ground
> Animals I never saw
>
> I with no voice
>
> Remembering names to invent for them
> Will any come back will one
>
> Saying yes
>
> Saying look carefully yes
> We will meet again (*P* 1:267)

Unlike Whitman, the poetic speaker has "no voice." His voice is as empty as the trackless ground. The "blind crosses" refer to the shadows cast by the window blinds, and suggest the "meaningless [and I add violent] crucifixions" of animals.[14] Animals no longer nurture Merwin's voice like they did for Whitman, and it is very difficult for the body of an animal to reappear in a poem if that animal does not exist.

To give this poem more weight, I turn to the arguments of Paul Shepard and David Abram. Both thinkers recognize the human indebtedness to animals regarding human imagination, intelligence, and culture. Shepard's driving thesis is that "human intelligence is bound to the presence of animals," and he discusses how this intelligence emerged: "Hunter and hunted are engaged in an upward, reciprocal spiral of consciousness with its constituents of stratagem and insight."[15] As prey and predators read each other's markings, scents, and bodily *poiesis* in order to survive, they become increasingly intelligent. Shepard argues that animals are essential to the human imagination. A lack of animals and of interspecies interactions depletes the human mind. Abram also argues that the increasing extinction of animals depletes language:

> As technological civilization diminishes the biotic diversity of the earth, language itself is diminished. As there are fewer and fewer songbirds in the air, due to the destruction of their forests and wetlands, human speech loses more and more of its evocative power. For when we no longer hear the voices of warbler and wren, our own speaking can no longer be nourished by their cadences. . . . as we drive more and more of the land's wild voices into the oblivion of extinction, our own languages become increasingly impoverished and weightless, progressively emptied of their earthly resonance.[16]

Provocatively, Abram uses the term *weightless* to describe this impoverished language. It is difficult to listen to the *weight of the language as it moves* if it has little material heft. As Merwin emphasizes, the loss of animals is a loss of language: "with the animals dying around us / . . . with the words going out like cells of a brain" (*P* 1:649).

Prior to both Shepard and Abram's arguments, Merwin recognized how a depletion of animals depletes the poetic voice. Rather than inventing a form/architecture of a poem as part of the process of engaging an animal, the poetic speaker contemplates the alternative: "Remembering names to invent for them." Two poems readily expose Merwin's shift from naming animals to naming the absence of animals: "Leviathan" from *Green with Beasts* and "For a Coming Extinction" from *The Lice*. "Leviathan" is the first poem of part 1 in *Green with Beasts*, the "Physiologus: Chapters for a Bestiary." In part 1, Merwin gravitates toward a poetics interested in the physiological characteristics of a given animal, but this physiology is enmeshed within the rich tradition of myth—especially in "Leviathan." In light of zoopoetics, the weight of the whale's body moving through oceans emerges in the weight of the language is it moves through sonorous words and long sentences spanning several alliterative lines across the poetic page:

> This is the black sea-brute bulling through wave-wrack,
> Ancient as ocean's shifting hills, who in sea-toils
> Traveling, who furrowing the salt acres
> Heavily, his wake hoary behind him,
> Shoulders spouting, the fist of his forehead
> Over wastes gray-green crashing, among horses unbroken
> From bellowing fields, past bone-wreck of vessels,
> Tide-ruin, wash of lost bodies bobbing
> No longer sought for, and islands of ice gleaming,
> Who ravening the rank flood, wave-marshaling,
> Overmastering the dark sea-marches, finds home
> And harvest.

The heavy lines continue in later phrases such as "The hulk of him is like hills heaving" and "Like land's self by night black-looming, surf churning and trailing / Along his shores' rushing, shoal-water boding / About the dark of his jaws" (*P* 1:99). Later, the poem echoes Old Testament passages that similarly use a heavy language when writing about the Leviathan (*Genesis, Job, Jonah*), but Merwin's language seems heavier. Just as Whitman used many verb-ful, augmenting adjectives in his prose piece on the locust-song, so Merwin does here. Instead of a *whirring, emitting, droning* energy, however, Merwin's language heaves: *bulling, shifting, traveling, furrowing, spouting, crashing, bellowing*. To give further weight to the language, Merwin hyphenates many words (such as *sea-brute, wave-wrack, gray-green*). But one of Merwin's innovative moves occurs through hyphenating a descriptor to one of the verb-ful adjectives, such as *wave-marshaling, black-looming, wind-combed.* "Leviathan" rivals anything within the literary tradition of whale-writing, including Edmund Burke's treatise on the sublime and Melville's *Moby-Dick*,[17] for the poem epitomizes zoopoetics: the heaving of the poetic lines resonates with the whale's heavy motion through the seas. "Leviathan" is one of the more obvious moments of iconicity in Merwin's *oeuvre*.

Amidst the growing awareness of mass extinctions, though, there are fewer animals for Merwin to turn toward in *The Lice*. The zoopoetic dynamic shifts to an attentiveness toward the absence of animals. The highly anthologized and much discussed "For a Coming Extinction" epitomizes Merwin's poetic break-throughs (in all their anguish) that emerge from an attentiveness toward absence. Unlike "Leviathan," the words and lines in "For a Coming Extinction" require little breath to read aloud:

> Gray whale
> Now that we are sending you to The End
> That great god
> Tell him
> That we who follow you invented forgiveness
> And forgive nothing
>
> I write as though you could understand
> And I could say it
> One must always pretend something
> Among the dying
> When you have left the seas nodding on their stalks
> Empty of you
> Tell him that we were made
> On another day
>
> The bewilderment will diminish like an echo
> Winding along your inner mountains
> Unheard by us
> And find its way out
> Leaving behind it the future
> Dead
> And ours
>
> When you will not see again
> The whale calves trying the light
> Consider what you will find in the black garden
> And its court
> The sea cows the Great Auks the gorillas
> The irreplaceable hosts ranged countless
> And foreordaining as stars
> Our sacrifices
>
> Join your word to theirs
> Tell him
> That it is we who are important (*P* 1:304–305)

Like "Leviathan," Merwin alludes to the Genesis myth of creation, but as he does so, he re-writes the myth.[18] The dominion of Genesis becomes the palimp-sest upon which Merwin erases and writes anew.[19] The speaker imagines the gray whale telling the creator that the coming extinction is justified since hu-mans "were made / On another day." The stanza break allows the reader to linger in the "justification" before learning that someone is utterly bewildered. Hank Lazer suggests that the whale is bewildered; however, his read does reconcile how the bewilderment "will"—that is, after the whale speaks to the great god—"diminish like an echo / Winding along [the whale's] inner mountains."[20] The whale *listens* to the bewilderment of someone else. Even though the whale could be bewildered by the coming extinction, he observes someone else's utter shock. And even though the tone of the poem is that of bewilderment, anguish, and angst, the bewilderment of line fifteen is "Unheard by us" humans. This leaves only one "person" left to be bewildered: the "great god."

In Merwin's myth, the impetus for the great god's bewilderment is the gray whale's message. Merwin enters into the creation myth to subvert it, suggesting that the great god is utterly perplexed why humans feel entitled to drive other species into extinction. The garden of Eden becomes the "black garden" full of extinct species or those near extinction: "The sea cows the Great Auks the gorillas."

Admittedly, the form of "For a Coming Extinction" is part of a much larger movement in Merwin's *oeuvre* toward sparseness, emptiness, and silence—a movement that gained much force in *The Moving Target* (1963) and continued through *The Lice* (1967) and beyond. An attentiveness toward the absence of animals contributed to the shift in form, though, which comes to fruition in "For a Coming Extinction." It is worth lingering in the aforementioned line—"The sea cows the Great Auks the gorillas"—as it demonstrates a specific breakthrough in form that emerges from an attentiveness toward the absence of an animal. The line exhibits palimpsest qualities, for vestiges of the alliterative verse from "Leviathan" return—but without the heaviness. The alliteration and assonance cross-stitches the animals together: the *s*'s throughout; the *khh* in *cows* and *Auks*; the *ghh* in *Great* and *gorillas*; and the *ahh* in *cows, Auks, gorillas*. The weight of the line, though, emerges not from the subtle musicality that is present; rather, it comes from the caesuras, the absences. As one *listens to the weight of the language as it moves* through the line, the pauses between each animal in the list augment. At first, one may hear just a comma separating each species—"the sea cows, the Great Auks, the gorillas"—but the bewilderment at the coming extinction calls for something more: "the sea cows . . . the Great Auks . . . the gorillas. . . ." A greater bewilderment, anguish, and angst charges the absent ellipses following "the Great Auks" as the emblem gesture of capital letters emphasizes the finality of their extinction. And the gorillas are next. The innovative breakthroughs in poetic form push the reader to listen to the weight of absence, and of silence, and of the coming extinction as it moves in language, thereby cultivating a similar sense of bewilderment, anguish, and angst already established in the poem's earlier stanzas. And so the heavy alliterated lines from "Leviathan" are erased and written over with a much more subtle alliteration, and instead of engaging the heaving movement of a whale through language, the reader confronts the bewildering absence. The juxtaposition of "Leviathan" and "For a Coming Extinction" exposes the interrelationship between biological and linguistic extinction. The language of "Leviathan"—like the whales—faces extinction. Merwin preserves vestiges of that rich language in "For a Coming Extinction," but the heaviness of the alliterative line dissipates in an elegant but anguish-filled subtlety.

Biological and Linguistic Extinction

To further explore the interrelationship between biological and linguistic extinction, I return to Bryson's insight regarding the "place-space synergy" in Merwin's work, specifically his claim that an "ever-present space-consciousness" is "perhaps the most prominent characteristic of Merwin's *oeuvre*."[21] Both extinctions increase the "space-consciousness" of an increasing sense of emptiness and absence. For instance, the poem "Place" from *The Rain in the Trees* (1988) epitomizes how Merwin often cultivates a profound identification with nonhuman nature (place) in the context of an increasing extinction, exploitation, and deforestation (space). "Place" sits amongst several of the poems in *The Rain in the Trees* that explore biological and linguistic extinctions such as "Conqueror," "Native," "Witness, "Chord," "Losing a Language," and "The Lost Originals" (*P* 1:661, 662, 663, 664, 664–65, 666). It is already the last day of the world:

> On the last day of the world
> I would want to plant a tree
>
> what for
> not for the fruit
>
> the tree that bears the fruit
> is not the one that was planted
>
> I want the tree that stands
> in the earth for the first time
>
> with the sun already
> going down
>
> and the water
> touching its roots
>
> in the earth full of the dead
> and the clouds passing
>
> one by one
> over its leaves (*P* 1:663)

This poem captures Merwin's resolve to plant trees in Hawaii as he has since the 1970's, but it also captures his poetic disposition. Merwin is a planter-poet, for his poems cultivate a strong sense of identification with many of the dynamic relationships within the ecosphere. "Place" directs attention to the simple but ineffable ecology of water, roots, earth, decomposition, clouds, leaves, sun, and a planter's hands. The shadow of *The Lice*, though, re-emerges in the phrase "earth full of the dead"—that is, the earth full of the completed extinctions.

The context of the surrounding poems from *The Rain in the Trees* further casts the sense of "place" as something fragile and tenuous. "Witness" confronts readers with how deforestation depletes language:

> I want to tell what the forests
> were like
>
> I will have to speak
> in a forgotten language (*P* 1:663)

Two pages later, Merwin laments "Losing a Language": "many of the things the words were about / no longer exist" (*P* 1:665). The immediate context coupled with the shadow of *The Lice* infuse "Place" with bewilderment, anguish, and a sense of hopelessness. The cultivation of "place" is inextricably bound up with, as Bryson suggests, a looming sense of space.

When Merwin turns toward the presence of animals, it is rarely outside the looming sense of space and the shadow of *The Lice*. This occurs even in *The Lice*, when, for instance, Merwin turns toward birds in "How We Are Spared":

> At midsummer before dawn an orange light returns to the mountains
> Like a great weight and the small birds cry out
> And bear it up (*P* 1:296)

Merwin infuses the midsummer dawn with anguish, the "great weight" of *The Lice*, and yet the birds "bear it up" through their song. A poem from *The Rain in the Trees* exhibits a similar dynamic. The title "After the Alphabets" casts a shadow over Merwin's celebration of the language of insects:

> I am trying to decipher the language of insects
> they are the tongues of the future
> their vocabularies describe buildings as food
> they can depict dark water and the veins of trees
> they can convey what they do not know
> and what is known at a distance
> and what nobody knows
> they have terms for making music with the legs
> they can recount changing in a sleep like death
> they can sing with wings
> the speakers are their own meaning in a grammar without horizons
> they are wholly articulate
> they are never important they are everything (*P* 1:652)

The title places the poem in the context of a post-human extinction. The insects will be the poets of the (human-less) future, undergoing the many facets of their bodily *poiesis*.

In his essay "The Winter Palace," Merwin recounts his journey to the Transvolcanic Range in Mexico where thousands of monarchs migrate. The essay places his identification with the butterflies in the context of the increasing challenges facing the monarch butterflies due to environmental devastation along the migration route as well as at the migration's ending place. Like his poetry, Merwin's prose refuses to separate an attentiveness toward animals from the coming extinction. He marvels at the sheer distance of the butterflies' migration (2,500 miles) and at their collective *poiesis* at the journey's end where they arrive at the oyamel firs in the Transvolcanic Range. The collective group undergoes the *poiesis* of the swarm:

> There are advantages to being part of a large assembly, and the first groups that settle into the oyamel firs obviously welcome still larger congregations: They have been seen above their trees in spiraling columns a thousand feet high, signaling to other groups, "Here is the place."

And at the essay's close, Merwin describes a continuity of languages between species: "we stood in the afternoon sunlight in the sound of them, a sound of words before words, a whisper of one syllable older than language, continuing like a pulse." However, such moments are, as mentioned, never isolated from the coming extinction: "If the reduction of the forest continues, the larger eastern population of the monarch species, at the end of its vast migrations, will be edged out of existence."[22]

The line quoted from "The Winter Palace"—"a whisper of one syllable older than language"—echoes a poem from *The Rain in the Trees*, "Utterance":

> Sitting over words
> very late I have heard a kind of whispered sighing
> not far
> like a night wind in pines or like the sea in the dark
> the echo of everything that has ever
> been spoken
> still spinning its one syllable
> between the earth and silence (*P* 1:647)

Merwin's work suggests that the "utterance" and the "spinning" of that "one syllable" includes the language of insects, the song of birds, the swarming spirals of butterflies, and the heavy motions of a whale who faces extinction. The poem reaches back to the elemental origins of language. It is an act of recovery in light of the extinctions underway, both biological and linguistic.

Finding the Islands and the Saunter of *The Vixen*

If Merwin only made occasional breakthroughs in poetic form through his attentiveness to animals and their absence, then zoopoetics could be seen merely as a
minor (though no less important) dynamic in his *oeuvre*. Two books of poems
after *The Lice*, however, further demonstrate how the continual turning toward
existing animals initiated breakthroughs in poetic form: *Finding the Islands*
(1982) and *The Vixen* (1996). *Finding the Islands* began as a discipline to distill
the poetic moment into as brief a moment as possible. "I wanted to see what it
was that made a poem complete as a small, if not the smallest, unit." Merwin
continues, "It was a way of discovering what was the single thing that would
stand by itself."[23] Throughout the duration of this exercise, Merwin wrote hundreds of haiku-esque tercets and compiled them into *Finding the Islands*. Even a
cursory glance at *Finding the Islands* exposes the sheer abundance of animals:
mice, a dove, a plover, owls, crows, mayflies, lizards, crickets, jays, tree toads,
chipmunks, nuthatches, beetles, wasps, a horse, grasshoppers, swallows, a cat,
bees, moths, a blackbird, and many more. Merwin, though, is not interested in
merely describing these animals; rather, he turns toward them to better understand what makes a poem complete. One could see the animals as simply poetic
material—something thematic —but I suggest that turning toward the bodily
poiesis of many animals contributed, necessarily so, to the breakthroughs of that
poetic exploration.

One of the breakthroughs involves a new way of listening:

> Rain on the tin roof
> lizard hands on the tin ceiling
> listening (*P* 1:545)

Though I can only surmise what counted as a success for Merwin, this poem
seems to epitomize the exercise. The three lines stand by themselves, but they
would not if they were a word shorter or if he timed the line breaks differently.
The silence of the line breaks helps the reader listen along with the lizard. The
first line establishes the image of rain on the tin roof; the lizard's hands emerge
in the beginning of the second line. The image morphs in the latter half of the
second line, for the hands are *inside* the structure, pressed up against the "tin
ceiling" from below. The third line delivers the success of the poem: *listening*.
The poem directs attention to a *listening* not through the ears, but through the
haptic vibrations felt through the hands. An attentiveness to the lizard's way-of-
being enhances Merwin's "setting down of a way of hearing how poetry happens in words."[24] The zoopoetic dynamic becomes complete as an attentiveness
to this lizard's motionless engagement with the rain led to the line break that
places "listening" by itself in all of its resonance. Merwin learns to listen
through an attentiveness to the lizard's listening posture, and the reader learns to
listen through an attentiveness to the *weight of the language as it moves* across
the line breaks.

When Merwin experiments with a form, he often does so for the duration of an entire book. Such is the case with *Finding the Islands*, and such is the case in *The Vixen*. Like *Finding the Islands*, myriad animals populate *The Vixen*, and much of the content involves an habitual attentiveness toward animals. Many of the titles foreground liminal moments—"Gate"; "Threshold"; "Entry"; "In the Doorway"; "Emergence"—and the poems often crisscross the threshold between the speaker and other animals. Similar to Cummings' emphasis on the green bird looking at him, Merwin writes about a "green snake lying in the sunlight watching me" or the reciprocity of looking back and forth: "I looked up a bank straight into the small eyes / of a boar watching me and we stared at each other / in that silence before he turned and went on" (*P* 2:24, 8). Though the majority of the book cultivates an identification with animals in a rural, pastoral setting, the shadow of *The Lice* persists. "Green Fields" continues the urgency of *The Lice*, for the attentiveness toward animals occurs less and less in "this part of the century":

> By this part of the century few are left who believe
>   in the animals *for they are not there* in the carved parts
> of them served on plates and the pleas from the slatted trucks
>   are sounds of shadows that possess no future
> there is still game for the pleasure of killing
>   and there are pets for the children but the lives that followed
> courses of their own other than ours and older
>   have been migrating before us some are already
> far on the way . . . (*P* 2:41, italics added)

The poem suggests, then, that part of the vision of *The Vixen* is to reclaim a "belie[f] / in the animals" and to discover where "they are."

The zoopoetic dynamic in *The Vixen* differs from Whitman and Cummings before him. Vestiges of an animal's bodily *poiesis* do not readily resurface in an iconicity, and yet I suggest that the form has still been shaped by his attentiveness toward animals. The form, though, has much more to do with cultivating a posture necessary to look and look again at animals. To make this argument, I meander through a series of important observations.

The Vixen is a curious form. The lines are not iambic pentameter, though they often have five strong beats. The lines are all similar in length, spanning roughly ten to fifteen syllables with occasional exceptions. Merwin indents lines 2, 4, 6, and so forth throughout the duration of the book, giving a flow-and-ebb momentum to the progression of a poem. What is more, Merwin utilizes this form in his book-long, epic poem *The Folding Cliffs: A Narrative of 19th Century Hawaii* published in 1998, two years after *The Vixen*. In *The Vixen*, he seems to return to the longer, heavier line of "Leviathan" after many years of writing sparser lines as in "For a Coming Extinction." In the 1982 interview "Fact Has Two Faces," Merwin provides a valuable perspective regarding palimpsests and the poetic line—one that pertains to his accomplishment in *The Vixen*. He shares:

You know, meter is never something permanently absent. I think that line is re-
lated to the Middle English line of *Piers Plowman*, which to me is the basic line
of English, overlaid—we talked about palimpsests—overlaid, as I said earlier,
by the Italianate iambic pentameter. But the caesura in the iambic pentameter is
like a ghost of the old Middle English line asserting itself all the time, saying
I'm here all the time. I think it's there under what we hear in iambic pentameter.
And as the iambic pentameter becomes harder and harder to hear or to stay
awake through in contemporary poetry, I think the other, the deeper, older line
is something one, with the slightest effort, might be able to hear again.[25]

Here, Merwin suggests that it may be possible to hear the "deeper, older line"
again, even in contemporary poetry. I suggest that if one *listens to the weight of
the language as it moves* through the lines of *The Vixen*, one hears that older line.

In the greater context of Merwin's work informed by "Witness" and "Place"
discussed above, reinventing this older line fights against its extinction. The
forgotten language awakens. Many of the titles in *The Vixen* point toward this
older language, such as "Ancestral Voices"; "Old Sound"; "Old Question"; "Old
Walls"; and "Oak Time." As Matthew Zapruder puts it, "centuries can go by in a
few lines."[26] Merwin reaches back to an older language and an older line to reclaim one's connectedness to what is still present.

Poem after poem cultivates an identification with the speaker's environment
and with the animals within that environment, and the form contributes to this
identification. As the lines flow and ebb, they generate a rhythm of walking, of
sauntering—to echo Thoreau.[27] The indented lines enhance the caesura of the
line break, and the weight of the line shifts as if to the other foot. Each line reads
complete up to the pause . . . but continues on the next. One step, a shift, then
another step. Merwin, then, effectively places the reader in the posture of one
whose attentiveness toward animals takes place while *sauntering* through the
poems. The sauntering rhythm qualifies Jeanie Thompson's observation that
"the construction" of the lines in *The Vixen* "teaches us how to be still and listen"; rather, they teach us how to listen through sauntering.[28] In *The Vixen*'s
"Walkers," the speaker shares "Then I could walk for a whole day" (*P* 2:8).
Readers reading *The Vixen* walk the whole day, too.

To demonstrate how the sauntering form coincides with an attentiveness
toward animals, I cite three of the poems in full, beginning with "Ancestral
Voices":

> In the old dark the late dark the still deep shadow
>   that had travelled silently along itself all night
> while the small stars of spring were yet to be seen and the few
>   lamps burned by themselves with no expectations
> far down through the valley then suddenly the voice
>   of the blackbird came believing in the habit
> of the light until the torn shadows of the ridges
>   that had gone out one behind the other into the darkness
> began appearing again still asleep surfacing in their

dream and the stars all at once were gone and instead the song
of the blackbird flashed through the unlit boughs and far
out in the oaks a nightingale went on echoing
itself drawing out its own invisible starlight
these voices were lifted here long before the first
of our kind had come to be able to listen
and with the faint light in the dew of the infant
leaves goldfinches flew out from their nests in the brambles
they had chosen their colors for the day and they sang
of themselves which was what they had wakened to remember (*P* 2:40)

The poem attentively traces the emergence of the voice of blackbirds, nightingales, and goldfinches. Characteristic of the entire book, the lines in this poem end on a word that completes a vivid image before turning to the next progression of the narrative. Exceptions include "few / lamps"; "their / dream"; and "far / out." In some lines, the end grants a sense of completion, but after the break, still contributes energy to the following line in a pseudo-enjambment: ". . . before the first / of our kind." The indented form intensifies the caesura of each line break, and it encourages the reader to attend to the fullness of each line. The indented form, that is to say, generates a different kind of energy than poems like "Leviathan" that use no indentation. They are a different prime gesture, to echo Cummings.

The line breaks in "Snake" also intensify the caesuras. This narrative poem directs attention toward a snake, but it leaves room for the ways in which the snake attentively observes the human:

When it seemed to me that whatever was holding
me there pretending to let me go but then bringing
me back each time as though I had never been gone
and knowing me knowing me unseen among those rocks
when it seemed to me that whatever that might be
had not changed for all my absence and still was not changing
once in the middle of the day late in that time
I stood up from the writings unfinished on the table
in the echoless stone room looking over the valley
I opened the door and on the stone doorsill
where every so often through the years I had come
upon a snake lying out in the sunlight I found
the empty skin like smoke on the stone with the day
still moving in it and when I touched it and lifted
all of it the whole thing seemed lighter than a single
breath and then I was gone and that time had changed and when
I came again many years had passed and I saw
one day along the doorsill outside the same room
a green snake lying in the sunlight watching me
even from the eyes the skin loosens leaving the colors
that have passed through it and the colors shine after it has gone (*P* 2:23–24)

Thompson acutely observes how "the syntax of 'The Snake' coils for nearly seven lines before the actual story begins," and she emphasizes the "coiled energy" of the poem.[29] Without using the word, her reading identifies a zoopoetic dynamic. Additionally, the poetic form requires patience to write and to read—but it is this patience that cultivates an attentiveness toward another species' bodily *poiesis*. Near the poem's end, Merwin breaks a line at the verb "saw," and he includes a complete line before one reaches the direct object: ". . . and I saw / one day along the doorsill outside the same room / a green snake. . . ." Merwin shapes the form of the poem around the moment of attentiveness, placing pressure on the word "saw" and on "a green snake" by separating the two with a line that generates suspense. The reader must wait to discover what she or he saw. The tempo of the line breaks coincides with the tempo of the encounter with the snake, which is a subtle form of temporal iconicity. An attentiveness toward the snake shapes the pacing of the poem as well as its "coiled energy," thereby demonstrating two facet of zoopoetics.

In "Threshold," the poem's speaker enters a new dwelling; moreover, the swallows and bats usher him into a creative space:

> Swallows streaking in and out through the row of broken
>   panes over the front door went on with their conversations
> of afterthoughts whatever they had been settling
>   about early summer and nests and the late daylight
> and the vacant dwellings of swallows in the beams
>   let their dust filter down as I brought in my bed
> while the door stood open onto the stone sill smoothed to water
>   by the feet of inhabitants never known to me
> and when I turned to look back I did not recognize a thing
>   the sound of flying whirred past me a voice called far away
> the swallows grew still and bats came out light as breath
>   around the stranger by himself in the echoes
> what did I have to do with anything I could remember
>   all I did not know went on beginning around me
> I had thought it would come later but it had been waiting (*P* 2:6)

The form of the poem saunters through this space, giving the reader time to linger on each image of the narrative. Like the other poems discussed from *The Vixen*, the line breaks place the reader in an attentive posture; the swallows and the bats unexpectedly change the space of the dwelling into the strange and the unknown—the space of the initial stirrings of *poiesis*. And I cannot help but draw the similarity between this moment and the moment articulated in Cummings' "i'd think 'wonder" (*CP* 354)—the moment when the sighting of a bat *opened a door* to "think things / which / where supposed to / be out of [his] / reach." In both cases, an encounter with a bat stirred the poets toward *poiesis*. Furthermore, Merwin's phrase "all I did not know went on beginning around me" resurfaces in a later publication of Merwin's: "The Nomad Flute" from *The Shadow of Sirius*. "The Nomad Flute" is the book's first poem, and it is an apostrophe to Merwin's muse. Rephrasing the title exposes how the poem revisits *sauntering*—"The Nomad Flute" is the song of the one who walks:

> You that sang to me once sing to me now
> let me hear your long lifted note
> survive with me
> the star is fading
> I can think farther than that but I forget
> do you hear me
>
> do you still hear me
> does your air
> remember you
> o breath of morning
> night song morning song
> I have with me
> all that I do not know
> I have lost none of it
>
> but I know better now
> than to ask you
> where you learned that music
> where any of it came from
> once there were lions in China
>
> I will listen until the flute stops
> and the light is old again (*P* 2:543)

Even here, animals impact the song and listening to the song. The line "once there were lions in China" epitomizes a musical flute with the complex constellation of *n's* and the *n* and an *s* (o*n*ce, lio*n*s, *in*, Chi*n*a), long *i's* (l*i*ons, Ch*i*na), and internal rhyme of *lion* and *in*. The word "once" suggests again the past and carries with it the shadow of extinction from *The Lice*. And the line's surprise (for it almost seems like a *non sequitur*), points us toward *all that we do not know* and therefore that moment where *poiesis* can begin. In the second to last line of "Threshold," "all I did not know" also becomes the first stirrings of the poetic moment as it "went on beginning around" the speaker. It is the unexpected visitation of the swallows and the bats that ushers Merwin into that space.

The sauntering form of *The Vixen* encourages an attentiveness to bats, swallows, snakes, goldfinches, nightingales, blackbirds, and many more species, but an earlier poem helps illuminate what, precisely, is at stake concerning the *saunter*: "An Encampment at Morning" from *The Compass Flower* (1977). The short poem exhibits an attentiveness toward spiders, and the speaker of the poem is walking—that is, "learning [his] steps"—amongst another nomadic species, a "migrant tribe of spiders." If there is any "hope" in Merwin's poetry and poetics, it is found "not in the inscriptions of a settled people" but rather from the "words on a journey"—the steps that are taken by the nomad, the one who migrates, the one who is willing to *learn new steps*:

> A migrant tribe of spiders
> spread tents at dusk in the rye stubble
> come day I see the color
> of the planet under their white-beaded tents
> where the spiders are bent
> by shade fires in damp September
> to their live instruments
> and I see the color of the planet
> when their tents go from above it
> as I come that way in a breath cloud
> learning my steps
> among the tents rising invisibly like the shapes of snowflakes
> we are words on a journey
> not the inscriptions of a settled people (*P* 1:476)

These are not the steps of Gerald Manley Hopkins' "Generations have trod, have trod, have trod."[30] In the context of Merwin's poetics of migration, walking, listening, and planting, *learning new steps* cultivates humility, and it is a humility that emerges out of the anguish of environmental devastation and mass extinction. The ambition of "learning my steps" comes to full fruition in *The Vixen*, for an attentiveness toward animals shapes a sauntering form that has the potential to cultivate a way-of-being in the midst of multiple species.

"but here"

As hinted at above, Merwin's genius for sauntering emerges again throughout *The Shadow of Sirius* (2008), as does his attentiveness toward animals—and the absence of animals—amidst mass extinction.[31] By way of conclusion, I explore just one poem from *The Shadow of Sirius*, "The Mole," where the *poiesis* of humans and animals merge but in a surprising way. An attentiveness toward the absence of the mole pervades the poem (paradoxically) through the speaker's attentiveness toward the presence of the material signs left over from the mole's activity. The mole is never present in the poem nor along the speaker's (and his beloved's) walks. The poem also extends the paradox of the "place-space synergy" at work throughout Merwin's *oeuvre*, for the speaker's sense of identification with the mole (place) occurs through emphasizing the vast distance between humans and the mole (space).[32] "The Mole" also exhibits one innovative gesture that emerges, I suggest, from an attentiveness to these paradoxes surrounding that place where the mole's sphere merges with the human's:

> Here is yet one
> more life that we see only from outside

from the outside

not in itself but later
in signs of its going
a reminder
in the spring daylight

it happened when we were not noticing
and so close to us
that we might not have been here
disregarded as we were

see where we have walked
the earth has risen again
out of its darkness
where it has been recognized
without being seen
known by touch
of the blind velvet fingers
the wise nails
descendants of roots and water

we have seen them
only in death and in pictures
opened from darkness afterward

but here the earth
has been touched and raised
eye has not seen it come
ear has not heard
the famous fur
the moment that finds its way
in the dark without us (*P* 2:577–78)

The zoopoetic dynamic where an innovation in poetic form emerges, in this case, from an attentiveness to "the moment that finds its way / in the dark without us" occurs in the line break between "we have seen them / only in death and in pictures" and in the emphatic "*but here.*" The stanza begins with place, "we have seen them," only for the next line to cancel out the moment of positive identification, replacing it with absence, distance, and therefore space, "only in death and in pictures / opened from darkness afterward." The following stanza break accentuates a caesura in which the reader can linger in the paradox. If readers *listen to the weight of the language as it moves*, the next stanza begins with an emphatic attentiveness to this site of a present absence, "*but here.*" The "here" refers to the place where the mole "touched and raised" the earth as well as to the paradox of a present absence. I use "place" in Gary Snyder's sense, for it is "like a mirror" and "can hold anything, on any scale." This mirror holds past and present markings, for Snyder suggests that the earth is a "palimpsest," a "great tablet holding the multiple overlaid new and ancient traces of the swirl of forces." He continues, "Each place is its own place, forever (eventually) wild. A place on earth is a mosaic within larger mosaics."[33] The "signs" of the mole—created by the "blind velvet fingers / the wise nails"—is merely a micro-mosaic etched momentarily on the earth's "great tablet." But for Merwin, it is a moment charged with the paradoxes outlined above, and it is explored in a poetics that gestures toward the walk. The breaks across "only in death and in pictures / opened from darkness afterward . . . // But here" mime the posture of one who engages the present absence of an animal while *sauntering*, with all of its observations, pauses, reflections, silent musings, and the original energy of the first stirrings of *poiesis*.

In *The Shadow of Sirius*, Merwin is still "learning [his] steps"—cultivating a way-of-being amidst and amongst other species on a planet in the midst of mass extinction. The form of his poetry often mimes the rhythm of these steps. To read Merwin is to walk with him too. Merwin, though, is not the only poet to attentively engage animals with an awareness of mass extinction. A younger contemporary poet, Brenda Hillman, does so as well, and though Merwin can be seen as a political poet (especially in *The Lice*), he is much more reserved in comparison to Hillman.

Notes

1.   Henry David Thoreau, *The Essays of Henry D. Thoreau*, ed. Lewis Hyde (New York: North Point Press, 2002), 149.

2.   W. S Merwin, "On Open Form," in *Regions of Memory: Uncollected Prose, 1949-82*, ed. Ed Folsom and Cary Nelson (Urbana: University of Illinois Press, 1987), 299.

3.   Merwin does, for instance, use punctuation in "The Last One" from *The Lice* (*P* 1:271–73).

4.   W. S Merwin, Ed Folsom, and Cary Nelson, "'Fact Has Two Faces': Interview," in *Regions of Memory: Uncollected Prose, 1949-82* (Urbana: University of Illinois Press, 1987), 357.

5.   Though I trace a continuity from Whitman, through Cummings, to Merwin, there are crucial differences. Concerning Whitman and Merwin, Thomas Byers articulates a sharp difference. Whitman's "most fitting relationship to nature" depends upon speech, while Merwin's relationship calls for silence and therefore "a speech that is self-negating." Thomas B. Byers, "Believing Too Much in Words: W. S. Merwin and the Whitman Heritage," *The Missouri Review* 3, no. 2 (1980): 87. Indeed, in the interview with Nelson and Folsom "Fact Has Two Faces," Merwin shares his unease with Whitman's overbearing celebration of westward expansion ("Fact Has Two Faces," 321). And as a later note highlights in this chapter, *The Lice* subverts Whitman's vision through several clear allusions to *Leaves of Grass*. However, the similarity I trace has to do with an attentiveness toward animals and toward the materiality of the poetic page despite the fact that Whitman seemed to listen more through his voice while Merwin seems to listen first with the roots of his hair.

6.   Merwin, Folsom, and Nelson, "Fact Has Two Faces," 355.

7. Ibid., 356.

8. Jeanie Thompson and Jonathan Weinert, "Raw Shore of Paradise: A Conversation with W. S. Merwin," in *Until Everything Is Continuous Again: American Poets on the Recent Work of W. S. Merwin*, ed. Jonathan Weinert and Kevin Prufer (Seattle: WordFarm, 2012), 117, 118.

9. It is beyond the scope of this chapter to articulate and encompass the full extent of the emergent term *ecopoetics*. Here, I use it in the spirit of Jed Rasula's discussion of the poet-as-bat, where poetry is a "kind of echo-location" that can cultivate a profound awareness of both place and space within the biosphere (*This Compost*, 8). J. Scott Bryson's *Ecopoetry: A Critical Introduction* offers a helpful, three-fold definition of ecopoetry: ecocentricity, an "imperative toward humility," and activism. J. Scott Bryson, "Introduction," in *Ecopoetry: A Critical Introduction*, ed. J. Scott Bryson (Salt Lake City: University of Utah Press, 2002. 5–6. For a more current discussion of ecopoetics, see Brenda Iijima's edited collection *)((eco(lang)(uage(reader))* (Brooklyn: Portable Press, 2010); and Angela Hume, "Imagining Ecopoetics: An Interview with Robert Hass, Brenda Hillman, Evelyn Reilly, and Jonathan Skinner," *Interdisciplinary Studies in Literature and Environment* 19, no. 4 (2013): 751–66.

10. W. S. Merwin, *The Collected Poems of W. S. Merwin*, ed. J. D. McClatchy, 2 vols. (New York: Library of America, 2013), 1:294; hereafter cited parenthetically as *P*.

11. J. Scott Bryson, *The West Side of Any Mountain: Place, Space, and Ecopoetry* (Iowa City: University of Iowa Press, 2005), 104, 111, 109.

12. Jarold Ramsey, "The Continuities of W. S. Merwin," in *W. S. Merwin: Essays on the Poetry*, ed. Ed Folsom and Cary Nelson (Urbana: University of Illinois Press, 1987), 37.

13. In "'I have Been a Long Time in a Strange Country': W. S. Merwin and America," in *W. S. Merwin: Essays on the Poetry*, ed. Cary Nelson and Ed Folsom (Urbana: University of Illinois Press, 1987), Ed Folsom explores how *The Lice* subverts Whitman's vision for an abounding, ever expanding, all encompassing self: "*The Lice* is Merwin's anti-song of the self. Here, instead of the Whitmanian self expanding and absorbing everything, naming it in an ecstasy of union, we find a self stripped of meaning, unable to expand, in a landscape that refuses to unite with the self, refuses to be assimilated, in a place alien and unnameable" (235). He observes that the first poem begins with a "ruined American Adam" who has no animals left to name; likewise, the final poem of *The Lice* subverts the end of "Song of Myself." Whereas Whitman ends with the notion of "finding," Merwin ends with the notion of looking (242).

14. Byers, "Believing Too Much in Words," 86.

15. Shepard, *Thinking Animals*, 249, 6–7. In light of Donna Haraway's *When Species Meet*, we recognize that intra- and interspecies "play" can also generate this reciprocal spiral toward intelligence.

16. Abram, *Spell*, 86.

17. Burke discusses the leviathan in his section on "Power" in *A Philosophical Enquiry into the Origin of Our Ideas of the Sublime and Beautiful*, 5th edition (London: Printed for J. Dodsley, 1767), 114–115.

18. Jane Frazier suggests that Merwin confronts the Judeo-Christian paradigm with his own "theologically laden homily" (101–102), but I prefer the term "myth." It is not only that Merwin is an "ecoprophet . . . confronting us with what we are doing to the animals of the planet and our subsequent denial of responsibility," but moreover that "For a Coming Extinction" erases and then recasts one of the troubling myths of creation. Jane

Frazier, *From Origin to Ecology: Nature and the Poetry of W. S. Merwin* (Madison: Associated University Press, 1999), 101.

19. The term "palimpsest" refers to the process of erasure and reinscription. When scribes scraped text off of a manuscript made of parchment (skin of a cow) or of vellum (the skin of a calf) in order to clear space for a new inscription, they created a palimpsest. One can detect vestiges of the old text beneath the new, rendering the manuscript a multi-layered and fascinating artifact. Within Merwin studies, the palimpsest concept serves as a trope for the ways in which the text alludes to, subverts, and rewrites a particular story, tradition, or idea. For instance, Walter Kalaidjian describes Merwin's poetry as an intertextual "web of fragments, a palimpsest, where what can be read is either never entire or a dialogic effect of other utterances it simultaneously reveals and effaces." Walter Kalaidjian, "Linguistic Mirages: Language and Landscape in W. S. Merwin's Later Poetry," in *W. S. Merwin: Essays on the Poetry*, ed. Cary Nelson and Ed Folsom (Urbana: University of Illinois Press, 1987), 204. Also, in the interview "'Fact Has Two Faces,'" Merwin, Folsom, and Nelson discuss the "feeling of inhabiting a palimpsest" while driving through the country and while engaging Merwin's poetry and poetics ("Fact Has Two Faces," 328).

20. Hank Lazer, "For a Coming Extinction: A Reading of W. S. Merwin's *The Lice*," *ELH* 49, no. 1 (1982): 268.

21. Bryson, *West Side*, 111, 104.

22. W. S. Merwin, *The Ends of the Earth: Essays* (Washington D.C.: Shoemaker & Hoard, 2004), 180, 189, 188.

23. Merwin, Folsom, and Nelson, "Fact Has Two Faces," 334.

24. Merwin, "On Open Form," 299.

25. Merwin, Folsom, and Nelson, "Fact Has Two Faces," 357–58. As the implications of Merwin's palimpsest poetics unfold, I note Cary Nelson's and Ed Folsom's observations in the first appendix from *W. S. Merwin: Essays on the Poetry* (Urbana: University of Illinois Press, 1987). In the subsection "Writing as Revision," they summarize how Merwin, at times, follows a "rather palimpsestic writing practice" as he makes new compositions upon the "reverse side of his own earlier manuscripts" (332). This "palimpsestic writing practice" dovetails well with issues surrounding the role of poetry amidst biological and linguistic extinction. Though the planet (and poetics) are scraped, so to speak, vestiges of a present-absence remain.

26. Matthew Zapruder, "Most of the Stories Have to Do with Vanishing," in *Until Everything Is Continuous Again: American Poets on the Recent Work of W. S. Merwin*, ed. Jonathan Weinert and Kevin Prufer (Seattle: WordFarm, 2012), 80.

27. Thoreau, *Essays*, 149.

28. Jeanie Thompson, "To Shine after It Has Gone: Resonance in W. S. Merwin's *The Vixen*," in *Until Everything Is Continuous Again: American Poets on the Recent Work of W. S. Merwin*, ed. Jonathan Weinert and Kevin Prufer (Seattle: WordFarm, 2012), 89.

29. Ibid., 94, 95.

30. Hopkins' line comes from "God's Grandeur," and despite Hopkins' optimism that "nature is never spent," the trodding upon the earth—where "all is seared with trade; bleared, smeared with toil; / And wears man's smudge and shares man's smell"—*has*, in a radical and perhaps irredeemable way, "spent" nature. Gerard Manley Hopkins, *Poems and Prose of Gerard Manley Hopkins*, ed. W. H. Gardner (New York: Penguin Books, 1985), 27.

31. In "The Silence of the Mine Canaries" for instance, the mine (which stands for the planet) and the canaries (who stand for all species extinct or on their way toward extinction) revisit Merwin's sense of urgency (*P* 2:589–90). At the poem's end, Merwin lists many species who no longer return to familiar places, which ought to generate a similar kind of urgency as Carson's *Silent Spring* (Boston: Houghton Mifflin, 2002). Though more personal, "Calling a Distant Animal" revisits the ideas from *The Lice*'s "The Animals" (*P* 2:566–67; 1:267), and therefore an attentiveness toward the absence of animals, in this time the speaker's companion species. And yet, poems such as "One of the Butterflies" further explore the stirrings that occur when and where species meet in all of their presence (*P* 2:592–93).

32. Bryson, *West Side*, 111.

33. Gary Snyder, *The Practice of the Wild: Essays* (San Francisco: North Point Press, 1990), 25, 27.

Interlude
Elephants

Elephants often pause on their migratory routes at the precise places where other elephants died. Curious to learn more, I discovered G. A. Bradshaw's *Elephants on the Edge: What Animals Teach us about Humanity*. Bradshaw focuses on the elephant-human conflict in places such as Nepal where much human force and violence is needed to keep elephants away from the human sphere where they damage crops and homes. As habitat shrinks, elephants lash out. Bradshaw, though, offers an intriguing insight:

> Elephants have trespassed against physical and psychological boundaries and have flouted human privilege by damaging houses, consuming crops, and showing commitment to kill. . . . Much like other cultures that have refused to be absorbed by colonialism, elephants are struggling to survive as an intact society, to retain their elephant-ness, and to resist what modern humanity has tried to make them—passive objects in zoos, circuses, and safari rides. . . .[1]

They retaliate, in part, due to the vanishing of the places that are intimately connected to their social ways of being. Helena Feder suggests that the elephant's violence emerges from the herds' "cultural breakdown" caused by "mass culling [and] habitat loss."[2]

Part of the cultural breakdown occurs when a matriarch dies prematurely. Bradshaw highlights how the matriarch's remarkable memory and her ability to process "complex social and ecological information" make her a crucial figure within the social fabric of the larger group.[3] Her study includes the work of Cynthia Moss who traced a group of elephants who lost the matriarch, named Emily, in 1989. Along with performing mourning rituals, the group returned to the matriarch's bones for years afterward. I cite Moss' recounting of her observations in full, for she identifies the bodily *poiesis* of the very clear material semiotics (or emblem gestures) of an animal whose grief emerges through the motions of her trunk:

> The three animals stopped and cautiously reached their trunks out. They stepped closer and very gently began to touch the remains with the tips of their trunks, first light taps, smelling and feeling, then strokes around and along the larger bones. Eudora and Elspeth, Emily's daughter and granddaughter, pushed through and began to examine the bones, and soon after Echo and her two daughters arrived. All the elephants were now quiet and there was a palpable tension among them. Eudora concentrated on Emily's skull, caressing the smooth cranium and slipping her trunk into the hollows in the skull. Echo was feeling the lower jaw, running her trunk along the teeth—*the area used in greeting when elephants place their trunks in each other's mouth*. The younger

animals were picking up the smaller bones and placing them in their mouths, before dropping them again. . . . Several years before, I had also seen [this group of elephants] start to bury the carcass of a young female from another family who had died of natural causes.[4]

Moss identifies a gesture that not only communicates a very clear meaning for elephants, but also, as it is used as a greeting, strengthens the sense of belonging and therefore the culture amongst elephants. And the emblem gesture of running the trunk along the skull's teeth suggests that Eudora experienced a complex array of emotions in that moment. It is fascinating that she gestures along the teeth of the dead matriarch's skull, and it suggests (and I do not think this is anthropomorphizing) a sense of loss, a desire to say hello, and an existential grappling with the absence of Emily through grappling with the presence of her remains. It could be a gesture toward the poetic tradition of elegy: a moment of *poiesis* that demonstrates another species' desire to grapple with deep feeling through an embodied act.

Moss' work exposes how elephants grieve through a bodily *poiesis*, and though such a moment fascinates, the context of Bradshaw's work generates anguish. The elephants are conscious of their genocide and cultural collapse amidst a shrinking planet. There are no easy answers to the elephant/human conflict, but it is a start to recognize how the polis in India is already multispecies regardless if recognized by humans. The elephants, in all of their agency, transgress their "proper place" through violent uprisings. History, unfortunately, demonstrates that those with power in a polis often do not consider the uprisings of the marginalized. Oppressed peoples are often discounted through a mindset that casts them as "less than human," that is, as mere bestial brutes "below" the human. What, then, shall the powerful make of the uprisings of an animal?

Notes

1. G. A. Bradshaw, *Elephants on the Edge: What Animals Teach Us About Humanity* (New Haven: Yale University Press, 2009), 41–42, 71.

2. Helena Feder, "Review of *Elephants on the Edge: What Animals Teach Us About Humanity*," *Interdisciplinary Studies in Literature and Environment* 17, no. 2 (2010): 440.

3. Bradshaw, *Elephants*, 11.

4. Qtd. in Bradshaw, *Elephants*, 12, italics added.

Chapter 5
The Zoopoetics of a Multispecies Polis:
Brenda Hillman's *Practical Water*

The first
Water Poet
Stayed down six years.
[She] was covered with seaweed.
The life in [her] poem
Left millions of tiny
Different tracks
Criss-crossing through the mud.

Gary Snyder
from "As for Poets"

But poets have been challenged to resign the civic crown to reasoners. . . .

Percy B. Shelley
from "A Defence of Poetry"

Gary Snyder, when discussing further the characteristics of the water poet, emphasizes the water poet's "calligraphy," her form, defined as "the trails and tracks we living beings leave in each other."[1] Such thinking becomes yet another seed for what I call zoopoetics as well as a vital perspective for reading Brenda Hillman's *Practical Water*.

Hillman's expansive tetralogy returns to and emerges out of the four elements.[2] And even though the form of her poetics has more in common with

Dickinson's lyric flights than Whitman's heavier verse, she continues the work of engaging the elemental forces of the earth and of the body.[3]

Concerning the arc of zoopoetics explored in this argument, Hillman's *Practical Water* envisions a political sphere where humans recognize the animals already in that space, weaving themselves into the social fabric of the polis. The zoopoetic dynamic explored in Whitman, Cummings, and Merwin continues, for several of Hillman's innovative breakthroughs in form emerge from an attentiveness to another species' bodily *poiesis*, but her work opens new directions for zoopoetic thought. Like Merwin, Hillman explicitly confronts the bewildering mass extinction underway in the twentieth and twenty-first century, and like Merwin, Hillman's poems renew one's attentiveness to animals in these urgent times—but *Practical Water* locates the work of the poet directly in the civic sphere. Merwin has many eco-political poems too, but the difference is that many of Hillman's "progressive, post-pastoral lyrics" in *Practical Water* take place on the front steps of the state capitol, or in a congressional hearing, or in the "neighborhoods of the resisters," or on the lawn of the White House.[4] *Practical Water* epitomizes Timothy Morton's *Ecology without Nature*, for Hillman gravitates to the complex interrelationships (ecology) between water, plants, animals, humans not "over there" in "nature," but in the cityscape of power, politics, society, and culture.[5] The concept of "nature" threatens to isolate human activity from an ecological interrelatedness, but *Practical Water* exposes how the natural sphere and the political sphere are (and have always been) merged within the ecosphere. One way Hillman arrives at an ecological and political poetics is through her attentiveness toward animals.

In the first section of this chapter, I establish a frame for the zoopoetics of Hillman's multispecies polis through a review of multiple disciplines all tending toward a civic space in which animals have a greater social and political presence. Ethologists, rhetoricians, ecocritics, and theorists contribute to a revisioning of the civic space in light of the ways animals 1) demonstrate agency; 2) sustain a social fabric through a very clear rhetoric—clear, that is, once it has been identified; and 3) instigate, cultivate, and sustain their own cultures. Hillman's *Practical Water* contributes the needed poetic perspective to this interdisciplinary work, for as Snyder suggests (and will be discussed later), poetry gets work done as it cultivates a profound sense of dwelling on the earth and as it confronts readers with the political implications of such a dwelling. One may *know* that animals coexist with humans in that dwelling, but poetry shapes the ontological implications of that knowledge. After the discussion of the interdisciplinary revaluation of animals in culture, I turn to a thorough exploration of *Practical Water.* Animals infuse Hillman's daringly political poetics; they are not at the periphery of the poetic nor the political sphere, but integral throughout both.

Rethinking the Polis

Cary Wolfe suggests that the humanities "are struggling to catch up with a radical revaluation of the status of nonhuman animals" in culture and society.[6] Part of the drive for the revaluation emerges from how animals often instigate interspecies interactions. Regardless of what humans call it (rhetorical energy, material-semiotic exchange), animals already cross species-lines, weaving themselves into the fabric of human sociality through innovative breakthroughs in *poiesis*. For example, in the 2012 article "An Asian Elephant Imitates Human Speech" published in *Current Biology* and widely circulated by NPR, YouTube, Facebook and other forms of social media, the scientists provide comparative spectrograms of both species' frequencies when vocalizing a given word. The elephant, Koshik, innovatively discovered a new way to vocalize: "putting a body part, in Koshik's case the trunk, inside the mouth, thereby modulating the vocal tract in order to manipulate formants, is a wholly novel method of vocal production" (Stoeger et al. 2145). The study explains that the trainers became aware of Koshik's imitation of human speech in August of 2004, and it suggests that a need for social interaction at a crucial moment of Koshik's adolescent development drove the innovation: "the determining factors for speech imitation in Koshik may be social deprivation from conspecifics during an important period of bonding and development when humans were the only social contact available." They continue, "this hypothesis may also hold for other known examples of speech imitation in mammals, Hoover the seal and the beluga Logosi, and also most talking birds."[7] Koshik's innovative breakthrough demonstrates at least one animal's agency to initiate a more-involved sociality with another species, this time *homo sapiens*.

Several current theorists offer ways to understand interspecies interactions that originate in animal spheres. In *Animal Spaces, Beastly Spaces*, Philo and Wilbert seek a "new animal geography" that takes into account 1) the ways "animals themselves . . . inject what might be termed their own agency into the scene"; 2) the ways animals "transgress the imagined and materially constructed spatial orderings of human societies; and 3) the ways animals "*resist* these orderings."[8] Koshik's innovative vocal *poiesis* reinforces the need for this kind of theory. Donna Haraway also explores interspecies interactions. She gravitates to the places where animals and humans co-invent a "material-semiotic exchange." She extends Mary Louise Pratt's trope of "contact zones" to include the inventive space when and where species meet. She sees the contact zone of interspecies interaction as an "ecotone" with its "edge effects" where "species assemblages intermix, producing extraordinary complexity." The richness of such semiotic ecotones involves an "embodied communication which takes place in entwined, semiotic, overlapping, patterning over time."[9] When Haraway argues for the "ontological and semiotic invention" that occurs in the ecotone, she is not waxing poetic. Koshik's story epitomizes the semiotic invention an elephant discovered where and when he met with humans.

One of the implications Haraway traces concerns envisioning the polis anew. She sees the civic space as an "intra-acting crowd of players that include, people, organisms, and apparatuses all coming together in the history of animal psychology." Moreover, she exposes how the etymology of *companion* necessarily recasts the human sphere. *Companion* comes from the Latin *cum panis*, meaning "with bread," or rather, "messmates at the table together, breaking bread," and Haraway suggests *companion species* raise fundamental, ontological questions such as "Who are you?" and "Who are we?"[10]

Along with theorists in animal studies, scholars working on animal rhetoric—who extend George Kennedy's theory of rhetorical energy—call for a revaluation of the civic space. In "Domesticating Animal Theory," John Muckelbauer recognizes that animal rhetoric entails "nothing short of a fundamental reorientation of the intellectual lineage associated with rhetoric." One implication of this reorientation would be "loosening the stranglehold that communicative rationality still maintains on rhetoric's sense of the *civic imaginary*," and he suggests, as a starting point for such a reorientation, a "nonhuman sociality of multiple forces and effects."[11] In "Toward a Bestial Rhetoric," Debra Hawhee lingers in the "remarkable theoretical possibilities . . . [and] tantalizing suggestions of what animality can do to—and for—rhetorical theory."[12] These possibilities include transforming the sphere of rhetoric, and thus the civic imaginary, to include animals. Additionally in *Inessential Solidarity*, Diane Davis further extends Kennedy's theory of a universal rhetoric:[13]

> In the pages that follow, the primary goal will be to expose a sort of commonality oblivious to borders . . . that precedes and exceeds symbolic identification and therefore any prerequisite for belonging; or, put another way: the goal is to expose an originary (or preoriginary) rhetoricity . . . that is the condition for symbolic action.

This "originary" moment, Davis suggests, emerges at the "intersection of rhetoric and solidarity."[14] And this is what Koshik demonstrates. His innovative, vocal *poiesis* strengthened his sense of solidarity with humans. Koshik, in a sense, validates Davis' theory. His new rhetoric emerged, so it seems, out of a desire to cultivate a fuller sense of belonging with humans.

Similar findings emerge in the field of ethology. Kevin Laland and Bennett Galef compiled several essays that explore and debate *The Question of Animal Culture*. Recognizing that "culture" is often defined as something uniquely human, Laland and Galef asked contributors to first define culture and then to discuss whether their field work supports the notion that animals have culture. Frans de Waal and Kristin Bonnie suggest that culture is a "way of life shared by members of one group but not necessarily with the members of other groups of the same species." To deepen their definition, Bonnie and de Waal provide the acronym BIOL, standing for "Bonding- and Identification-based Observational Learning." Simply put, it is the "form of learning born out of the desire to belong and fit in." Later in the article, Bonnie and de Waal discuss the innovative emblem gesture of handclasp grooming amongst a subgroup of chimpanzees. While grooming each other, two chimpanzees clasp hands high above their head, in what looks like a frozen "high-five."[15] The gesture does not improve the efficiency of grooming, but rather cultivates a deeper sense of solidarity—like a secret handshake. It is, to echo Cummings' theory discussed in chapter 3, a prime gesture. Bonnie and de Waal's work on BIOL resonates with Davis' work on the intersections between rhetoric and solidarity, for the innovative rhetoric myriad species develop emerges from a desire to belong. Again, Koshik epitomizes BIOL, but he pushes it further. The desire to "belong and fit in" pushed him to develop a rhetoric that initiates the dizzying steps necessary to enter into another species' rhetorical sphere.

In the field of ecocriticism, Helena Feder contributed "Rethinking Multiculturalism: Theory and Nonhuman Cultures" to *ISLE*'s 2010 "Special Forum on Ecocriticism and Theory." She sees the need to "rethink '*the social*'" and calls for a "broader concept of culture." She cites Laland and Galef's collection of essays and the many studies in the journal *Nature* as evidence of other disciplines exploring how "many species . . . learn socially and pass on traditions of knowledge." Rather than seeing animals as part of the environment, she foregrounds an animal's agency to exist within and shape that environment through social activity:

> Concern for the welfare of ecosystems requires learning more about the lives of the beings which not only inhabit but, in a sense, create them. For this reason, attention to biological work on nonhuman social worlds may intervene in the question of theory and ecocritical practice.[16]

Feder tends toward a (post)humanities and therefore beyond the assumption that the subject is a human. The humanities, erudite in the ways of culture, ought to extend paradigms to become more versed in the ways other species create and sustain their social worlds. These "nonhuman social worlds" are always already woven into the sphere of human social worlds. Yann Martel in *The Life of Pi* captures this well:

> If you took the city of Tokyo and turned it upside down and shook it, you would be amazed at the animals that would fall out. It would pour more than cats and dogs, I tell you. Boa constrictors, Komodo dragons, crocodiles, piranhas, ostriches, wolves, lynx, wallabies, manatees, porcupines, orangutans, wild boar—that's the sort of rainfall you could expect on your umbrella.[17]

Animals already infuse urban spaces, and they are already undergoing their own rhetoric and bodily *poiesis* regardless if humans notice.

The shift toward a multispecies polis is further apparent in animal rights theory. In *Zoopolis: A Political Theory of Animal Rights*, Sue Donaldson and Will Kymlicka call for a "citizenship theory approach" in order to grapple with and understand the "complexity of the relationships humans have with animals."

They help "shift the debate" surrounding animal rights "from an issue in applied ethics to a question of political theory," and they envision a polis where humans see domesticated animals as co-citizens, wild animals as sovereign, and liminal animals as denizens.[18] A zoopolis provides a way of thinking through "our obligations" to animals as it calls for a re-visioning of the "shared spaces" of the polis on "multiple levels." The category of denizenship for liminal animals is particularly intriguing. The myriad animals in urban and suburban spaces—who are "neither wilderness animals nor domesticated animals"—are often overlooked despite how they pervade human dwellings.[19] Many of the animals populating the poetry of Whitman, Cummings, Merwin, and Hillman fall into the liminal/denizen category: Whitman's locusts, spiders, and chickadees; Cummings' green bird, grasshopper, and bat; Merwin's reptiles and foxes; and as will be explored, Hillman's sparrows, earthworms, and blackbirds. The Euro-American poetic tradition resonates with Dickinson's self-evident stance that animals such as butterflies and lizards who live amongst humans already posses political status: "Are not those your Countrymen?"[20]

In a sense, the interdisciplinary revaluation of animals begins to accept, and yet address, the crime that Edgar Allan Poe exposes so brilliantly in "The Murders in the Rue Morgue." The real crime of this detective story is not the murder; it is the failure of the sailor to understand the orangutan's many attempts to turn the human space into a shared space. To expand, the crime is that humans refuse to see the bodily *poiesis* of other species. In "No Human Hand? The Ourang-Outang in Poe's 'The Murders in the Rue Morgue,'" Stephanie Rowe highlights how the orangutan attempts to bridge the cultural gap between him and the sailor through the gesture of grooming—a social activity full of a rhetoric that sustains solidarity amongst primates. The orangutan observed the sailor shaving, and later, with the razor in hand, the orangutan attempts to bridge the species gap through mimicking the ritual of shaving. When the sailor sees the orangutan wielding it, he reads it as a weapon. Rowe's analysis then exposes how the orangutan could escape if he wanted to, but he chooses otherwise. He risks being caught in an effort to reach some sort of understanding through a series of gestures.[21] These gestures seek to cultivate an interspecies solidarity, but the sailor sees them as meaningless. Rowe further highlights the orangutan's effort to bridge the species barrier when he singles out the room with a light on it, climbs in, and attempts to groom Mdm. L'Espanay, in Poe's words: "flourishing the razor about her face, in imitation of the motions of a barber."[22]

These gestures are not understood, and the grooming session turns into a hideous bloodbath. Rowe's analysis continues as she exposes assumptions concerning hands, agency, humans, and orangutans, but what strikes me is Poe's use of grooming. Long before ethologists debated the question of animal culture in today's era, Poe casts an orangutan as a rhetorical being who possesses the agency to seek solidarity with humans—not unlike Koshik. Like so many other attempts of animals who do not speak human words, the orangutan's inventive efforts fail. If Koshik remained "mute," the trainers may not have recognized the profundity of the many other, more subtle, moments of bodily *poiesis* Koshik invented out of his desire for solidarity with another species.

The interdisciplinary sources outlined above coalesce into a joint effort to re-imagine the human polis to include animals in an unprecedented way. As with all radical change, not much is accomplished without addressing the political sphere, and it is perhaps this re-envisioning of the polis that is most difficult to attain. Early in *When Species Meet*, Haraway emphasizes how her work is bound up with such a re-visioning: "To hold in regard, to respond, to look back reciprocally, to notice, to pay attention, to have courteous regard for, to esteem: all of that is tied to polite greeting, to constituting the polis, where and when species meet."[23] For Haraway, animals are no longer "out there" with "nature," but rather integral species "constituting the polis." Many of the ethologists, rhetoricians, and theorists would agree with Haraway's direction.[24] The magnitude of the shift toward a multispecies polis—and all of its implications—cannot be accomplished by one discipline, nor by one theorist. In what follows, I examine the ways that Hillman contributes to the interdisciplinary shift. For Hillman, the multispecies polis begins by recognizing the bodily *poiesis* of earthworms on the front steps of a state capitol building.

The Zoopoetics of *Practical Water*

Glimpses of Hillman's zoopoetics can be found when she discusses her ecopoetics. In Angela Hume's "Imagining Ecopoetics: An Interview with Robert Hass, Brenda Hillman, Evelyn Reilly, and Jonathan Skinner," Hillman articulates the challenge and the possibility of poetry's contribution to the ethical and political discussions surrounding "our degraded relationships with the planet" including the "disappearance of species":

> The problem for the poet is always how to present these things in a nondidactic and imaginative way. For me, the situation calls for both an intense, unpredictable poetry and an imaginative activism, as writers and as citizens.

As I will argue, part of Hillman's "unpredictable poetry" emerges from her stance, explicitly stated in the interview, that "ecopoetics is about nonhuman bodies, too." Hillman provides a three-fold understanding of place: the "local bioregion," "symbolic realms," and crucially for the zoopoetic dynamic, the "site of the material syllable, the composition."[25] In ecopoetics, one of the crucial locales of place is the materiality of the poetic page and the body who reads the syllables aloud.

Through an "unpredictable poetry" that includes "nonhuman bodies" and that emphasizes the material sphere of the poetic page, *Practical Water* provides a poetic perspective to the revaluation of animals within the polis. As the zoopoetic dynamic is necessarily bound up with the political vision of *Practical Water*, I establish some of the many instances where an attention to another species' bodily *poiesis* leads to an innovation of poetic form. Two preliminary, shorter passages demonstrate Hillman's turning toward other species. In "Reportorial Poetry, Trance & Activism," Hillman turns toward bees as a source of other ways of being:

> If bees can detect ultraviolet rays, there are surely more possibilities in language & government. The possible is boundless. (*PW* 33)

Hillman's "possible" echoes Dickinson's well-known dwelling place, and to discover such boundless ways-of-being in language, Hillman suggests that humans ought to pay attention to the ontology of other species. In a second shorter passage, Hillman conflates the form of a poem with the form of a wing:

> A poem doesn't fail when you set your one good wing on the ground
>
> It is the wing
> It doesn't abandon you (*PW* 47)

In this way, Hillman ascribes an animal ontology to the form of a poem—*poem as wing*—thereby continuing the line of thought prevalent in Cummings' work. Cummings and Hillman recognize how the "fluent technique" of many species "comprises certain untranslatable idioms, certain innate flexions, which astonishingly resemble the spiritual essence of poetry."[26]

In some poems from *Practical Water*, Hillman demonstrates a very basic zoopoetic dynamic. For instance, in "April Moon" Hillman turns the ampersand into an ideogrammatic sign, not unlike Cummings:[27]

> The non-you enters
> the you, & morning
>
> also has a dusk,
> a texture behind
> the hermit thrush,
>
> italic ampersands
> in the brush,
> *&&& &*
>
> a form of now
> alright all right
> a form of then
> so bright so bright (*PW* 64)

The space after the third ampersand suggests a tiny hop, and the line in its entirety—"*&&& &*"—becomes a "form of now" just like the thrush hopping about the bush. Comparing thrush to italic ampersands is a small, but no less significant example of a water poet's "calligraphy" that contains the "the trails and tracks" of other "living beings"—to echo Snyder. In the titular poem "Practical Water," the zoopoetic dynamic intensifies as Hillman uses several layers of iconicity to reenact the emergence of a thrush. I include the stanza just prior, for it demonstrates how her political poetry is bound up with the zoopoetic dynamic. One level of "Practical Water" is simply to provoke political involvement, which can be "uncomfortable." She follows her rhetorical question—"If not you who"—with the thrush who drinks water :

> You should make yourself uncomfortable
> If not you who
>
> Thrush comes out from the cottony
>   coyote bush glink-a-glink
>   chunk drink
>   trrrrrr
>   turns a golden eyebrow to the ground (*PW* 5)

The sounds of the thrush emerge through innovative spelling "glink-a-glink," while the indentation of "chunk drink" draws attention to the material space of the poetic page. The line breaks coincide with the movements of the bird, thereby adding the visual, spatial, and temporal moments of iconicity, where form mimes meaning.

Another example of a slightly more complex zoopoetic dynamic is found in "May Moon":

> Officer, i was speeding
> because light sped
> like crushed bits of God
>
> seeking more energy
>
> i understand the horse
> who broke her front
> legs trying to run
> i understand that horse
>
> all women understand her
> we all understand that
> horse we all understand
>
> her all of us do (*PW* 65)

The innovative line breaks in the poem's final stanzas emerge from an attentiveness to the horse "who broke her front / legs trying to run." As the line breaks generate pauses, the repeated phrase breaks. The sentence stumbles, and as it stumbles, possibilities emerge:

i understand that horse

all women understand her
we all understand *that*
horse, we all understand (italics added)

The line breaks generate resonance in the word *that*, and moreover, they allow the reader to turn with the speaker of the poem toward the horse in a moment of empathy.

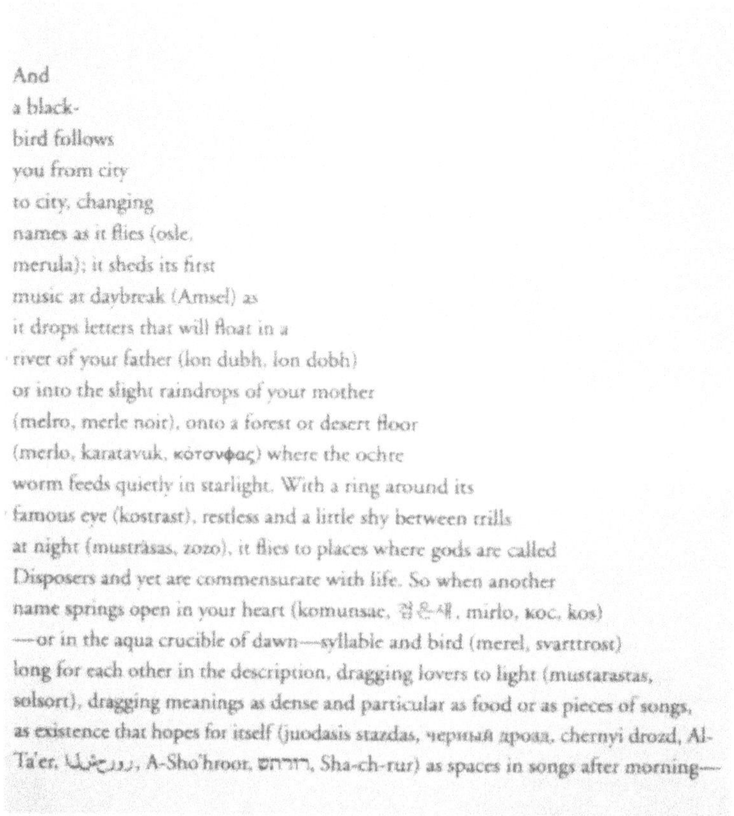

And
a black-
bird follows
you from city
to city, changing
names as it flies (osle,
merula); it sheds its first
music at daybreak (Amsel) as
it drops letters that will float in a
river of your father (lon dubh, lon dobh)
or into the slight raindrops of your mother
(melro, merle noir), onto a forest or desert floor
(merlo, karatavuk, κότσυφας) where the ochre
worm feeds quietly in starlight. With a ring around its
famous eye (kostrast), restless and a little shy between trills
at night (mustràsas, zozo), it flies to places where gods are called
Disposers and yet are commensurate with life. So when another
name springs open in your heart (komunsac, 검은새, mirlo, кос, kos)
—or in the aqua crucible of dawn—syllable and bird (merel, svarttrost)
long for each other in the description, dragging lovers to light (mustarastas,
solsort), dragging meanings as dense and particular as food or as pieces of songs,
as existence that hopes for itself (juodasis strazdas, черный дрозд, chernyi drozd, Al-
Ta'er, الشحرور, A-Sho'hroor, שחרור, Sha-ch-rur) as spaces in songs after morning—

Figure 5.1. A scanned preservation of the multiple languages within—and the form of—Brenda Hillman's "Rhopalic Aubade."

"Rhopalic Aubade" reflects the most complex display of zoopoetics in *Practical Water* as the form of the poem is shaped by an attentiveness to the ways blackbirds fly through the air, fly through language, and therefore fly through culture (*PW* 12, see Fig. 5.1.). The title emphasizes the poem's form, for rhopalic verse proceeds either by adding an additional syllable with every successive word, or, in this case, adding an additional syllable with every successive line—but the impetus behind the added syllables is the flight of the blackbird. As the blackbird flies "from city / to city," new syllabic constellations are added to myriad human languages, including the Old English "osle," the Latin "merula," the German "Amsel," the Gaelic "lon dubh," and so forth. Hillman includes thirty-one languages in "Rhopalic Aubade"—a palindromic nod and therefore homage to Wallace Stevens' "Thirteen Ways of Looking at a Blackbird." Here, the poem includes "Thirty-One Ways of Saying Blackbird" (thirty non-English spellings plus *blackbird*). The rhopalic progression of each augmenting line compliments the sense that with each new city, each new culture, each new language, the flight of the blackbird enriches human languages. With each new word for *blackbird*, humans demonstrate an attentiveness to another species. Like Dickinson's whippoorwill discussed in this book's introduction, the blackbirds continue to burst into human language.

David Abram's work on language and birds further illuminates this attentive dynamic. In *The Spell of the Sensuous*, Abram discusses how an attentiveness toward birds shaped the language of the Koyukon Indians in northwest Alaska. As a result of "listen[ing] attentively to subtle nuances and variations in the calls of birds," their names for birds became "highly onomatopoetic" much like the name whippoorwill. When one "speak[s] their names," she or he "echo[es] their cries." Abram concludes, "As we ponder such correspondences, we come to realize that the sounds and rhythms of the Koyukon language have been deeply nourished by these nonhuman voices."[28] The process by which the Koyukon people created their words for many birds epitomizes zoopoetics, for an attentiveness to those birds gave rise to innovative forms for echoing back their cries in the language itself.

Some of the syllabic constellations that say *blackbird* in "Rhopalic Aubade" may have onomatopoetic echoes as well—but regardless, the poem demonstrates how the presence of *blackbirds* enriches myriad human languages and cultures. Hillman emphasizes this process in the content of the poem:

> it sheds its first
> music at daybreak (Amsel) as
> it drops letters that will float in a
> river of your father (lon dubh, lon dobh)
> or into the slight raindrops of your mother
> (melro, merle noir), onto a forest or desert floor
> (merlo, kartavuk,   .   .   .) where the ochre
> worm feeds quietly in starlight.

Hillman casts the blackbird as possessing agency, for blackbirds are the ones who "drop letters" through their songs into human languages. And in the span of a few lines, Hillman emphasizes the interconnectedness of the blackbirds, their songs, human traditions, generations, language, raindrops, forests, deserts, worms.

Hillman recognizes that the morning song of the blackbird still generates new names: "So when another / new name springs open in your heart . . . / —or in the aqua crucible of dawn—syllable and bird . . . long for each other in the description." The blackbird's song also contributes to the long tradition of the morning song of lovers, the "aubade" implied in the unity of Steven's man, woman, and blackbird—who are all "one."[29] The blackbird's song across myriad human cultures continues "dragging lovers to light." And as the blackbird contributes to the rarified and intimate sphere of lovers, the birds further enrich human existence one syllable at a time.

The Multispecies Polis

However, more so than Whitman's, Cummings', or Merwin's works, Hillman embeds the zoopoetic dynamic of *Practical Water* inextricably within the political sphere. Some of the poems discussed above, such as "Practical Water," already hint at how the poetic form shaped by an attentiveness toward animals grows out of questions concerning how to live, and live well, in civic spaces. For Hillman, animals always already infuse the civic space, and her political poetics, therefore, includes many species. She explicitly establishes her political poetics in many ways. First, the collection includes overt political titles, including "Ballad at the State Capitol"; "Reportorial Poetry, Trance & Activism: An Essay"; "In a Senate Armed Services Hearing"; "Economics in Washington"; "From the White House Lawn"; "In a House Subcommittee on Electronic Surveillance"; and "Request to the Berkeley City Council Concerning Strawberry Creek." Second, many poems take place in overt political settings such as the steps of a state capitol building or a congressional meeting. Third, Hillman includes epigraphs that explicitly direct readers toward the political sphere, such as Hanna Arendt's quote from *The Human Condition*: "To be political, to live in a polis, meant that everything was decided through words and persuasion and not through force and violence" (qtd. in *PW* 31). And fourth, poetry, politics, nature, culture intersect one another continuously, such as the (sub)urban, post-pastoral elegy for sparrows in the "neighborhoods of the resisters" (*PW* 3).

For Hillman, living in a polis means recognizing the innumerable species that cohabit that space. Indeed, animal presences permeate the political spaces. In "January Moon," Hillman writes, "in town, *thwack* of politics / on pavement. Soon, sparrows / will come from their districts" (*PW* 61). And not just sparrows, but "Ballad at the State Capitol" suggests earthworms have already arrived:

> When we climbed the steps of the Capitol in the middle
> of winter the middle of main, there were pale new
> earthworms washed up on the steps, flat pink circles
> around their necks as we passed . . .

*   *   *   *   *

> in the middle of rain, the earthworms adjusted the alphabet so
> the next thing may not be the next thing, they wrote.
> They spelled in calligrammes & codes. When they
> brought back Ishtar's cuneiform. For the love of myrtle,
> cedar & rose that came from dust. The vine sisters
> twisted in stone as they turned in earth to speak to us. (*PW* 10–11)

The permeable skin of the earthworms reminds us just how *practical* water is, and when water becomes toxic, the earthworms' presence on the steps of the state capitol becomes charged with implications. As will become clear, these earthworms *legislate* through the mere presence of their bodies. The ballad is not zoopoetic, *per se*, for the form does not emerge from an attentiveness to the shapes of an earthworms' *poiesis*, but the content tends toward zoopoetics. Hillman suggests that the earthworms' bodily *poiesis* is akin to the "calligrammes & codes" of a "cuneiform" or script. In the notes, Hillman shares that the poem "intersperses quotes from Hammurabi's Code of Law, 1750 BCE"—such as the line "If any / man put out the eye of another his eye shall be put out etc." (*PW* 101, 10). The integration of Hammurabi's Code of Law establishes how the activist pushes against a tradition of laws written primarily for one species: *homo sapiens.* The earthworms-as-calligrammes, though, turns attention to the other species within civic spaces, suggesting that their presence is something that lawmakers ought to listen to as well. Instead of limiting the communal "ballad" to the human sphere alone, Hillman includes earthworms whose presence could affect laws. "The vine sisters," Hillman writes, "twisted in stone as they turned in earth to speak to us"—or rather, to speak to those who would listen.

The multispecies, political poetics emerges again in "A Violet in the Crucible." Like the ballad, "A Violet" alludes to a text from the past, thereby embedding the present day's political poetics in a dynamic historicity. In "A Violet," Hillman intersperses the poem with four quotes from Percy Shelley's "A Defence of Poetry." However, she only includes phrases from longer passages. The longer passages contextualize not only the short phrases, but moreover, "A Violet in the Crucible" as a whole. The first several lines establish two intersections between "A Violet," "A Defence," and a political poetics inclusive of animals:

> Shelley wants you to visit Congress when he writes
> *a violet in the crucible* & when he notes
>   *imagination is enlarged by a sympathy*
> that you may intuit environments
> as endangered creatures do when 7 million pounds
>   of nitrogen flow into the Chesapeake—; (*PW* 42)

First, the phrase "*a violet in the crucible*" emerges from Shelley's well-known passage on the futility of translation:

> Hence the vanity of translation; it were as wise to cast a violet into a crucible that you might discover the formal principle of its colour and odour, as seek to transfuse from one language into another the creations of a poet. The plant must spring again from its seed, or it will bear no flower.[30]

Hillman, though, applies this principle toward political activism. It is just as fruitless to rely on someone else to "visit Congress" on one's behalf as it is to seek the "formal principle" of the "creations of a poet" through reading a translation of his or her work. One must undergo the organic process of beginning with the seed in order to apprehend the growth of a flower. One must make the argument in his or her own embodied presence at Congress—as suggested by the lines from "Practical Water": "You should make yourself uncomfortable / If not you who" (*PW* 5). Second, for Shelley, the "pains and passions" of sympathy are "mighty" (20), and as Hillman alludes to, such *sympathy* can *enlarge* and expand the *imagination*.[31] Unlike Shelley's monospecies "A Defence," though, Hillman's sympathy expands further due to her attentiveness toward and empathy with the many animals facing extinction, including those impacted by "The cogs . . . selling credits to the dams / for phosphorous to go into the sea" (*PW* 42).

The third allusion to Shelley's work integrates the final words of "A Defence": "Poets are the unacknowledged legislators of the world."[32] If one still maintains that poetry and politics ought not inhabit the same sphere, Hillman reminds us that Shelley, for one, saw the act of writing poetry to be essential to the political process of lawmaking. Hillman suggests that poets legislate not unlike the earthworms on the front steps of the capitol building:

> When Shelley says ‹ the poet is the legislator › he means as
>   the duskytail darter from Tennessee legislates or
> the Indiana bat, *myotis sodalist*, the dwarf wedgemussel
>   half buried in Maryland with your bivalve
>   in silt of your wetland habitat, as you, the vanishing
> northeastern bulrush from Massachusetts
>   legislate by shrinking; (*PW* 42)

The growing absence of these species ought to increasingly affect legislation. The poem suggests, though, that one of the root issues hindering such legislation is the lack of imagination due to a lack of sympathy.

The fourth allusion to Shelley's "A Defence" occurs in the final lines of "A Violet," and it also benefits from contextualization. Hillman writes,

> When Shelley notes ‹ the poet is meant to cheer › he means
>   your name is on the list right here, he means

> if you don't survive this way there are others,
> he means send the report with your body— (*PW* 43)

At first, the allusion does not seem to carry political implications, for Shelley argues,

> A poet is a nightingale, who sits in darkness and sings to cheer its own solitude with sweet sounds; his auditors are as men entranced by the melody of an unseen musician, who feel that they are moved and softened, yet know not whence or why.

However, shortly after this passage, Shelley discusses the work of "Homer and his contemporaries," suggesting that they *"were the elements of that social system which is the column upon which all succeeding civilization has reposed."*[33] In the larger context of the passage, "to cheer" means to sway listeners to be active in defining and sustaining the "column[s]" of the "social system." "A Violet" suggests that the civic space—the social system—ought to enlarge its imagination to include the innumerable species already within that sphere.

And this brings us to a discussion of the poem's innovative form. As demonstrated by the shorter passages quoted already, "A Violet in the Crucible" generates energy through indentations. Other poems in *Practical Water* exhibit this form, such as "In a House Subcommittee on Electronic Surveillance" (but with more space between each line) and "Dragonskin" (that has, unlike "A Violet," stanza breaks as well). Each of these three poems merges the poetic and political spheres, and the indentations are a way of disrupting poetic language to find the form for an overt political argument. In "Dragonskin" (which is the name for a material proposed for armor in desert warfare), Hillman merges the form of indented lines with the effort to find a language that can push against a political system:

> There's a useful panic like the secret script
> sent between women in villages. Right now
>   it's a series of marks i'm making ··· :::: ::: ::
>   during a subcommittee hearing
>
>   *   *   *   *   *
>
> & each time someone says *Dragonskin* i feel the panic
>   or subpanic as from school when certain
> steady voices had set in & we made light natural dots
>   in a string :::: ···..··· or a set of *therefores* (:: :: :)
>
>   *   *   *   *   *
>
> The calm in adult talk sets this going if
>   there are no modulating tones around it—;
> my heart makes tiny confidential dots ··· ::·:: ··

> & i've read that women in remote villages in China
>   invented script men couldn't read ···:::::··
>   breathprints of a neutrino entering
>   earth through a rain cloud ···· sending whispers
>   with it . . . (*PW* 39)

The dots represent a way for women to circulate a coded language amidst the language of a dominant, patriarchal, power-ridden system. It is a way to resist within (and through) that language. Hillman playfully reminds readers that writing technologies are a form of power, constricting thought, for as she makes the set of *therefores*, she remarks "which, when i'm placing parentheses now, / Microsoft keeps changing to a happy face— (:: ☺ " (*PW* 39). The "happy face" illustrates how writing technologies are embedded within systems of power, and as one pushes against such systems, the system exerts its own, seemingly benign, agenda. To write within and push against the language of the political sphere, Hillman seeks new forms of poetry.

In this way, Hillman brings to fruition the essence of Emerson's call for a new poetry: "For it is not metres, but a metre-making argument that makes a poem—a thought so passionate and alive that like the spirit of a plant or an animal it has an architecture of its own."[34] Throughout *Practical Water*, Hillman includes myriad forms—and variants of those forms—and the *argument* organically drives the architecture of these innovations. From the small scale of the string of dots and colons to the larger scale of each poem, the merging of the political, poetic, and animal spheres opens up a wide range of poetic forms. An attentiveness to animal ways-of-being contributes to this process, for as mentioned, Hillman finds "more possibilities in language & government" by observing how "bees can detect ultraviolet rays" (*PW* 33). A string of dots is one such possibility, as is a poem with seemingly random indentations.

And so, the zoopoetic dynamic in "A Violet in the Crucible" emerges through recognizing that its form is bound up with an attentiveness to the ways that endangered species "legislate." Out of the three poems that similarly use indentation, animals permeate "A Violet." I suggest that the form, then, as it breaks open space with each indentation, is a statement concerning how one might envision "more possibilities in language & government"—specifically, the implications of a political sphere always already permeated with animals. The line breaks and indentations merge the reader with the animal, for instance, by placing pressure on the animal and the merged sphere of the "you":

> When Shelley says ‹ the poet is the legislator › he means as
>   the duskytail darter from Tennessee legislates or
>   the Indiana bat, *myotis sodalist*, the dwarf wedgemussel
>   half buried in Maryland with your bivalve
>   in silt of your wetland habitat, as you, the vanishing
>   northeastern bulrush from Massachusetts
>   legislate by shrinking; (*PW* 42)

If one applies Merwin's discipline of *listening to the weight of the language as it moves*, the line break after "wedgemussel" and "bivalve" followed by the indentations places pressure on those words. And when Hillman turns from the wedgemussel to the bulrush, the transition occurs in the "as you." At that moment, an ambiguity emerges. In various moments of the line's unfolding, the "you" refers to the wedgemussel, the bulrush, or to the reader. The "you," therefore, becomes a sphere where humans ought to include animals in the civic space of lawmaking.

Hillman, of course, is not the first to suggest animals ought to be integrated into the political sphere on a much more practical level. In the well-known interview "The Real Work," Gary Snyder and Paul Geneson discuss the possibilities of a civic space inclusive of nonhuman nature. In the interview, though, it seems that Snyder is hesitant. Snyder suggests that a democracy is one in which "trees and rocks should be able to vote in Congress, that whales should be able to vote." He continues, "We can see it has been one of the jobs of poetry to speak for these things, to carry their voice in the human realm. . . . Everyone has been consulted except the porpoises. At that point we call on the poet from the marine mammals. What do the porpoises feel about that? So he gets up and does his dance." And yet, the interview includes a parenthetical after this statement: Snyder and Geneson exhibit "(*Sustained laughter*)." The laughter begins earlier when they discuss the possibility of having poets be "the spokesmen for the short grass prairies of Montana, and we'll all have seats in Congress. (*He laughs*)."[35] The laughter becomes a cryptic emblem gesture, but it seems to emerge from the absurd impossibility of such talk.

But voting matters. It may seem impossible for a democracy to include, in a practical way, the voices of animals, but the nineteenth century abolitionist, William Wilberforce, fought against the "impossible" ideal that the slave trade ought to cease. What is more, Wilberforce saw a relationship between all forms of oppression, including the plight of animals: "His pedigree reveals how the animal liberation movement is premised on the idea of an increasingly extended circle of rights: first the emancipation of the unpropertied and the poor, then that of women and children, next of slaves, and so to animals."[36] Since Wilberforce, animals have had an increased presence within legislation, from the spotted owl, to other animals represented by the Endangered Species Act, to the rights extended by Spanish Parliament to Great Apes. But is such progress enough? In the conclusion to *Before the Law: Humans and Other Animals in a Biopolitical Frame* (2013), Cary Wolfe discusses how the Spanish Parliament's decision is nonetheless "shadowed, indeed, haunted, by the mechanized killing of billions of animals each year, in factory farming, in aquaculture, in the fishing of the seas to the point of collapse, in the sixth largest extinction event in the history of the planet." In this context, he, and others, call for the "biopolitical point" of a "newly expanded community of the living and the concern we should all have with where violence and immunitary protection fall within it, because we are all, after all, potentially animals before the law."[37]

Though Snyder cloaked similar ideas with laughter, he recognized that the plight of animals must, eventually, impact the political sphere in the same ways that other oppressed groups found voice. Snyder also provides insight as to how the poet contributes to the "increasingly extended circle of rights": the poet must "get his [and her] poetry reading down there," that is, to the "center of power."[38] Hillman's *Practical Water* does this and more, for it emerged from the poet "send[ing] the report with [her] body" to that center of power.

The opening poem of *Practical Water*—"Partita for Sparrows"—establishes many of these themes. *Partita* is a musical composition without words, and the people in the poem create music "with found instruments" to accompany the burial of sparrows in the "neighborhoods of the resisters." The poem, then, is a (sub)urban, post-pastoral elegy, comprised of one sentence, stretching across two stanzas each with twelve lines. A semi-colon ends the first stanza, and several words/phrases echo across that boundary including "neighborhoods of the resisters," "average," "half-spinning," "princely," and "unmarked":

> We bury the sparrows of Europe
> with found instruments,
> their breasts light as an ounce of tea
> where we had seen them off the path,
> their twin speeds of shyness & notched wings
> near the pawnbroker's house by the canal,
> in average neighborhoods of the resisters,
> or in markets of princely delphinium & flax,
> flying from awnings at unmarked rates
> to fetch crumbs from our table half-spinning
> back to clefs of grillwork on external stairs
> we would descend much later;
>
> in rainy neighborhoods of the resisters
> where streets were taken one by one,
> where consciousness is a stair or path,
> we mark their domains with notched sticks
> of hickory or chestnut or ash
> because our cities of princely pallor
> should not have unmarked graves.
> Lyric work, flight of arch, death bridge
> to which patterned being is parallel:
> they came as if from the margins
> of a painting, their average hearts half-spinning
> our little hourglass up on the screen. (*PW* 3)

The poem's content establishes the starting place for zoopoetics, for the speaker exhibits an attentiveness to the sparrows' bodily *poiesis*. The movement of their bodies—and not just their vocalizations—is musical, for the body is a note on the "clefs of grillwork." In the first stanza, the bodies of the sparrows are "half-spinning" as they "fetch crumbs from our table," whereas in the second stanza, the sparrows' "average hearts" are in the act of "half-spinning" the "little hour-glass upon the screen." The attentiveness to the sparrows has driven the poet to the computer, to wait for the hourglass to disappear so she can write. "Average," in the first stanza, refers to the "neighborhoods," while in the second, it refers to the "hearts" of the sparrows—a repetition that merges the human sphere with the sphere of the sparrow's interiority. Hillman suggests that "Lyric work" is a place where "patterned being is parallel," and the parallel dynamic between the two stanzas establishes a "patterned being" where a concern for animals permeates the human sphere: "because our cities of princely pallor / should not have un-marked graves." Hillman's respect for this liminal animal resonates with the zoopolis shift in animal rights toward seeing sparrows as *denizens*, and she ex-pands the polis as well as the poetic tradition through her elegy.[39]

These observations lead to a subtle zoopoetic moment in the poem: the sparrows' action of "half-spinning" directly relates to the image of the hourglass of the computer. The sparrow's hearts are "half-spinning," but their hearts are also actively "half-spinning / our little hourglass." The overall form of the poem, too, functions like an *hourglass*. I do not suggest that the poem's silhouette bears a resemblance to the curvature of the hourglass; rather, in a subtle move, the stanzas mirror one another (each with twelve lines). The repeated words in the second stanza (the bottom of the hourglass) "travel" as bits of sand having already flowed from the first stanza (the top of the hourglass), through the semi-colon and stanza break, and into the lower half of the hourglass where they settle into a new constellation of words. The innovative move of one long sentence spanning two equal stanzas, where words seem to sift into new arrangements as the poem progresses, emerges in part from an attentiveness to a sparrow's body—a note—"half-spinning / . . . to clefs of grillwork" that parallels the "half-spinning hourglass" of the poem itself. The attentiveness toward the sparrow in a (sub)urban and political context leads to an "unpredictable poetry."

Politics, a Poetics of Across, and Animals

In an interview with Tod Marshall "A Range of What's Possible" (2000), Hill-man acknowledges how "making political statements . . . is very hard to do in poetry without falling into terrible cliché or smugness."[40] And yet, nine years later, Hillman publishes *Practical Water* where she makes innumerable political statements. One way she resists "cliché or smugness" is through her use of allu-sion. The integration of lines, for instance, from Hammurabi's Code and Shel-ley's "A Defence of Poetry" places responsibility upon the reader to make the connections, the leaps, the insights. Her multimodal use of images, too, requires that the reader make leaps between the visual rhetoric of the photographs and the text of the poems. Her "lyric work" (to quote "Partita for Sparrows") further calls on the reader to participate in the "flight of arch." The conclusions, there-fore, are not didactic but rather emerge from the reader's efforts to grapple with and explore the poetry.

Her 2003 essay, "Split, Spark, and Space: A Poetics of Shared Custody," provides a glimpse into the evolution of her political poetics. In it, Hillman articulates how the split of divorce and the liminal space her daughter crossed between parents accompanied new trajectories of poetic thought:

> In the mid-Eighties, my poetry and poetics began to evolve unexpectedly. By "poetics," I mean the theoretical aspects of poetic procedure inherent in, linked to, the poems themselves. The sense of the single "voice" in poetry grew to include polyphonies, oddly collective dictations, and the process of writing itself.

The intensity of the parting, in all of its subtle nuances, called for a new language. Hillman continues,

> It seemed crucial to pay attention to the micromovements of the thought-language-space-shape continuum so that such a reality might become bearable. A new set of *betweennesses* happened in language as her body came and went through time and distance. Individual words fell apart. Colors became letters. Yellow was plural, was daughters of yellow. Red was too much. Words like "see" "you" "soon" grated themselves into the air. A poetic method, which had heretofore been based on waiting for insight, suddenly had to accommodate process, an indeterminate physics, a philosophy that combined spiritual searching with detached looking. In this procedure of baffled decenteredness, my daughter and I shared a method of *across*.

This longer quote, retained for its unity, exposes Hillman's utter attentiveness to "the micromovements of the thought-language-space-shape continuum" when parting from her daughter. Language became the borderland, the time and space of "*betweennesses.*" In the essay's "(a minifesto)," Hillman suggests that a "poem is the rescue of a vanishing body," and the aphorism readily applies to the "rescue" of her vanishing daughter, who walks across time and space.[41]

I suggest that the zoopoetic dynamic in *Practical Water* emerged from a similar attentiveness to "micromovements" of beings who are likewise vanishing. Provocatively, in "Split, Spark, and Space," Hillman observes how "Tiny bats between Berkeley double-you'd the air"—an indication of Hillman's attentiveness to how the micromovements of another species, likewise, travels across the "thought-language-space-shape" continuum. Like Cummings and Merwin before her, seeing a bat sparks new ways of seeing the possibilities of language.[42]

Between 2003 and 2009, Hillman's attentiveness to "micromovements" extends from her daughter and the bat to include many other beings: sparrows "half-spinning" through a poem; endangered species who legislate; blackbirds who fly through myriad languages and cultures, shaping poems as they "drop letters"; earthworms who protest through the presence of their bodies; bees who detect ultraviolet rays; thrush who shift their bodies over to the right, "*&&& &*"; and a horse who broke her front legs from a desire to run that much faster.

Poiesis and the Imagination

Many fields contribute to the revaluation of animals within culture. Ethologists debate the question of culture amongst animals; rhetoricians establish how animals are rhetorical beings; and theorists following Darwin unravel the HUMAN/animal divide in favor of continuity, a "ANIMAL↔HUMAN" framework. These fields open up new ways to envision animal presences within the civic sphere. They help address the crime of humanity, suggested by Poe's "The Murders of the Rue Morgue," of failing to recognize the ways that animals are rhetorical, cultural, and poetic beings, the crime of limiting the polis to one species.

Hillman's *Practical Water* contributes to this shift as well, but whereas other fields foreground epistemological processes, her poetry foregrounds ways-of-being within the polis. New ways-of-being in relation to animals emerge through discovering new ways of existing in the materiality of the poetic page. The poetry becomes a borderland where many spheres merge: the poetic, the political, and animal ways-of-being.

In the context of this argument, Hillman's *Practical Water* places the zoopoetic accomplishments of Whitman, Cummings, and Merwin through yet another needed iteration. Hillman's zoopoetics, her post-pastorals, her morning songs, occur in the very "center of power" of the human sphere (to echo Snyder) in a way unprecedented in the tradition of American poetry. Concerning the arc of this argument, Hillman's 2009 *Practical Water* further demonstrates that zoopoetics is not a minor event in American poetry. From Whitman's 1855 *Leaves of Grass*; to Cummings' *oeuvre*; to Merwin's *The Lice*, *The Vixen*, and *The Shadow of Sirius*; and to Hillman's *Practical Water*, zoopoetics helps illuminate a crucial dynamic within the Euro-American poetic tradition, and its implications. This zoopoetic dynamic can be found in other poets from the long-twentieth century: the line breaks of William Carlos Williams' "Poem" keep in stride of the cat who climbs downward; the time it takes to read Elizabeth Bishop's "The Fish" corresponds to the length of time a fish can survive out of water; the timing of a long bus ride and a short encounter with the moose in Bishop's "The Moose" corresponds with twenty-one-and-a-half stanzas of exposition and the brief six-and-a-half stanzas with the bewildering creature—and there are more examples.[43] The in-depth exploration of zoopoetics in the featured poets of this argument provides a context for further exploration of the zoopoetic dynamic in the poetry and poetics of the long-twentieth century and beyond.

More urgently, the zoopoetic dynamic in these four poets contributes to the revaluation of animals in culture in a crucial way. They help recover the reality that has been deflected through—to use Kenneth Burke's phrase—"terministic screens" that limit an understanding of animals.[44] Zoopoetics constructs other "screens" that help identify the innovative *poiesis* in myriad species. The poems explored here—including Whitman's spider, eagle, and locust poems; Cummings' cat, grasshopper, and bird poems; Merwin's whales, insect, lizard, and "sauntering" poems; Hillman's sparrow, earthworm, and blackbird activist poems—exemplify innovative forms that emerge from an attentiveness to animal ways of poetic being. Through their innovative, material forms, the poems gesture as well, and as the language embodies the forms of both animals and humans, a multispecies event occurs.

The poetry explored here cultivates an imagination to see the rich borderland that occurs when and where species meet. In comparison to the fields of ethology, rhetoric, politics, and animal rights, poetry may seem the least practical—until recognizing how a "failure of / imagination" is perhaps the most damning accusation one can make of *homo sapiens*. And the earth is already in the "palm of [our] hand."[45] It is my hope that zoopoetics contributes to an imagination that does not fail.

The poets explored in this argument cultivate an imagination that sees animals as much more than a "nicety" or a "metaphorical convenience" in the poetic tradition and in human culture. Animals, in all of their agency, animate the human sphere and rarify that space where and when species meet—rarify, that is, for beings with a disposition willing to *stretch toward* another species.

Notes

1.   Gary Snyder, *Turtle Island* (New York: New Directions, 1974), 114, 87.
2.   The tetralogy includes *Cascadia* (2001), *Pieces of Air in the Epic* (2005), *Practical Water* (2009), and *Seasonal Works with Letters on Fire* (2013).
3.   In an interview with Tod Marshall, Hillman discusses Dickinson's poetics:

> It sort of seems like the incremental examination of the conditions of the mind is all most poets are good for, and Dickinson's genius lies in her language of agony and enduring what it means. The ones that are most about the impossibility of knowing how to exist. The titlelessness of her work is connected to her concept of heaven, and having a heaven that exists both as an absolute and not at all, she gives us this vacancy 'above.' She looks up into the beyond and sees a faceless eternity that isn't reflecting the self back to her. But of course, she couldn't do it all; poets after her had to continue this work. (114)

Hillman is one such poet continuing the work of lyrical flights. Brenda Hillman and Tod Marshall, "A Range of What's Possible: A Talk with Brenda Hillman," *Denver Quarterly* 35, no. 3 (2000): 111–131.
4.   Brenda Hillman, *Practical Water* (Middletown: Wesleyan University Press, 2009), 3; hereafter cited parenthetically as *PW*. In an email exchange with Hillman, she used the phase "progressive post-pastoral lyric" to describe not only her work but other poets involved in the emergent theory and practice of ecopoetics.
5.   Morton, *Ecology Without Nature*, 125.
6.   Wolfe, *Zoontologies*, xi.
7.   Angela S. Stoeger et al., "An Asian Elephant Imitates Human Speech," *Current Biology* 22, no. 22 (2012): 2145, 2146. Koshik's innovation, though, is bittersweet. We humans learn of this incredible breakthrough only as a result of the shrinking planet,

captivity, and Koshik's isolation. If Koshik had other elephants to engage with socially, he would have little impetus to reach out toward humans.

8.   Philo and Wilbert, "Introduction," 5, 14, 15.

9.   Haraway, *Species*, 206, 217, 26. Kristin Abbey's "Dog Theory" compliments Haraway's *When Species Meet.* Abbey artfully sets forth a thorough, interspecies rhetorical exploration of the "material-semiotic exchange" that occurs when she heads out on a walk with her greyhound. Kristen L. Abbey, "Dog Theory," *Interdisciplinary Studies in Literature and Environment* 17, no. 4 (2010): 777–780.

10.   Haraway, *Species*, 211, 208.

11.   John Muckelbauer, "Domesticating Animal Theory," *Philosophy and Rhetoric* 44, no. 1 (2011): 99, italics added.

12.   Hawhee, "Bestial," 83.

13.   For a discussion of Kennedy's "rhetorical energy," see this argument's introduction.

14.   Davis, *Inessential*, 2, 3.

15.   De Waal and Bonnie, "In Tune," 21, 22, 33.

16.   Feder, "Multiculturalism," 776.

17.   Yann Martel, *Life of Pi: A Novel* (Harcourt Books, 2001), 52–53.

18.   Donaldson and Kymlicka, *Zoopolis*, 8, 12, 21.

19.   Ibid., 123, 131, 210.

20.   Emily Dickinson, *The Letters of Emily Dickinson*, ed. Thomas H. Johnson (Cambridge: Belknap Press of Harvard University Press, 1958), 2:412.

21.   Stephanie Rowe, "No Human Hand? The Ourang-Outang in Poe's 'The Murders in the Rue Morgue,'" in *Animals and Agency: An Interdisciplinary Exploration*, ed. Sarah E. McFarland and Ryan Hediger (Boston: Brill, 2009), 113.

22.   Qtd. in ibid., 116–17.

23.   Haraway, *Species*, 19.

24.   Timothy Morton is another theorist who recognizes the implications of a multispecies polis. In *Ecology without Nature*, Timothy Morton argues that the concept of nature "militates *against* ecology" through casting "nature" as something "'over there'— a pristine wilderness beyond all trace of human contact." The concept of "nature," then, "re-establishes the very separation it seeks to abolish" (125). By getting rid of the baggage of "nature," Morton opens space for theory to illuminate the ecological relationships anywhere in the ecosphere, including urban and political spaces. One of the crucial implications of an ecology without nature, is that animals are no longer kept at the margin:

> *Margin* . . . denotes a border or an edge, hence "seashore." Indeed, if current industrial policies remain unchecked, these very spaces, such as coral reefs, and liminal species (Latin, *limen*, boundary) such as amphibians, will be increasingly at risk of being wiped out. . . . As a matter of urgency, we just *cannot* go on thinking of [liminal species] as "in between." We must choose to include them on this side of human social practices, to factor them in to our political and ethical decisions (51).

Though Morton uses "liminal" differently than Donaldson and Kymlicka in *Zoopolis*, he contributes to the work of "choos[ing] to include" animals in social, political, and ethical spheres. Hillman's poetry, too, directs the imagination to find ways "to choose." See also Cary Wolfe's *Before the Law: Humans and Other Animals in a Biopolitical Frame.*

Wolfe foregrounds the problem that "animals are things and not persons under United States law—things that may or may not have legal status depending on whether or not they have a property relation to an entity designated a 'person,' who thus has a legal interest in, and standing to argue on behalf of, the animal in question" (13). For Wolfe, the polis must extend through the practical way of legislation.

25. Hume, "Imagining Ecopoetics," 759, 760, 764 .

26. Cummings, *Miscellany*, 114.

27. In Cummings' "(im)c-a-t(mo)" discussed in chapter 3, the ampersand visually suggests the path of the falling, acrobatic cat, and in another acrobat poem, two ampersands visually suggest two trapeze artists meeting in midair after a series of aerial somersaults and flips: "&meet&" (*CP* 655, 536).

28. Abram, *Spell*, 147.

29. Stevens, *Collected Poems*, 93.

30. Percy Bysshe Shelley, *Essays, Letters from Abroad, Translations and Fragments*, ed. Mary Shelley, 2 volumes (London: Edward Moxon, 1852), 1:10.

31. Ibid., 1:20.

32. Ibid., 1:49.

33. Ibid., 1:14, italics added.

34. Emerson, *Essential Writings*, 290.

35. Gary Snyder, *The Real Work: Interviews & Talks, 1964-1979* (New York: New Directions, 1980), 74, 74–75, 75, 74.

36. Jonathan Bate, *The Song of the Earth* (Cambridge: Harvard University Press, 2000), 177.

37. Wolfe, *Law*, 105. In *Before the Law*, Wolfe traces a similar line of thought as Paul Shepard. Wolfe speaks of how "contemporary practices of factory farming" not only cause "pain and suffering" amongst animals, but also contribute to the "deadening and diminishing of 'animality' itself in all its vitality, creativity, and multiplicity, which would in turn forestall our own ability to discover the multiplicity in ourselves via animality as a creative force for our own evolution" (41). Wolfe, like Shepard, recognizes the crucial role of animals in the evolution of human creativity and intelligence.

38. Snyder, *Real Work*, 74.

39. Cummings has several poems that epitomize a pastoral elegy for animals, such as the bee that is enfolded in his grave of petals and in the lines of the poem (*CP* 691), his mouse elegy immediately following "r-p-o-p-h-e-s-s-a-g-r" *(CP* 397), and his poem about a fly that spins into death (*CP* 692). Along with "For a Coming Extinction," Merwin wrote the terse, one-line poem, "Elegy." It is an "anti-elegy" or "post-elegy" in its gesture of erasure, and it laments the plight of all species on the planet: "Who would I show it to" (*P* 1:400). Perhaps because of the unfounded sense of the perpetual abundance of animals in nineteenth century North America, Whitman has few (if any) pastoral elegies for animals. As Hillman demonstrates, one way to extend the polis is through a post-pastoral, (sub)urban elegy for animals (who are not pets) that die within a neighborhood.

40. Hillman and Marshall, "A Range of What's Possible," 115.

41. Brenda Hillman, "Split, Spark, and Space: A Poetics of Shared Custody," in *The Grand Permission: New Writings on Poetics and Motherhood*, ed. Patricia Dienstfrey and Hillman Hillman (Middletown: Wesleyan University Press, 2003), 246, 247, 250.

42. Ibid., 245. For a discussion of Cummings' and Merwin's sightings of a bat, see chapter 3 and chapter 4.

43. Williams, *Collected Poems*, 1:352; Elizabeth Bishop, *The Complete Poems, 1927-1979* (New York: Farrar, Straus and Giroux, 1983), 42–44, 169–173.

44. See Kenneth Burke, *Language as Symbolic Action: Essays on Life, Literature, and Method* (Berkeley: University of California Press, 1966), 44–62.

45. Brian Andreas, *Still Mostly True: Collected Stories & Drawings* (Decorah: Story People, 1994).

Postlude
Owls

one owl dead—
      the other perches
on a yellow line

Wipers frantically sloshed the heavy rain from the windshield as we headed home that night. Up ahead, a couple of pulled-over cars flashed their safety lights, and the traffic slowed. Still clipping along at forty miles an hour, we briefly glimpsed two owls in the middle of the road, right before a turn lane. When I could, I turned around, came back to the scene, and parked the car at the back of the turn lane with my headlights facing away from the owls.

Someone had already called the Greenwood Wildlife Rehabilitation Center, for it looked like one owl still lived. Blood from the other owl slowly seeped onto the asphalt, mixing with the heavy rain.

Was the owl that lived stunned? Had a car hit him or her too? Could that owl fly away? Why did that owl remain with his or her presumed mate?

I grew nervous each time a semi-truck passed us. Nervous for the owl. Nervous for my car. Nervous for myself. Through the heavy rain, wind—pressed from the grill of a semi—ruffled the feathers of both owls. But the owl perched on the yellow line never moved. I began to wonder if both owls were dead.

Derrida, in his passionate vindication for animals, recognizes how extremely difficult it is for a human to glimpse the interiority, or abyss, of an animal.[1] I can speculate. I can suggest that the perched owl grieved the sudden loss of a mate. I can cite instances where two eagles, reunited after two separate injuries, erupted into passionate vocalizations and gestures upon seeing each other again. I can argue that the perched owl's motionless poise exemplifies a bodily *poiesis* that is utterly stoic. I can even give my hand at making sure that there are no unmarked graves in our neighborhood by writing my own pastoral elegy for the owl—even if it is only three lines.

Despite the prevalent shift in our culture toward seeing much more continuity between humans and animals than ever before, I know many people still think of owls as animals in the derogatory sense: instinct-driven brutes who are not capable of any sensitivity or emotional pain when a death disrupts the social fabric of their lives. Owls, for some, are nothing more than an inconvenience that hinders human economic growth, when, for instance, an owl inspires legislation that affects the harvesting of trees. Fortunately, though, rhetoricians, ethologists, theorists, philosophers, and poets argue otherwise. Their work brings to mind well-known poem by Emily Dickinson concerning sanity, insanity, madness, wisdom, and insight: "Much Madness is divinest Sense." Often, it is the minority perspective that offers the clearest insight—but such radical thought is "straightaway dangerous" and calls for a "Chain" to control.[2] The "Chain" implies a wild animality for those who think differently from the majority. Though once a perspective of a few radicals, an increasing number of people recognize the agency of innumerable animals. The "mad" perspectives of earlier poets such as Whitman who saw humans and animals as sharing *the same old law* is now cogent. A multispecies polis is already underway.

When the animal rescuers arrived, they gently nudged the live owl into a carrier. Then, one of them respectfully wriggled their hands beneath the cold owl, lifted the owl up slowly, and carefully lowered the body into another box.

Drenched, we turned to go our separate ways, and within moments, hundreds of cars whirred past the now empty scene.

Notes

1. Derrida, *Animal*, 29–30.
2. Dickinson, *Poems*, 620.

Bibliography

Abbey, Kristen L. "Dog Theory." *Interdisciplinary Studies in Literature and Environment* 17, no. 4 (2010): 777–780.

Abram, David. *The Spell of the Sensuous: Perception and Language in a More-than-Human World*. New York: Pantheon Books, 1996.

Andreas, Brian. *Still Mostly True: Collected Stories & Drawings*. Decorah: Story People, 1994.

Aristotle. *History of Animals, Books VII–X*. Translated and edited by D. M. Balme. Cambridge: Harvard University Press, 1991.

———. *The Complete Works of Aristotle: The Revised Oxford Translation*. Edited by Jonathan Barnes. Princeton: Princeton University Press, 1984.

Bate, Jonathan. *The Song of the Earth*. Cambridge: Harvard University Press, 2000.

Berger, John. *Why Look at Animals?* London: Penguin, 2009.

Bishop, Elizabeth. *The Complete Poems, 1927–1979*. New York: Farrar, Straus and Giroux, 1983.

Blackmur, R. P. *Language as Gesture: Essays in Poetry*. New York: Harcourt Brace & Company, 1952.

Blake, William. *The Complete Poetry and Prose of William Blake*. Edited by David V. Erdman. Berkeley: University of California Press, 2008.

Boggs, Colleen Glenney. "Emily Dickinson's Animal Pedagogies." *Publications of the Modern Language Association of America* 124, no. 2 (2009): 533–541.

Bradshaw, G. A. *Elephants on the Edge: What Animals Teach Us About Humanity*. New Haven: Yale University Press, 2009.

Bryson, J. Scott. "Introduction." In *Ecopoetry: A Critical Introduction*, edited by J. Scott Bryson, 1–13. Salt Lake City: University of Utah Press, 2002.

———. *The West Side of Any Mountain: Place, Space, and Ecopoetry*. Iowa City: University of Iowa Press, 2005.

Burke, Edmund. *A Philosophical Enquiry into the Origin of Our Ideas of the Sublime and Beautiful*. 5th ed. London: Printed for J. Dodsley, 1767.

Burke, Kenneth. *Language as Symbolic Action: Essays on Life, Literature, and Method*. Berkeley: University of California Press, 1966.

Byers, Thomas B. "Believing Too Much in Words: W. S. Merwin and the Whitman Heritage." *The Missouri Review* 3, no. 2 (1980): 75–89.

Carson, Rachel. *Silent Spring*. Boston: Houghton Mifflin, 2002.

Cummings, E. E. *A Miscellany Revised*. Edited by George J. Firmage. New York: October House, 1965.

———. *Complete Poems, 1904–1962*. Edited by George J. Firmage. New York: Liveright, 1991.

———. *EIMI: A Journey through Soviet Russia*. Edited by George J. Firmage. New York: Liveright, 2007.

———. *Etcetera: The Unpublished Poems of E. E. Cummings*. Edited by George J. Firmage and Richard Kennedy. New York: Liveright, 1983.

———. *No Thanks*. Edited by George J. Firmage. Typescript ed. New York: Liveright, 1978.

———. *Selected Letters of E. E. Cummings*. Edited by F. W. Dupee and George Stade. New York: Harcourt, 1969.

Darwin, Charles. *From so Simple a Beginning: The Four Great Books of Charles Darwin*. Edited by Edward O. Wilson. New York: W. W. Norton & Co., 2006.

Davis, Diane. "Creaturely Rhetorics." *Philosophy and Rhetoric* 44, no. 1 (2011): 88–94.

———. *Inessential Solidarity: Rhetoric and Foreigner Relations*. Pittsburgh: University of Pittsburgh Press, 2010.

De Waal, Frans B. M., and Kristin E. Bonnie. "In Tune with Others: The Social Side of Primate Culture." In *The Question of Animal Culture*, edited by Kevin N. Laland and Bennett G. Galef, 19–40. Cambridge: Harvard University Press, 2009.

Deleuze, Gilles, and Félix Guattari. *A Thousand Plateaus: Capitalism and Schizophrenia*. Minneapolis: University of Minnesota Press, 1987.

Derrida, Jacques. *The Animal That Therefore I Am*. Edited by Marie-Louise Mallet. Translated by David Wills. New York: Fordham University Press, 2008.

Dickinson, Emily. *The Letters of Emily Dickinson*. Edited by Thomas H. Johnson. 3 vols. Cambridge: Belknap Press of Harvard University Press, 1958.

———. *The Poems of Emily Dickinson*. Edited by Ralph William Franklin. Massachusetts: Harvard University Press, 1999.

Donaldson, Sue, and Will Kymlicka. *Zoopolis: A Political Theory of Animal Rights*. Oxford: Oxford University Press, 2011.

Edwards, Jonathan. *Puritan Sage: Collected Writings of Jonathan Edwards*. Edited by Vergilius Ferm. New York: Library Publishers, 1953.

Emerson, Ralph Waldo. *The Essential Writings of Ralph Waldo Emerson*. Edited by Brooks Atkinson. New York: Modern Library, 2000.

Estok, Simon. "Theorizing in a Space of Ambivalent Openness: Ecocriticism and Ecophobia." *Interdisciplinary Studies in Literature and Environment* 16, no. 2 (2009): 203–225.

Faulkner, William. *As I Lay Dying*. New York: Random House, 1964.

Feder, Helena. "Rethinking Multiculturalism: Theory and Nonhuman Cultures." *Interdisciplinary Studies in Literature and Environment* 17, no. 4 (October 1, 2010): 775–777.

———. "Review of *Elephants on the Edge: What Animals Teach Us About Humanity*." *Interdisciplinary Studies in Literature and Environment* 17, no. 2 (2010): 440–42.

Folsom, Ed. "'I Have Been a Long Time in a Strange Country': W. S. Merwin and America." In *W. S. Merwin: Essays on the Poetry*, edited by Cary Nelson and Ed Folsom, 224–249. Urbana: University of Illinois Press, 1987.

———. "Whitman Making Books/Books Making Whitman: A Catalog and Commentary." *The Walt Whitman Archive*. Lincoln: Center for Digital Research in the Humanities, University of Nebraska, 2005.

Fothergill, Alastair. *Planet Earth*. BBC Worldwide Americas Inc., 2007.

Frazier, Jane. *From Origin to Ecology: Nature and the Poetry of W. S. Merwin*. Madison: Associated University Press, 1999.

Friedman, Norman. "Not 'e. e. cummings.'" *Spring: The Journal of the E. E. Cummings Society* no. 1 (1992): 114–121.

———. "Not 'e. e. cummings' Revisited." *Spring: The Journal of the E. E. Cummings Society* no. 5 (1996): 41–43.

Frost, Robert. "The Figure a Poem Makes." In *Twentieth-Century American Poetics: Poets on the Art of Poetry*, edited by Dana Gioia, Meg Schoerke, and David Mason, 11–12. Boston: McGraw-Hill, 2004.

Gannon, Thomas C. "Complaints from the Spotted Hawk: Flights and Feathers in Whitman's 1855 Leaves of Grass." In *Leaves of Grass: The Sesquicentennial Essays*, edited by Susan Belasco, Kenneth M. Price, and Ed Folsom, 141–78. Lincoln: University of Nebraska Press, 2007.

Garrard, Greg. *Ecocriticism*. 2nd ed. New York: Routledge, 2012.

Garrison, Jim. "Walt Whitman, John Dewey, and Primordial Artistic Communication." *Transactions of the Charles S. Peirce Society: A Quarterly Journal in American Philosophy* 47, no. 3 (2011): 301–318.

Gioia, Dana, David Mason, and Meg Schoerke, eds. *Twentieth-Century American Poetry*. Boston: McGraw Hill, 2004.

Gonzalez, Ray. *Consideration of the Guitar: New and Selected Poems, 1986–2005*. Rochester: BOA Editions, 2005.

Gordon, Karen Elizabeth. *The Deluxe Transitive Vampire: The Ultimate Handbook of Grammar for the Innocent, the Eager, and the Doomed*. New York: Pantheon Books, 1993.

Griffin, James. "The Pregnant Muse: Language and Birth in 'A Song of the Rolling Earth.'" *Walt Whitman Quarterly Review* 1, no. 1 (1983): 1–8.

Haraway, Donna. *Simians, Cyborgs, and Women: The Reinvention of Nature*. New York: Routledge, 1991.

———. *When Species Meet*. Minneapolis: University of Minnesota Press, 2008.

Hawhee, Debra. "Language as Sensuous Action: Sir Richard Paget, Kenneth Burke, and Gesture-Speech Theory." *Quarterly Journal of Speech* 92, no. 4 (2006): 331–354.

———. "Toward a Bestial Rhetoric." *Philosophy and Rhetoric* 44, no. 1 (2011): 81–87.

Hill, Carolyn Eriksen. "Changing Times in Composition Classes: *Kairos*, Resonance, and the Pythagorean Connection." In *Rhetoric and* Kairos: *Essays in History, Theory, and Praxis*, edited by Phillip Sipiora and James Baumlin, 211–225. Albany: State University of New York Press, 2002.

Hillman, Brenda. *Practical Water*. Middletown: Wesleyan University Press, 2009.

———. "Split, Spark, and Space: A Poetics of Shared Custody." In *The Grand Permission: New Writings on Poetics and Motherhood*, edited by Patricia Dienstfrey and Brenda Hillman, 245–253. Middletown: Wesleyan University Press, 2003.

Hillman, Brenda, and Tod Marshall. "A Range of What's Possible: A Talk with Brenda Hillman." *Denver Quarterly* 35, no. 3 (2000): 111–131.

Homer. *The Odyssey*. Translated by Robert Fitzgerald. New York: Vintage Books, 1989.

Hopkins, Gerard Manley. *Poems and Prose of Gerard Manley Hopkins*. Edited by W. H Gardner. New York: Penguin Books, 1985.

Huang-Tiller, Gillian. "One Art: Intuition and Typography in E. E. Cummings' Original Analysis of 'r-p-o-p-h-e-s-s-a-g-r' (1935)," 2012.

———. "Review of E. E. Cummings' Erotic Poems." *Spring: The Journal of the E. E. Cummings Society* 18 (2011): 167–171.

———. "The Iconic Meta-Sonnet, Manhood and Cultural Crisis in *No Thanks*." In *Words into Pictures: E. E. Cummings' Art Across Borders*, edited by Jiří Flajšar and Zénó Vernyik, 27–57. Newcastle: Cambridge Scholars Publishing, 2007.

Huffard, Christine L., Norah Saarman, Healy Hamilton, and W. Brian Simison. "The Evolution of Conspicuous Facultative Mimicry in Octopuses: An Example of Secondary Adaptation?" *Biological Journal of the Linnaean Society* 101, no. 1 (2010): 68–77.

Hume, Angela. "Imagining Ecopoetics: An Interview with Robert Hass, Brenda Hillman, Evelyn Reilly, and Jonathan Skinner." *Interdisciplinary Studies in Literature and Environment* 19, no. 4 (2013): 751–66.

Iijima, Brenda, ed. *)((eco(lang)(uage(reader))*. Brooklyn: Portable Press, 2010.

Jiménez, Eva Maria Gómez. "Review of E. E. Cummings' Erotic Poems." *Spring: The Journal of the E. E. Cummings Society* 18 (2011): 164–66.

Kalaidjian, Walter. "Linguistic Mirages: Language and Landscape in W. S. Merwin's Later Poetry." In *W. S. Merwin: Essays on the Poetry*, edited by Cary Nelson and Ed Folsom, 198–223. Urbana: University of Illinois Press, 1987.

Kennedy, George A. "A Hoot in the Dark: The Evolution of General Rhetoric." *Philosophy and Rhetoric* 25, no. 1 (1992): 1–21.

Kennedy, Richard. *Dreams in the Mirror: A Biography of E. E. Cummings*. New York: Liveright, 1980.

Killingsworth, M. Jimmie. "'As if the beasts spoke': The Animal/Animist/Animated Walt Whitman." *Walt Whitman Quarterly Review* 28, no. 1–2 (2010): 19–35.

———. *Walt Whitman and the Earth: A Study in Ecopoetics*. Iowa City: University of Iowa Press, 2004.

———. "Whitman's Physical Eloquence." In *Walt Whitman: The Centennial Essays*, edited by Ed Folsom, 68–78. Iowa City: University of Iowa Press, 1994.

Kilyovski, Vakrilen. "The Nude, the Grasshopper and the Poet-Painter: A Reading of E. E. Cummings' 'r-p-o-p-h-e-s-s-a-g-r'." Presented at a Conference in Sofia, 2009.

Kraitsir, Charles V. *Glossology: Being a Treatise on the Nature of Language, and on the Language of Nature*. New York: George Putnam, 1852.

———. *Significance of the Alphabet*. Boston: Peabody, 1846.

Kristeva, Julia. *Revolution in Poetic Language*. Translated by Margaret Waller. New York: Columbia University Press, 1984.

Laland, Kevin N., and Bennett G. Galef, eds. *The Question of Animal Culture*. Cambridge: Harvard University Press, 2009.

Lanham, Richard. *The Electronic Word: Democracy, Technology, and the Arts*. Chicago: University of Chicago Press, 1993.

Lazer, Hank. "For a Coming Extinction: A Reading of W. S. Merwin's *The Lice*." *ELH* 49, no. 1 (1982): 262–285.

Le Guin, Ursula K. *Buffalo Gals and Other Animal Presences*. Santa Barbara: Capra Press, 1987.

Lippit, Akira. *Electric Animal: Toward a Rhetoric of Wildlife*. Minneapolis: University of Minnesota Press, 2000.

Lowell, Amy. "Preface to Some Imagist Poets." In *Twentieth-Century American Poetics: Poets on the Art of Poetry*, edited by David Mason, Meg Schoerke, and Dana Gioia, 15–17. Boston: McGraw-Hill, 2004.

Martel, Yann. *Life of Pi*. Harcourt Books, 2001.

McFarland, Sarah E., and Ryan Hediger. "Approaching the Agency of Other Animals: An Introduction." In *Animals and Agency: An Interdisciplinary Exploration*, 1–20. Boston: Brill, 2009.

Melson, L. Gail. *Why the Wild Things Are: Animals in the Lives of Children*. Cambridge: Harvard University Press, 2001.

Merwin, W. S. *The Collected Poems of W. S. Merwin*. Edited by J. D. McClatchey. 2 vols. New York: Library of America, 2013.

———. "On Open Form." In *Regions of Memory: Uncollected Prose, 1949–82*, edited by Ed Folsom and Cary Nelson, 298–300. Urbana: University of Illinois Press, 1987.

———. *The Ends of the Earth: Essays*. Washington D.C.: Shoemaker & Hoard, 2004.

Merwin, W. S., Ed Folsom, and Cary Nelson. "'Fact Has Two Faces': Interview." In *Regions of Memory: Uncollected Prose, 1949–82*, 320–361. Urbana: University of Illinois Press, 1987.

Miller, Carolyn R. "Foreword." In *Rhetoric and* Kairos*: Essays in History, Theory, and Praxis*, edited by Phillip Sipiora and James Baumlin, xi–xiii. Albany: State University of New York Press, 2002.

Moe, Aaron. "Autopoiesis and Cummings' Cat." *Rupkatha Journal: On Interdisciplinary Studies in Humanities* 3, no. 1 (2011): 110–120.

———. "Chaos & the 'New' Nature Poem: A Look at E. E. Cummings' Poetry." *CT Review* 32, no. 1 (2010): 11–24.

———. "Cummings' Urban Ecology: An Exploration of *EIMI*, *No Thanks*, & the Cultivation of the Ecological Self." *Interdisciplinary Studies in Literature and Environment* 18, no. 4 (2011): 737–762.

———. "Toward Zoopoetics: Rethinking Whitman's 'original energy.'" *Walt Whitman Quarterly Review* (forthcoming).

———. "Two Converging Motifs: E. E. Cummings' *l!ook*." *Spring: The Journal of the E. E. Cummings Society* 18 (2011).

———. "Zoopoetics: A Look at Cummings, Merwin, & the Expanding Field of Ecocriticism." *Humanimalia: A Journal of Human/Animal Interface Studies* 3, no. 2 (2012).

Morton, Timothy. *Ecology Without Nature: Rethinking Environmental Aesthetics*. Cambridge: Harvard University Press, 2007.

Muckelbauer, John. "Domesticating Animal Theory." *Philosophy and Rhetoric* 44, no. 1 (2011): 95–100.

Nänny, Max. "Iconic Dimensions in Poetry." In *On Poetry and Poetics*, edited by Richard Waswo, 111–135. Swiss Papers in English Language and Literature 2 (1985). Tübingen: Gunter Narr Verglag, 1985.

———. "Iconic Features in E. E. Cummings' Poetry." In *The Idea and the Thing in Modernist American Poetry*, edited by Cristina Giorcelli, 209–234. Palermo: ILA Palma, 2001.

Nelson, Cary, and Ed Folsom, eds. *W. S. Merwin: Essays on the Poetry*. Urbana: University of Illinois Press, 1987.

Olson, Charles. "Projective Verse." In *Twentieth-Century American Poetics: Poets on the Art of Poetry*, edited by Dana Gioia, Meg Schoerke, and David Mason, 174–181. Boston: McGraw-Hill, 2004.

Outka, Paul. "(De)composing Whitman." *Interdisciplinary Studies in Literature and Environment* 12, no. 1 (2005): 41–60.

Paget, Sir Richard. *Human Speech: Some Observations, Experiments, and Conclusions as to the Nature, Origin, Purpose and Possible Improvement of Human Speech*. London; New York: Harcourt Brace & Company, 1930.

———. *This English*. London: K. Paul , Trench, Trubner & Co., 1935.

Patton, Paul. "Language, Power, and the Training of Horses." In *Zoontologies: The Question of the Animal*, edited by Cary Wolfe, 83–99. Minneapolis: University of Minnesota Press, 2003.

Perloff, Marjorie. *Differentials: Poetry, Poetics, Pedagogy*. Tuscaloosa: University of Alabama Press, 2004.

Philo, Chris, and Chris Wilbert. "Animal Spaces, Beastly Places: An Introduction." In *Animal Spaces, Beastly Places: New Geographies of Human-Animal Relations*, edited by Chris Philo and Chris Wilbert, 1–34. New York: Routledge, 2000.

Poe, Edgar Allan. *Collected Works of Edgar Allan Poe, Tales and Sketches, 1831–1842*. Edited by T. O. Mabbott. Vol. 2. Cambridge: Harvard University Press, 1978.

Pollock, John. "Appreciating Cummings' '(im)c-a-t(mo).'" *Spring: The Journal of the E. E. Cummings Society* 10 (2001): 44–47.

Ramsey, Jarold. "The Continuities of W. S. Merwin." In *W. S. Merwin: Essays on the Poetry*, edited by Ed Folsom and Cary Nelson, 19–44. Urbana: University of Illinois Press, 1987.

Rasula, Jed. *This Compost: Ecological Imperatives in American Poetry*. Athens: University of Georgia Press, 2002.

Reiss, Edmund. "Whitman's Debt to Animal Magnetism." *Publications of the Modern Language Association of America* 78, no. 1 (1963): 80–88.

Ridgway, Sam, Donald Carder, Michelle Jeffries, and Mark Todd. "Spontaneous Human Speech Mimicry by a Cetacean." *Current Biology* 22, no. 20 (2012): 860–61.

Rothenberg, Jerome, and Pierre Joris, eds. *Poems for the Millennium: The University of California Book of Modern and Postmodern Poetry*. 2 Vols. Berkeley: University of California Press, 1995.

Rotman, Brian. *Becoming Beside Ourselves: The Alphabet, Ghosts, and Distributed Human Being*. Durham: Duke University Press, 2008.

Rowe, Stephanie. "No Human Hand? The Ourang-Outang in Poe's 'The Murders in the Rue Morgue.'" In *Animals and Agency: An Interdisciplinary Exploration*, edited by Sarah E. McFarland and Ryan Hediger, 107–128. Boston: Brill, 2009.

Rueckert, William. "Literature and Ecology: An Experiment in Ecocriticism." In *The Ecocriticism Reader: Landmarks in Literary Ecology*, edited by Cheryll Glotfelty and Harold Fromm, 105–123. Athens: University of Georgia Press, 1996.

Rukeyser, Muriel. *The Life of Poetry*. New York: Kraus, 1968.

Sargeant, Brooke L., and Janet Mann. "From Social Learning to Culture: Intrapopulation Variation in Bottlenose Dolphins." In *The Question of Animal Culture*, edited by Kevin N. Laland and Bennett G. Galef, 152–173. Cambridge: Harvard University Press, 2009.

Scott, Shelly R. "The Racehorse as Protagonist: Agency, Independence, and Improvision." In *Animals and Agency: An Interdisciplinary Exploration*, edited by Sarah E. McFarland and Ryan Hediger, 45–66. Boston: Brill, 2009.

Shelley, Percy Bysshe. *Essays, Letters from Abroad, Translations and Fragments*. Edited by Mary Shelley. 2 vols. London: Edward Moxon, 1852.

Shepard, Paul. *Thinking Animals: Animals and the Development of Human Intelligence*. New York: Viking Press, 1978.

Sipiora, Phillip. "Introduction: The Ancient Concept of *Kairos*." In *Rhetoric and* Kairos*: Essays in History, Theory, and Praxis*, edited by Phillip Sipiora and James Baumlin, 1–22. Albany: State University of New York Press, 2002.

Snyder, Gary. *The Practice of the Wild: Essays*. San Francisco: North Point Press, 1990.

———. *The Real Work: Interviews & Talks, 1964–1979*. New York: New Directions, 1980.

153

———. *Turtle Island*. New York: New Directions, 1974.

Stein, Gertrude. "Composition as Explanation." In *Twentieth-Century American Poetics: Poets on the Art of Poetry*, edited by Dana Gioia, Meg Schoerke, and David Mason, 20–26. Boston: McGraw-Hill, 2004.

Stevens, Wallace. *The Collected Poems*. New York: Vintage Books, 1982.

Stoeger, Angela S., Daniel Mietchen, Sukhun Oh, Shermin de Silva, Christian T. Herbst, Soowhan Kwon, and W. Tecumseh Fitch. "An Asian Elephant Imitates Human Speech." *Current Biology* 22, no. 22 (2012): 2144–2148.

Terblanche, Etienne. *E. E. Cummings: Poetry and Ecology*. Amsterdam: Rodopi, 2012.

———. "That 'Incredible Unanimal/Mankind': Jacques Derrida, E. E. Cummings and a Grasshopper." *Journal of Literary Studies* 20, no. 3–4 (2004): 218–247.

Thompson, Jeanie. "To Shine after It Has Gone: Resonance in W. S. Merwin's *The Vixen*." In *Until Everything Is Continuous Again: American Poets on the Recent Work of W. S. Merwin*, edited by Jonathan Weinert and Kevin Prufer, 87–99. Seattle: WordFarm, 2012.

Thompson, Jeanie, and Jonathan Weinert. "Raw Shore of Paradise: A Conversation with W. S. Merwin." In *Until Everything Is Continuous Again: American Poets on the Recent Work of W. S. Merwin*, edited by Jonathan Weinert and Kevin Prufer, 113–127. Seattle: WordFarm, 2012.

Thoreau, Henry David. *The Essays of Henry D. Thoreau*. Edited by Lewis Hyde. New York: North Point Press, 2002.

Webster, Michael. "E. E. Cummings: The New Nature Poetry and the Old." *Spring: The Journal of the E. E. Cummings Society* no. 9 (2000): 109–124.

———. "How to Plot a Grasshopper: Reading E. E. Cummings' 'r-p-o-p-h-e-s-s-a-g-r' [to David Hendrickson, April 26, 1954–Feb. 15, 2012]." San Francisco, 2012.

———. "Poemgroups in *No Thanks*." *Spring: The Journal of the E. E. Cummings Society* 11 (2002): 10–40.

West, Michael. "Charles Kraitsir's Influence Upon Thoreau's Theory of Language." *ESQ: A Journal of the American Renaissance* 19, no. 4 (1973): 262–274.

White, Christopher T. "Animals, Technology, and the Zoopoetics of American Modernism." Dissertation. Pennsylvania State University, 2008.

Whitehead, Hal. "How Might We Study Culture?: A Perspective Form the Ocean." In *The Question of Animal Culture*, edited by Kevin N. Laland and Bennett G. Galef, 125–151. Cambridge: Harvard University Press, 2009.

Whitman, Walt. *Complete Prose Works in the Walt Whitman Archive*. Lincoln: Center for Digital Research in the Humanities, University of Nebraska, 1995.

———. *Leaves of Grass in the Walt Whitman Archive*. Lincoln: Center for Digital Research in the Humanities, University of Nebraska, 1995.

"Whippoorwill." *Oxford Dictionary of English*. Oxford: Oxford University Press, 2010.

Williams, William Carlos. *The Collected Poems of William Carlos Williams*. Edited by Christopher MacGowan. 2 vols. New York: New Directions, 1988.

———. "The Poem as a Field of Action." In *Twentieth-Century American Poetics: Poets on the Art of Poetry*, edited by Dana Gioia, Meg Schoerke, and David Mason, 51–57. Boston: McGraw-Hill, 2004.

Wolfe, Cary. *Animal Rites: American Culture, the Discourse of Species, and Posthumanist Theory*. Chicago: University of Chicago Press, 2003.

———. *Before the Law: Humans and Other Animals in a Biopolitical Frame*. Chicago: University of Chicago Press, 2013.

———. *Zoontologies: The Question of the Animal*. Minneapolis: University of Minnesota Press, 2003.

154

Zapruder, Matthew. "Most of the Stories Have to Do with Vanishing." In *Until Everything Is Continuous Again: American Poets on the Recent Work of W. S. Merwin*, edited by Jonathan Weinert and Kevin Prufer, 77–85. Seattle: WordFarm, 2012.

Index

About the Author

Aaron M. Moe earned his Ph.D. from Washington State University. His interests include the long-twentieth century of poetry and poetics, animals studies, and ecocriticism. Along with numerous conference presentations, his work has appeared in several literary and ecocritical journals. Passionate about the circulation of discussions of poetry, he co-founded and co-edits the online journal *Merwin Studies: Poetry | Poetics | Ecology*.

Lightning Source UK Ltd.
Milton Keynes UK
UKHW051557140223
416998UK00026B/539

9 781498 550437